CHANGING SCENES

CELEBRATING 150 YEARS OF THE TENBURY AGRICULTURAL SOCIETY 1858-2008

WRITTEN BY
JEN GREEN

FOREWORD SIR ROY STRONG

Published by The Tenbury Agricultural Society Ltd. 2008

ISBN 978-0-9559373-0-9

Cover Photograph
Jack Teague circa 1930
Kindly loaned by his daughter Veronica Hipkiss

Inside cover photograph of Jen Green
Peter Logan 2005

Research
Jen Green & David Spilsbury

Drawings
Joyce Spilsbury

Foreword
Sir Roy Strong

Design and Art Work
Orphans Press Ltd.

Printed and bound in Great Britain
by
Orphans Press Leominster, Herefordshire.
Email: info@orphanspress.co.uk

Published and Distributed
by
The Tenbury Agricultural Society Ltd.
16 Teme Street : Tenbury Wells : Worcestershire : WR15 8BA.
Email: tenbury.show@btopenworld.com

This book will bring a great deal of delight not to mention information to all those who love Tenbury Wells and the Teme Valley.

I love its pell-mell character, one minute we read of the impact of the First World War, the next about a character like Bill Dipper whose role was to kill the farm pig and joint it up for the family.

This is a kaleidoscope of social history in the main brought vividly to life through personal recollection. In celebration of the hundred and fiftieth anniversary of the Tenbury Agricultural Society a century and a half of change is caught both in large and in miniature.

Historian and writer Sir Roy Strong lives in Herefordshire where, with his late wife, stage designer Julia Trevelyan Omar he designed one of England's largest post-war formal gardens. His Herefordshire home also contains his library of Gardening History. The former Director of the National Portrait Gallery and later the Victoria and Albert Museum, Sir Roy, a passionate royalist was knighted in 1982 and remains a major voice in English history.

In large in the dissolution of the great estates, in small in cameos like the history of Bowkett's, the family butchers or the Beatles one night stand in 1963. There are gaps like what happened to local government or the Church but the aim was clearly never to be comprehensive but to present us with an enchanting *pot pourri* of history from the bottom up.

The result is a testament to the resilience and enterprise of the people of Tenbury Wells and the Teme Valley.

Roy Strong

LITTLE TOWN IN THE ORCHARD

On November 5 1832, Her Royal Highness The Princess Victoria, heir apparent to the throne, was on her way to Witley Court; she was 13 years old. The young Princess was accompanied by her mother, the Duchess of Kent, and protected by an escort of mounted troops from Shropshire. Before crossing into Worcestershire the carriage procession stopped at the Swan Hotel for a change of horses and for the Worcestershire escort troop to muster and accompany the Royals for the rest of the journey. It was a joyous occasion for the township and it seems for Her Royal Highness too, and the visit has left an indelible mark on Tenbury Wells. At the time the Royal visitor was but a child yet she appears to have been quite taken with the town and with the surrounding countryside, particularly the apple orchards, as she progressed through the Teme Valley towards Witley Court. It was while she was passing through Kyrewood that an interesting moment occurred; local farmer Mr. Nicholls stopped the procession and presented the little Princess with a basket of apples, previously known as 'Standardine', which she graciously accepted and by Royal command the name of the apple was changed to the 'Princess Pippin'.

That wasn't the only honour awarded to Tenbury Wells by the Princess; inspired by her visit she announced that Tenbury would thereafter be known as my "Little Town in the Orchard", an honour that survives with much pleasure today. For one old man in Tenbury it was a special day. Richard Mantle was a cannel coal moulder, a profession that has virtually disappeared. In anticipation of the Princess becoming his future Queen he had been quietly crafting a few gifts for her; these included a necklace, a brooch, a model of Windsor Castle, an inkwell and one or two other small pieces of 'exquisite workmanship'. When he knew she was to pass through the town he was determined to present them to her. Alas! It was not to be. As he dashed over the Teme Bridge to greet the Royal party parked up outside the Swan Hotel, the inkwell fell from the pocket of his apron. He ran back for it but by the time he had found it the entourage had moved on and poor Mr. Mantle was left standing in the centre of the highway staring after the disappearing carriages. However, "all's well that ends well" and some years later an overjoyed Richard Mantle received a Royal Coat of Arms from the Princess which he displayed with great pride at his little house and workshop near Teme Bridge. Five years later Princess Victoria was crowned Queen; she was 18 years old. She eventually became the longest reigning monarch in British history and there was great rejoicing in her "Little Town in the Orchard" and thereafter on her Golden and Diamond Jubilees. Queen Victoria reigned over the Great British Empire for 64 glorious years, and she died aged 82 at Osbourne House, her private retreat on the Isle of Wight, on January 22 1901. She is buried at Frogmore in the Royal Mausoleum which she had built for her consort, Prince Albert, at Windsor. Her words engraved over the door read "Farewell best beloved, here at last I shall rest with thee; with thee in Christ I shall rise again".

A LONDONER'S VIEW

Lying on a branch line of the Great Western Railway, the small West Midland town of Tenbury is to many people hardly known, even by name. A few musical folk know of its St. Michaels, a few cyclists and motorists halt there, but by the ordinary holiday maker it is quite untouched. Yet it is the centre of a region of rare beauty, only three and half hours from London by train, the journey through the Thames valley, the Cotswolds, by the plum orchards of Evesham and Pershore, past Worcester Cathedral, on to the oak clad hills of the Wyre Forest and into the Teme Valley to Tenbury. In a country of uncommon richness – emerald pastures, green with vividness rare in England, orchards of apples and pear, plum and cherry; hop yards with long over-arched avenues like church aisles lie in the valley and ascend its slopes. The region is perhaps at its loveliest in April and May when the orchards are a sea of white and pink blossom; but in September and October, the time of fruit gathering, hop picking and cider making, it has a charm of luscious ripeness of overflowing plenty.

Tenbury lies between the river Teme and its little tributary, the Kyre brook. Entering the place from the station, and across a mediaeval bridge, sadly spoilt by recent widening, and pass up the broad main street, turn right into Market Street and you see the round red butter cross in the market square.

It is but a little place, the population is only 1,400; several charming old buildings have vanished in the last few years, but still a deal of 18th century brick remains, as well as typical black and white houses – notably, four old inns, the Royal Oak, the Kings Head, and the Hop Pole and across the river, the Rose and Crown. The college of St. Michaels, Tenbury, merits more than a passing mention; it was founded at a great cost in 1856 by that zealous churchman and excellent musician, the late Sir Frederick Gore Ouseley. He is buried in the churchyard, and his fine musical library of five thousand books and manuscripts (many of them rare and valuable) was bequeathed to the college.

The Manchester Guardian
March 1910.

5

Tenbury Agricultural Show
Committee Members - 1924

	Dorrell	A. Jones	Wilfred Morgan	Sir Archer Baldwin M.P.		J.W. Rose (Burford)	
Hill-Lowe	Jackson	Stanley Mattock	James Nott	H. Jones	Col. Prescott	Hill	J. Compton
	A.J. Dent		Stanley Baldwin . M.P	C.G. Partridge (Lambswick)	Col. Wheeler	W.M. Baldwin (Boraston)	Rev. Lea (Eastham)

Tenbury Agricultural Show
150th Anniversary Committee Members - 2008

Top left to right

Nick Champion,   Rosemary Prichard,   Stan Yapp,   David Powell,   Glyn Morgan,   David Hodges,   Will Morgan,
David Rawlings,   Rob Handley,   Gill Handley,   Ray Morris,   Dan Bradley,   Tony Patrick,   Geoff Beamand,   Will Davies

Bottom left to right

June Davies,   Rosemary Ayres,   Anne Durston-Smith,   David Spilsbury,   Edward Carpenter,
Burgess Adams,   Rosemary Adams,   Cyril Norman,   Margaret Morris,   Caroline Handley,   Sam Jacobs,

7

Field Map of Burford 1840

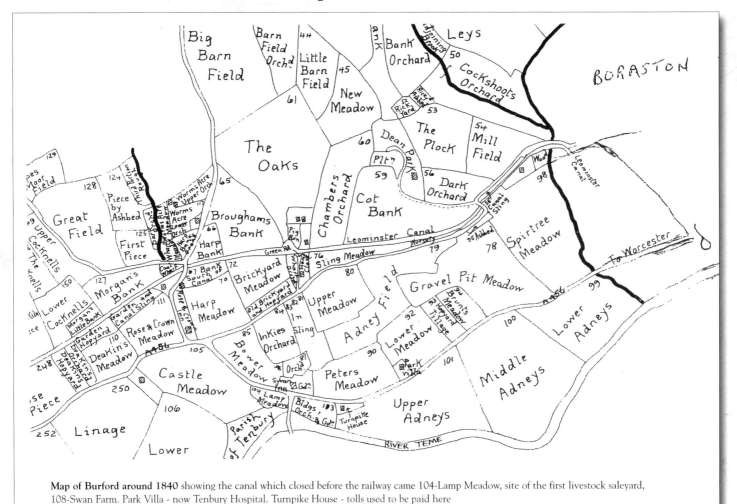

Map of Burford around 1840 showing the canal which closed before the railway came 104-Lamp Meadow, site of the first livestock saleyard, 108-Swan Farm. Park Villa - now Tenbury Hospital. Turnpike House - tolls used to be paid here

Burford Present Day

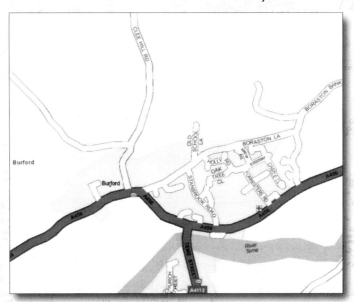

Contents

People, Places and Social Institutions

Heard Under The Bridge

Facts and Figures

Epilogue

Faces & Places

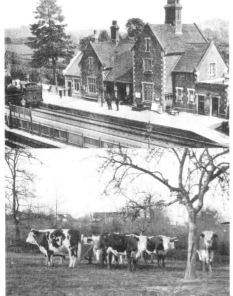

CHANGING SCENES IN THE TOWN IN THE ORCHARD

When the Tenbury Agricultural Society was founded in 1858 the town was very much smaller than it is today. Teme Street, Market Street, Cross Street and part of Berrington Road formed the basis of the town; the Victorian Round Market eventually replaced the old Butter Market.

The Pump Rooms and Spa, built a few years earlier, invited visitors to take the health giving waters but up until this time little had changed in Tenbury Wells for over two hundred years.

Teams of oxen worked the land, later followed by horses and apart from the plough, seed drill and harrows there were very few farm implements available. Until the arrival of the new fangled, steam powered mobile threshing machine, corn was hand-threshed by flail on the barn floor.

The coming of the railway saw a substantial rise in trade; livestock and produce markets were introduced and these played an important part in the economic development of market town commerce. Local auctioneer G.H. Winton built his new livestock market off Teme Street, adding to the market sites already established near to the railway station and at the Swan Hotel.

Butchers, poultry merchants, greengrocers and fruiterers from across the county were able to buy and take their purchases back by rail instead of relying on horse-drawn carts and wagons.

Nearly every farm in and around the Teme Valley grew hops and fruit and the acreage was greatly increased as the railway made it possible to supply midland and northern towns and cities with freshly grown food.

Economic decline hit hard in the late 1800s and agriculture went into depression until the First World War. This forced landlords to reduce rents to allow their tenants to keep on farming but eventually estates had to be sold up. Very few are left today.

The start of the Great War saw farming at a very low ebb. Most of the young men of Tenbury and the Teme Valley were called up to serve their country in the armed forces and most of the horses were commandeered by the army for gun carriage and ammunition supply duties on the front line leaving the estates and farms very short of labour and horsepower.

Greater effort was needed to grow more food; women replaced the men on the farms and in factories as the war took its toll with considerable loss of life and injuries in the struggle for freedom.

A cock crows on his own dunghill.

Better times soon followed with plenty of imported cheap food for everyone but this only served to cause a further deep depression in farming.

The invention of the motor car at the turn of the 20th century had brought in lorries and then bus transport. Water, electricity and the telephone came into the district around the same time and the old age pension was paid.

The threat of the Second World War in 1937 caused the government of the day to realise that agriculture would need to produce as much home grown food as possible to feed the military and the country at large.

The County War Agricultural Committee established a farm machinery depot complete with drivers who were contracted out to work for food producers and farmers. The growing Women's Land Army filled the labour gap caused by the men and women called into military service.

Enemy U-boats attacked and sunk the supply ships crossing the Atlantic and food for the country and the fighting forces was in very short supply. Everyone in villages, town and cities across the United Kingdom was encouraged to 'Dig for Victory' and wherever there was suitable space, allotments sprang up. This continued throughout the austere post-war years of the late 1940s and early 1950s.

By 1960 the railway had given way to road transport; the rail route through the Teme Valley scuppered by the Beeching report and four years later Tenbury station was finally closed.

An outbreak of Foot and Mouth disease in the latter part of the 20th century brought near disaster to rural areas; it was repeated early into the new millennium bringing to an end Mr Winton's original livestock market and adding another nail to the livestock coffin. It was also the site for the traditional holly and mistletoe sales, held annually on the Teme Street market site since Victorian times and when it was sold some three years ago - for what use is still a mystery - the town was left economically and emotional bereft.

It was a sad end for the rich, green and luscious Teme Valley, the 'historic little town in the orchard' and its close association with agriculture, hit yet again by devastating floods in the summer of 2007. But you can't keep a committed and optimistic agricultural society down. Despite government and EEC red-tape it continues to nurture and protect the local farming community and its agricultural wellbeing and as the society celebrates 150 years of farming history – what next for British agriculture?

Jen Green 2008

In the beginning

1930s FARMER

Stanley Baldwin M.P.

It all began at a meeting, convened at the Corn Exchange on July 20th 1858 chaired by Sir William Smith, Bart., to officially constitute the founding of "Tenbury Agricultural Society". It was resolved that "A Society should be formed forthwith to be called The Tenbury Agricultural Society and work ceaselessly in the Pursuit of Excellence in the Field of Agriculture using new and innovative ideas to forward and improve our noble aim in good husbandry to feed and nurture our island race".

For the first 41 years, 1858 to 1899, the Society organized a ploughing and hedging competition at different farms around Tenbury. Prizes were given to the man who had built his master's corn stacks and hayricks in the best manner and also to the best thatcher. These three classes were for a first and second prize and were judged on the farm. This part of the competition rewarded farm employees who, for generations, have been loyal servants, and a prize of two week's wages (£1.00) was awarded to the labourer who had brought up the largest family without parochial relief, except medical. There were also long service awards for both male and female.

Other prizes included the best crop of swedes (min 5 acres), mangolds (2 acres) and for the best cultivated tenanted farm; all competitions were open to persons living within 7 miles of the Corn Exchange. Later, classes were added for the best gallon of cider in a stone jar, butter, cheese, dried hops and fruit of all description, in fact anything to do with household and farm. For many years, the latter classes were judged at the Corn Exchange and when it closed they were moved to the Bridge Hotel ballroom where it is still held today as the Autumn Show.

The livestock classes were introduced in 1899 on Castle Tump meadow and the adjoining Swan saleyard. The show was held on this site for the next two years and then in 1902 moved to a permanent site on Palmers Meadow. The autumn produce shows were held at the Corn Exchange until 1919 and then at the Bridge Hotel ballroom from 1920 until 1950, with the exception of the Second World War years. In 1951 it was held at Lower Berrington with the ploughing match and from 1952 it was held in Tenbury Market; in more recent years it was back to the Bridge Hotel ballroom again.

When the society was first formed, most of the Teme Valley and the surrounding countryside was owned by large estates and let to tenants nearly all of whom grew hops and fruit as well as arable crops and also raised livestock. Most villages in the valley were self-contained within the estates with the village shop, the blacksmiths, post office, ale and cider houses and inns playing their part in village life; the school and the church were at the heart of the community. Although many farms had their own cider mills, travelling cider mills were also welcome in the villages; these allowed cottagers and householders with small orchards attached to produce their own brew. Forestry was also important for building fences, gates and hop poles, ash-beds were felled every 7 years and hedges pleached (laid) every few years. These conditions were insisted upon in the rent agreement between the estate and tenant farmer. Six-foot standard trees with wire tree guards around them to prevent damage by livestock and rabbits were planted in the orchards. In those days rabbits were plentiful and a serious pest that could inflict enormous damage to unprotected fruit trees as well as growing crops; a substantial workforce was employed to try to keep the rabbit population down to a manageable level but this was before nature intervened. Early in the 1950s myxomatosis swept across the countryside

A good wife makes a good husband.

destroying most of the rabbit population. It goes without saying that many estates were and had to be completely self-sufficient in their own right. Government and European subsidies were the future not the past and employing skilled labour was costly. Most estates also needed their own teams of carpenters, blacksmiths, wheelwrights, bricklayers, gamekeepers, forestry workers, stonemasons and thatchers. Seasonal workers were brought in to help with fruit picking and the hay making and corn harvest, all of which was carried out by hand. Armies of hop-pickers from the industrial Midlands invaded the valley by train and were taken by wagon to the numerous hop growing farms. They were usually accommodated in farm buildings, granaries and later purpose-built barrack type accommodation where they lodged until the hop harvest was gathered in – about four to six weeks. The tender, hand-picked hops were picked in hessian cribs and, for newcomers, training was essential; a man known as a busheler was always on hand to give advice and if not taken this resulted in a tirade of verbal abuse from other pickers on the correct way to pick a bushel of hops so as not to slow the picking process down. Although the Tenbury Show basically started out as a ploughing match, other agricultural competitions became attached to it including prizes for keeping some of the roads in South Shropshire repaired. Notably in the early years, leading families from the big estates along the Teme Valley provided the presidents of the Society.

The recession in farming from the 1880s and again in the 1930s meant that landowners had to accept lower rents from farmers to the point that they were forced to sell part or all of their estates. It is interesting to note that in the early days of the society; around 80% of the land in the Teme Valley was owned by estates. These days there has been a substantial reversal with the figure down to about 20%. In 1907 the show, which included exhibits from the Cottage Garden Society, had a balance of nine pounds, eleven shillings and seven pence, the gate money amounted to three pounds, five shillings and six pence. Members of the Agricultural Society were reminded that if the show was to be a success and worthy of the district and the visitors, then members must be prepared to bring forward new ideas and suggestions. These included driving and jumping competitions but there was no guarantee that prize money would be allocated. The Tenbury Horticultural Society became part of the Agricultural Show in 1921, the first show after the Great War.

It was also usual for farmers' sons and daughters to follow in father's footsteps and take over the family farm but with the changing face of rural England we now see many young people preferring to go to college or university with hopes of gaining more lucrative employment rather than staying at home to manage the family farm. Today a farmer no longer has the sole say on what he can do on his farm. Advisors such as the Department of Environment, Food and Rural Affairs (DEFRA) which replaced the more familiar Ministry of Agriculture in the 1990s, come up with new rules and the conflicting directives from Central Government at Westminster and the European Community sometimes make it difficult to understand what all the outpouring of legislation has done to help improve the farming community. Farmers have been the stewards of the land for hundreds of years; they work endlessly to ensure its safe keeping and it goes without saying that the Tenbury Agricultural Society will strive to collectively continue its stewardship and good works. Farming and horticulture is still rightly believed to be a most honourable profession, producing essential food to feed the world and, as they say, the show must go on.

A green Christmas makes a full churchyard.

Farming

DAIRYING

Ever since man domesticated cattle, milk products have been important to the health and wellbeing of the family not only as a drink but also for making butter and cheese. Back in the 1850s most farms had a few cows to rely on; in the winter they were housed in adjacent cowsheds or byres with chains around their neck, where they would be fed and milked. The cows would be let out for exercise while the manure and other waste was cleaned out and they always returned to their own familiar stalls without any prompting.

In the 1800s all milking was carried out by hand to the high pitched sound of the milk squirting into the empty bucket, the sound getting lower as the bucket filled up with frothy creamy white liquid. Occasionally there might be a clatter or two, particularly when the cow kicked the bucket or the stool from under the milker who watched the milk disappear down the drain usually accompanied by a few suitable adjectives!

It was customary for dairy farmers to travel around the towns and villages and by the early 1900s fresh milk was available daily. This was delivered to the door from a large churn carried on a milk float, a small cart drawn by a pony, ladled into a jug or can brought out by housewives and paid for on the spot; it is believed that for some years Tenbury Show held annual speed milking competitions.

Mr and Mrs Herring from Berrington were still delivering this way in the 1930s along with other local milk delivery farmers Clark Bros, Terrills Farm, and Mr Booton of Kyrewood and Kemps at Linnage Farm. Surplus milk was taken to the railway station in 17 gallon churns and sent by train to Birmingham and other Midland towns. In Tenbury there were at least three inns, the Pembroke, the King's Head and the Barn and Barrel in Berrington Road, which were small holdings and sold milk as well as ale and cider.

Around the 1930s the government, realising the importance of fresh milk in the daily diet of children, resolved to make free milk in one third pint bottles available to all school children. The milk had to be consumed on school premises and this coincided with the introduction of the glass milk bottle and the door step delivery as we know it today.

Interestingly, up to the 1900s there were many attempts to perfect a milking machine but it wasn't until the 1920s when the pulsator was invented and used with a vacuum system that it actually came about. This proved to effectively milk the cows without damaging the udders and worked so well that today's modern milking machines still use a similar system.

The first milking machines were moved from cow to cow, the units plugged into an overhead vacuum line and the teat cups attached and this method continued until the early1950s. As herd numbers increased, cows were loose housed in open sheds or cubicles and milked in a parlour. Today most modern milking parlours are computerised, particularly those with herds of several hundreds, and use a system whereby the animals come into the parlour with an identity collar attached and the correct amount of feed is dispensed while the cows are being milked.

Back in the 1950s most villages in the Teme Valley and Tenbury district would have had six or eight dairy farms milking around 10 to 20 cows. The milk was taken in churns for the road side collection and it's fair to say that the farmers made a reasonable living. Since the turn of the 21st century these same villages probably have only one dairy farm now producing twice as much milk

Milking by hand

A man of words and not of deeds is like a garden full of weeds.

as the others put together did yet finding it more difficult to make a worthwhile profit.

As with most small and large businesses, marketing and distribution always had its problems and dairying was no exception so, to help farmers meet their obligations, in 1933 the Milk Marketing Board was set up specifically to bring stability and price guarantees to the dairy farming sector and ensure that surplus milk for human consumption was sent for manufacturing into butter or cheese.

With the increase in the volume of milk came milk manufacturing plants, such as Cadbury's at Marlbrook in Leominster. Local haulage firms, such as O.P. Morgan of Miles Hope, took over the transport of the milk from farms to the factories in a fleet of lorries, to Birmingham based dairies, the Co-op, Wathes, Cattel and Gurden who were all able to cope with 10 and 12 gallon capacity churns. Most farms had a milk stand at the end of the farm drive or lane for collection, putting additional pressure on herdsmen to get the milking done and cooled off otherwise he missed the lorry, something of a sin for dairy farmers. Most of the milk produced to the east of Tenbury was despatched to Birmingham for human consumption and milk produced to the west was sent to Leominster for the manufacture of Cadbury's chocolate products. If a churn was returned during the summer months with the label still attached the farmer knew the milk was sour and as most farms kept a few pigs, it was never wasted.

Churns went out of fashion in the mid 1970s, to meet increased demand, bulk collection came in and farmers installed refrigerated tanks, meaning the milk was pumped directly into the refrigerated tankers.

Again this put more pressure on the small producers and herds were further increased to cover the overheads; these day it's not unusual to see hundreds of cows stroll into a milking parlour. When Automatic Cluster Removal (ACR) was introduced, a transponder was attached to a collar on the cow's neck, this activated the computer used to trigger off a measured amount of food for each individual animal. This was calibrated weekly depending on how much milk the animal was producing.

Over the last five years Robot Milkers have been introduced and cows are housed all year round; udders are washed and wiped, teat clusters put on and off and teats are dipped all automatically. But take heed, there's more to looking after cows than just milking them and good stockmanship will never be replaced. So much in dairying has changed over the years; when farmers kept a few cows that were all known by their individual names and most likely responded when called in but it's now all down to big, personal identity tags clipped to both ears. Each animal has its own passport which is used to inform the British Cattle Movement Schedule every time an individual animal is moved from one farm to another, taken to market or any other movements; this is generally referred to as 'traceability'.

No longer do we see cows with long horns; these were originally grown to protect themselves and their progeny from wolves and wild animals; the calves are now dehorned at a few weeks old to prevent injury to one another when being transported or in large herd situations.

When it comes to grazing systems there have been a few modifications. Years ago the livestock could freely graze all over the farm before moving on to 'strip grazing' behind an electric fence able to be moved once a day; this was done to utilise the grass more efficiently but in a wet season poaching would often occur. Paddock grazing was another option, but again with a lot of cows the passage ways leading to the paddocks became a quagmire. Set stocking was the next craze and this has stood the test of time, unless the farmer prefers zero grazing when the cows stay in all the time and you cart the grass to them.

Artificial Insemination has had a tremendous impact on cattle breeding; years ago most stock farms had a bull, generally a beef type, to do the business but nowadays there is much sire choice with each having different attributes.

Until the 1850s nearly all cows on dairy farms were Dairy Shorthorns, a good milking cow which, when crossed with a Hereford bull, produces a very good beef calf, usually brown in colour with a grey or mottled face. The early 20th century saw more Channel Island and Ayrshire cows introduced which helped improve the butterfat content of the milk.

Interestingly, it is possible that the first Friesian cattle brought into the Teme Valley was a herd belonging to Mr. Kerby of Hill Farm at Hanley Childe; he brought them in from his farm at Hall Green, now a suburb of Birmingham, when he moved into the area in 1923. It was a move which suited the herd and by 1928-1929 Mr. Kirby had won two cups for the highest milk yield in Worcestershire, amounting to some 1,040 gallons.

The big problem with the first Friesians was the butterfat, often as low as a 3.2% average but, strangely enough, today it would have been very acceptable to the public as most people have a preference for semi-skimmed or low fat milk.

Shallow stretch of water gave one farmer a chance to water his cattle - 1908

RIVER TEME, TENBURY.

If you want a job done well, do it yourself.

The Friesian bulls from good framed, high yielding and higher butterfat cows were imported to improve the breed, firstly from South Africa in 1922 and then Holland in 1936 and 1950. These bulls had a dramatic effect on the breed and went on to establish the British Friesian leading to a big increase in Friesian dairy herds, firstly by crossing onto the Shorthorn and Ayrshire cows. After several generations, a superb black and white animal emerged which went on to be bred purely for milk production or crossbred for beef and by the mid 1950s the Friesian was the most numerous dairy cow in this country. From the late 1940s artificial insemination helped bring change and most smaller dairy farmers used Friesian semen and a mixture of blue and black legged cows were seen on local farms and, after one or two generations of Friesian blood, the transformation was complete.

To improve milk yield and udders, Holstein blood was introduced and towards the end of the 20th century most dairy herds had several crosses, many pure Holstein. This modern dairy cow has been shown to produce phenomenal annual yields of good quality milk but yet remains inferior to the British Friesian when crossed with a beef bull.

Believe it or not, fifty years ago there were 200,000 dairy farmers in Britain. Today there are just over 12,000. Without farms there are no fields. Hedgerows and stone walls are the defining features of the landscape and farmers spend, on average, about two and a half weeks a year managing them as a shelter and boundary for livestock. They also provide an important habitat for birds, insects and mammals.

Ponder this, today dairy farmers are paid, on average, 17 pence per litre for milk. Nevertheless it costs 21p to produce a litre which is sold in supermarkets and on the door step for around 50p. Milk consumption is on the increase so every time milk is poured on cereal or in tea or coffee, just pause to remember where it comes from.

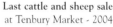

Last cattle and sheep sale
at Tenbury Market - 2004

A work ill done must be done twice.

19

Farming

Worcestershire Waggon.

OXEN TO COMBINE
150 years of power and machinery

When Tenbury Agricultural Society was formed in 1858, some working oxen were still being used, and small numbers continued to be used up to about 1900. There was an advertisement in the Tenbury Advertiser for someone wanting a team of oxen, broken in, to work in 1872. Most would have been of the Hereford breed, naturally docile animals, usually worked from 3 to 7 years old, after which they were sold on for fattening to go for meat. Oxen, mentioned in the Domesday Book, were mainly used for ploughing and cultivation and it was reckoned that a team of 8 would be kept for every 60 acres of arable land.

Horses were taking over from oxen in the 1850s, but previously they had been more important for pulling mail coaches, carriages, hunting and pack horses. These tended to be slightly built and quick moving, whereas the farm horse was of a heavier build and much slower, working at a steady pace all day and suited to ploughing, cultivation and pulling wagons and carts. The farm cart horse was improved by importing stallions from Europe, particularly Belgium. In 1891, the Tenbury Shire Horse Society was formed to further improve the working horse. The society hired or bought a Shire stallion of good breeding for the season, and it was travelled round the district, staying at different farms overnight, for a period of 8 to 10 weeks from April to June. Anything from 60 to 80 foals were born from a stallion each year. A great improvement in the quality of the heavy farm horse was seen up until about 1950 when horses were gradually replaced by tractors as the main source of pulling power on the farm. Horses not only did the general farm work, but were used to power machinery by walking round the Jinny ring, harnessed to a long pole which turned a series of gears and shafting to drive chaff-cutters, root-pulpers, corn mills and the early threshing machines until the steam engine took over.

For centuries, the corn crops (wheat, oats, barley, beans etc.) had been cut by sickle or scythe, gathered into bundles and tied into sheaves and put into stooks so the wind and sun could dry them. When dry enough the sheaves were carted and stored in the barn or outside corn stacks which were thatched. Up until about 1850 all corn was threshed by flail; two pieces of wood joined by a leather thong, and used to beat and dislodge the grain from the straw. This was usually done on the stone floor of the threshing barn with both sets of barn doors wide open, to create a flow of air through to carry the chaff away from the grain when both were tossed into the air on a shovel. To further clean the grain, a hand powered winnowing machine was used. This was a wooden fan, geared up to produce a good flow of air; the grain was passed in front of it, blowing away the lighter dust and chaff and leaving a good clean sample ready for milling.

Although some machinery such as the seed drill, cultivators and harrows had been invented many generations earlier, it was the horse drawn mower with the reciprocating blade powered by the land wheel which revolutionised hay making and harvesting. Before this, all grass for hay making was cut with the scythe and all the corn crops were cut with the sickle and scythe by hand.

By the 1860s several different makes of mowing machines were on the market, mostly invented by blacksmiths, and soon most county towns had their own manufacturers of farm implements. Almost immediately a reaper, similar to a mower, was made to cut cereals. The moving blade cut the straw and it fell onto a wooden frame and the man sitting on the seat guiding the horses had to pull the bundle of straw off with a rake when enough had accumulated to make a sheaf; this was then tied by hand, often by women.

An English summer - three hot days and a thunderstorm.

The reaper was further improved and lead to the invention of the self-tying binder, a machine that cut the crop of corn and elevated it by moving canvasses up to the packing platform. When the correct size sheaf was formed, a trip mechanism brought a needle, threaded with string round, which knotted it and cut it free, immediately a revolving arm pushed the sheaf onto the ground. Soon after, a sheaf carrier was invented whereby six sheaves could be carried before being deposited in a pile, making it much easier for the workers who put the stooks together. The stooks had to stand up to allow the rain to run off them and they usually stayed out for two or three weeks before they were dry enough to bring into the barn. By 1878, the national farming press stated that three quarters of the corn crop was being cut with the reaper.

Trevor Edwards horse power

During the 1850s, the threshing machine was perfected; one of the first manufacturers was Humphries of Pershore. Mr. E.V Wheeler of Kyrewood purchased one of these machines in 1861 for £93 and also a chaff-cutter for £12-5s. Although these items of machinery were first powered by horses turning the Jinny ring, steam engines soon took over as the main source of power well into the 1920s and 1930s.

In 1865 one of the leading farmers of this area, James Best of Hilltop Farm, Rochford, employed a steam cultivator from the Hereford Steam Cultivation Company. The next year, 1866, a group of farmers set up the Tenbury and Teme Valley Steam Cultivation and General Implement Co. Ltd. with a capital of £1,500 in 300 £5 shares. For some reason the company failed and was voluntarily wound up in 1870 and Mr. E.V. Wheeler was appointed liquidator. Although steam power had not been a success for cultivation in this area, it was very successful for haulage and as stationary engines, providing power for barn machinery and particularly the threshing machine. The steam traction engine was used for road rollers, timber hauling and pulling heavy transport wagons for delivery as the road system improved, and it powered some of the first lorries, but was eventually replaced by the petrol and then diesel engine.

In the early 1900s small petrol/paraffin engines were perfected and in time used on most farms, providing power for chaff cutting, root pulping,

Jimmy and Joey, two oxen photographed in Cirencester Park, 1945, with their herdsman, Mr. Smith. Oxen were used on the land until the beginning of this century, later in some districts, and recently a pair of oxen were "broken-in" to the plough on one farm where the ploughing is still done using a horse and single-handed plough.

Where there's muck, there's money.

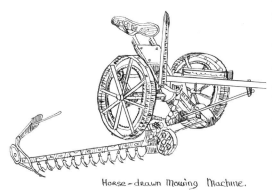

Horse-drawn Mowing Machine.

corn milling, cider making, wood sawing and very often on hop farms to drive fans for hop drying.

When the First World War started in 1914, the government commandeered a large number of horses for the army to transport supplies, guns and ammunition etc. Most of the able bodied men had joined the armed forces and with the loss of many of the young horses, farming was in great difficulty. A big acreage of land had to be ploughed to grow cereals and potatoes to take the place of food that had previously been imported. The formation of the Women's Land Army and the setting up of the War Agricultural Executive Committee, who hired machinery to farmers, helped to get through a very difficult period. By the end of the war, food was very scarce and the U.K. was near to starving.

During the war a few American tractors, mostly Fordson, were imported into this country and the first British tractors were made, the Austin being the most numerous in this district.

Tractors were being used more between the two world wars, but because of the great depression in agriculture in the late 1920s and most of the 1930s, farmers could not afford to invest in tractors or machinery. It is recorded in Gaut's History of Worcestershire Agriculture that in the period 1920 to 1938 working horses in this county decreased from 12,299 to 7,356.

By 1937, the government of the day could see that again war was inevitable and encouraged farmers to improve their land by the use of subsidised lime and basic slag, and to grow more cereals, potatoes and sugar beet.

At the outbreak of the Second World War, with lessons learned to increase food production in the First World War, the Ministry of Agriculture soon issued orders to farmers as to what crops they should grow, especially wheat, potatoes and sugar beet. If any farmer failed to obey these orders or did not manage his farm to a good standard of husbandry, the land was taken from him (even if he owned it), and managed and cropped by the local War Agricultural Executive Committee (WAEC), who also took over ploughed and cropped commons, golf courses, deer parks and any land that could be used for food production. With strict food rationing, enough food was grown to feed the nation through the war years.

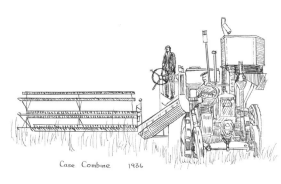

Case Combine 1936

The WAEC also set up local depots which had modern tractors and machinery of every description, employing mechanics and drivers who cultivated and cropped the derelict land and were hired out to the local farms for all seasonal work. This worked out very well because most farmers still only had horse drawn implements, and some of these were adapted for use with the tractor until more modern machinery was available.

Meantime, the Ford Motor Company of America had started to manufacture tractors in the U.K., which were available from 1938, and many farms owned a Standard Fordson by the end of the war. Also, at this time, imports of tractors from America included McCormack International, Case, Caterpillar, John Deere and others, as well as machinery.

The invention of the Ferguson tractor (T.E.20) in the late 1940s, along with its own hydraulic implements, revolutionised farming; it was the forerunner of all modern machinery. Up to this time most implements had been trailed behind the tractor, but now, with the hydraulic lift and depth control giving more traction to the wheels, it was very much more efficient. A few imported combine harvesters were used during the Second World War years, the first models being towed and powered by a tractor, the grain bagged off and dropped

22

onto the floor to be picked up by hand and loaded onto a trailer. In the 1950s and 1960s the self propelled combine was invented, with its large grain holding tank, which could be augered directly into a grain trailer. The first combines would have only cut a 6 to 8 foot width, whereas 12, 15 or 18 foot cut is normal nowadays.

Balers, starting with the stationary model, were wire tied, the wire threaded through the needle and tied by hand. These balers, first used in the 1930s, were mostly used for baling straw behind the threshing machine, replacing the old straw tyer. By the 1950s, pick up balers, mostly driven from the tractor power take off, were perfected and are used up to this day on small stock rearing farms. Around 1970 the big round baler was invented and has proved very successful for baling straw, hay and silage, the latter which is wrapped with plastic film to keep it airtight. This has been used widely on stock rearing farms.

Silage was first made as far back as 1880, and through the years was made as a salvage operation in a poor haymaking season, the end product often turned out to be foul smelling and acidic. All through these early years, silage making was very labour intensive: grass was forked on to carts and unloaded into a pit or concrete tower. During the Second World War the government encouraged farmers to make silage instead of hay because of the fear that enemy aircraft would use incendiary bombs to burn the barns and stacks full of hay. Not until some years later when wilting the grass was practised and the buck rake was invented to collect and transport the grass and plastic sheets came in to make it airtight, did silage making become the main way of conserving grass for feeding cattle and sheep. Later came power driven machines which picked up the wilted grass, chopped and blew it into the trailer; this speeded up the operation and now, big self propelled machines clear 30 acres in a day.

Cinders Farm Oldwood, early 50s:
Robert Davis on tractor by baby Andrew Miller
with Brian and Basil Tyler standing next to
Daphne Allen

Bob Brown's at Sutton Court - 1993

Bees that have honey in their mouths have stings in their tails.

Farming

APPLES

APPLES AND CIDER

Apples, cider and the Teme Valley go hand in hand but where would we be without the small apple-growers dotted about the county who for centuries have brought us 'seasons of mists and mellow fruitfulness'? In spring the valley is a patchwork of blossom; in summer, the apple orchards burst with a variety of ripe fruit and in autumn the heady aroma of fermenting fruit drifts across town and country as the latest brew is put to the press.

In the good old days, cider making was a cottage industry for farms and households who would harvest their orchards in October and November. Father would shake the apple trees with a stick or hook pole while the children scrambled in the wet long grass and nettles to collect them up and mother baked the traditional apple pies. Those without pressing facilities on site could call in dependable Bob Morgan and his portable cider press to crush enough apples for the family cider stock; the main crop was stacked up in hessian sacks and carted to the nearest cider mill for crushing and the pulp was then spread in layers on coconut matting. This was placed in the big press and screwed down until all the juice - the scrumpy - was squeezed out ready for the barrels. It took many weeks to mature, usually until January by which time it was powerful stuff, especially if extras like 'pot fruits' - cookers and eaters - were added to the flavour. According to local hearsay, "new cider would never be drunk - it will make you talk about friends you never had and anyone foolish enough to do so, it was with dire consequences."

In the winter when the cider was ready for tasting, the head of the family entertained his relations and friends. He would fill up a horn or two with his own brew and take the chill off with a red hot poker taken straight from the hot coals on the fire.

With tradition comes superstition and the apple orchards were not without their's; from New Years Day until Twelfth Night orchards were wassailed - a salutation or drinking toast made during festivities - with cider and song. Farm workers, their families and friends would slip into the orchards after dark carrying shot guns, drinking horns and a large pail of cider. The best apple tree in the orchard was chosen and the new brew of cider poured onto the roots, a

Apple picking - 1929

24

Brag is a good dog but holdfast is better.

specially baked cider-soaked cake was carefully placed in the fork of the tree and a few branches dipped into the cider pail. A blazing bonfire was lit to keep the guests warm and a traditional supper set out and eaten; afterwards the farmer would toast the chosen tree as if it were a person. After the feasting a song of admonition and blessing was sung, people danced through the orchards and general merriment carried on through the night.

On Twelfth Night the orchards were decorated and a traditional Twelfth Night cake was cut and served with tea. Inside the cake was a pea and a bean and those finding them became King and Queen for the night. However, tradition has it 'if a man split a pea or a woman bit into a bean they had to change roles immediately or strange things might happen. Perhaps it was a bit of old fashioned gender-bending to make the party go with a swing.

Today, apple-wassailing is largely regarded as a cheerful frolic associated with good luck; some farm-workers still drop by the orchards with a flagon or two, just in case.

Although in the early days cider was home-produced, today Tenbury and the Teme Valley apple orchards supply the growing number of small cider producers across the region and back in the late 1800s Hardimans made cider in Tenbury and for many years Robinsons, at the Rose and Crown (Wells Drinks) made cider and perry for specials occasions, later selling apple and black currant juice and other soft drinks. In 1970 they developed the nearby former railway station into a busy drinks company employing a large staff of some 300 local people. The company became an important supplier of a variety of soft drinks to most supermarket chains but transport difficulties forced a company move to Northhampton in 2000.

It is fair to say that the Tenbury Agricultural Society has seen a good few changes in the apple cider market but, as always fashion dictates the market, today cider making has grown from strength to strength and English apples and cider are acknowledged as 'simply the best' by connoisseurs and cider drinkers the world over.

Pressing apples

Horse drawn apple wagon

Thomas H. Graves
Fruit Merchant

Apple press - 1948

Careless shepherds make many a meal for the wolf.

A PASSION FOR TREES

Andrew Wright, Nick Dunne
and daughter Stephanie

Trials are underway for a dedicated Tenbury apple and two or three are expected to be short-listed in autumn 2009. This challenging project is rooted in the capable and experienced hands of the Frank. P. Matthews's team at Berrington and the new variety of apple is currently in the late stages of development.

Frank P. Matthews is a family run business. Frank Matthews began growing fruit trees and roses in 1901 at Hayes and Harlington, close to Heathrow airport and Andrew, his son-in-law and Adrye Dunn - nee Matthews, moved the business to Tenbury Wells in 1956; sadly they both passed away in 2007 at the age of 91.

In the late 1950s the nursery site at Hayes and Harlington was threatened by the expansion of Heathrow airport and the proposed M4 motorway; a move had to be made and the Teme Valley was chosen as a suitable location. The deep valley soils proved ideal for tree production and it was coincidental that the nursery specialised in fruit trees that are so much of historical influence in the Teme Valley.

During the 1960s and 70s, the nursery followed a consistent pattern producing bare root trees for fruit growers and nurseries. At this time, the United Kingdom led the world in fruit tree research; the company played a major part in the propagation of virus free material, exporting fruit trees to many parts of the world - especially fruit development programmes in developing countries. Seventy percent of the company's production was apple trees with the other fruits and just a few ornamentals making up the rest.

Throughout the 1980s, Frank P. Matthews continued to be fairly stable in the fruit industry and the bare root side of the business continued as before. The rapid development of the 'garden centre' industry created the opportunity to put trees in pots so the business started its expansion into 'Container trees' to compliment the field production. It was during this time that commercial orchard production began its decline so the business was able to maintain steady tree production and employment.

Decline in the fruit industry and expansion into tree production for the domestic market continued into the 1990s; additional opportunities to supply mail order companies helped the business expand further. The company also adopted the *'Trees for Life®'* trade mark and this has grown to be a significant brand leader in quality fruit and ornamental trees for gardens. The cider industry also had a surge of planting during this decade resulting in the family business growing trees for many cider and perry companies in the west of the country.

The company celebrated its centenary in 2001 with the publication of the first 'Tree Guide for Gardens' and since then the fruit industry has experienced a slow turnaround, firstly with dwarf cherry orchards, mounting interest in plums and apricots and latterly even an interest in apples with new orchard plantings. Most of this interest came on the back of the 'home grown and organic movements' as well as public enthusiasm for local food and home production. The garden centre and nursery business continues to evolve and has now become the main business activity, accounting for 80% of production.

FPM maintains strong links with local and traditional fruit varieties and many trees are raised to supply standard orchards through private and stewardship scheme initiatives, particularly in Herefordshire, Worcestershire and surrounding counties. Old, declining trees are often 'rescued' by a special propagation service the Matthews nursery provides.

Come day, go day. God send Sunday. (The lazy man's prayer).

The company works closely with breeders and other nurseries and enthusiasts in the development of new tree varieties to enable the introduction of exiting new trees to the orchard and garden industry. Most important is the work of apple breeder Hugh Ermen; his varieties are trialled on site for many years and so far several have had considerable success. These include Scrumptious and Herefordshire Russet. Ornamental trees are also important and additions are continually included within the existing wide range of Acer to Zelkova.

Ever keen to take on a challenge, the company are working towards producing a 'Tenbury Apple', an exciting idea conceived after the first successful Tenbury Apple Festival in 2005 and two or three varieties can expect to be short listed by autumn 2009. The select few will be put into trial and tastings will be undertaken within the local community to gain a consensus of opinion as to which is the most popular variety deserving of the honorary title of Apple 'Tenbury Wells'. Once decided upon it will be officially named and offered for sale in years to come. The apples selected for trial will initially come from the breeding programme of Hugh Ermen and it will take time and patience to produce such a unique apple, but it will be worth it in the end.

Passionate about trees is what Frank P. Matthews is all about, their well established propagation producing the large majority of what it sells 'in house'. It is fundamental to the self-imposed quality standards the business maintains through every stage of the production cycle of the tree. The highly dedicated, loyal and skilful staff is as important an asset to the company as is its location.

There is also a strong desire to preserve the fertility of the soil and the other natural resources that the Tenbury area provides, most important of which is the River Teme for its irrigation.

Nick Dunn, the founder's grandson, is the current Managing Director and his daughter Stephanie has recently joined the business making her the fourth generation of the Frank P. Matthews Ltd dynasty. Andrew Wright of St Michaels, soon to complete 25 years with the company, is Production Director and the business currently employs over seventy full time staff, all from Tenbury and nearby local communities and although the company's roots are in the past, its eyes are definitely on the future.

Apples at an autumn show

Apple picking

APPLES

THE MILLENNIUM ORCHARD

If an apple a day keeps the doctor away then it's fair to say that people living in a 'town in the orchard' can expect to enjoy good health. These days names like Golden Pippin, Hereford Beefing, William Crump, Peasgood Nonsuch and Lord Derby are among the many fine English apples missing from the market place, but for a touch of apple history take a stroll through Tenbury's Millennium Orchard, just off the A456 at Burford. The idea for a unique apple orchard as the town's millennium project was planted in 1998; it was one of a number of suggestions put forward by the public, but a major stumbling block was likely to be the purchase of a suitable piece of land reasonably close to the town and within a manageable budget. Reading about the proposed project in the local press, Burford House and Gardens offered a piece of unused land and an agreement was reached. A team of volunteers set about cutting down a mass of five-foot-high brambles and rough scrubland, burning it all up and digging out the age old roots. Berrington based fruit tree specialists Frank P. Matthews joined in the project and came to the rescue. They offered to rotavate the area and provide and look after the trees in the early stages. Thirty eight sponsors paid for planting costs and hopes were high that they would continue to take an interest as the trees grew. On a glorious May Bank Holiday Monday in 2001, the Rev. Keith Crouch from the local team ministry led about 60 people in a service of blessing on the site and Tenbury's adventurous millennium project was up and running. However, like many similar projects, day-to-day funding is often hard to come by and Peter Barrington, chairman of the Millennium Orchard Committee and his group of volunteers work hard organizing apple and plough-man's suppers, quizzes and other events to keep the orchard ticking over. They rely on the goodwill of the townspeople to keep it up to scratch - and it shows. Since the first planting, the Millennium Orchard has become a quiet spot in which to find peace of mind, rest on the benches provided by local people and enjoy the fruits of the labours of the people of Tenbury Wells.

A good English apple may be a fruit of the past but, growing, they are a sight worth seeing, especially at blossom time. In the autumn when the apple harvest is ready, visitors are welcome to taste a variety or two of these rare English apples but for history's sake, don't take more than you can eat on the day.

Destroy the lion while he is but a whelp.

THE BIRDS, THE BEES IN THE ORCHARDS

The birds, the bugs and the bees are back in the old orchards in the Teme Valley. Past decades have seen a dramatic drop in rare birds and insects which, like the truly English apple, have been lost in European red tape. It's not just that red tape has increased the number of trees being cut down, more that cheaper food is available from abroad. It is hard to make a living selling fruit from British orchards so farmers cut them down to make way for bigger grass fields or plough them up.

Caring for old orchards can reap much fruit for wildlife. Created and managed as part of the agricultural landscape, traditional orchards were unarguably an 'artificial' habitat for a wide variety of birds, bees, beetles and butterflies.

KINGFISHER.

A common sight in Worcestershire and the Teme Valley, perhaps more than in any other part of England, the old orchards help define the character of the county. They are a living part of our heritage and are much valued by residents and visitors.

It's no small wonder then that Tenbury Wells is considered 'the town in the orchard'. Street names like Dark Orchard and Orchard Close highlight areas of the town and the parasite mistletoe, clinging to the branches of the trees in the orchards attracts countless buyers and sellers to the annual auction sales, held in the town at Christmas time.

There is even a new orchard tucked away in Burford which has been planted with old fashioned apple trees to celebrate the turn of the 21st century.

Traditional orchards are of great value as habitats for several birds of the highest conservation concern, including the Tree-Sparrow, Spotted Flycatcher and the Bullfinch, numbers of which have dropped dramatically in recent decades. The ancient fruit trees have also become home to hole-nesting varieties like Woodpeckers and Owls and in the autumn and winter the fruits attract Thrushes, Fieldfares and Redwings. But it is not only in the orchards that birds are likely to be seen. Water attracts birdlife too; the Kingfisher, Dipper, Moorhen and Coot can be seen sharing water side environments with regular visitors like the Dabchick (Little Grebe), Mallards and Tufted ducks and Canadian geese. It's thanks to the conservation schemes encouraging more farm pools that the number of Kingfishers has increased over the past 30 years. They can be seen flying and following the streams and diving into the pools as well as perching on over hanging branches on the river bank.

The last few years have seen fewer House Martins, Swallows and Swifts nesting in the area, but Robins, Wrens various Tits, Hedge-Sparrows, Wagtails and Yellow Hammers are still about and happily feed on the woodland insects. The Nuthatch likes to take over disused Woodpecker holes, and Greater Spotted and Greater Green Woodpeckers nesting in decaying trees are common place but not so the Lesser Spotted.

Barn owls were more common when the corn harvest was stored in ricks and barns where they would enjoy feeding on the mice, but these days numbers are low; nesting boxes in converted barns have helped and with the increase in field margins providing extra feeding ground, numbers are said to be on the increase. Pleasingly, the Tawny owl is still around in good numbers, living mainly in woodland, ivy clad or old hollow trees.

There are odd pairs of skylarks on most farms but like most ground nesting birds they seem to have disappeared in recent years. The sight of a skylark rising almost vertically into the sky singing its song until it is out of sight is one of

Early to bed, early to rise, makes a man healthy, wealthy and wise.

nature's wonders. There are still a few pairs of Lapwing (Peewit) about, which in the winter are usually seen in flocks in riverside meadows, and a few years ago a nesting Curlew was a regular sight; they are rarely seen or heard now. The Cuckoo too is fast disappearing; its song the call of spring seems to be a distant memory but there are ample numbers of Magpie, Jackdaw, Rook, and Carrion Crow. The Raven, thought to be extinct in the area since 1924, has lately been seen and its distinctive call heard in some villages. In the early 20th century the Nightingale could be heard singing in the Teme and Kyre Valleys but not now. In a letter to a Tenbury paper in 1919, the Rev. Allan Ellison from Rochford rectory claimed to have heard a nightingale at 11pm singing across the valley in the direction of Newnham Bridge about a mile away. Coming from the Home Counties he was used to the sound and was delighted to hear it so far north as it was believed they were rarely heard west of the River Severn. The last reported sighting of a nightingale in the locality was at Lindridge and on Bromyard Downs in the 1930s.

Fieldfares and Redwings return in flocks during October after breeding in the northern woodlands and can be seen feeding on berries and the last of the apples towards the end of the year; in the winter they search the fields for food and leave for the north again in March.

Buzzards have recently returned to breed in the valley and the sight of them flying effortlessly on the thermal current is a joy to behold. Gold Finches breed in good numbers in the old orchards and large flocks of Greenfinches enjoy

Mistletoe in apple trees - 2007

Every time a sheep baas he looses a bite.

winter feeding on linseed and sunflowers. If a scheme could be arranged for a field of mixed seed to be grown in every village close to a public highway, the general public would be able to view many wild birds. It would also bring badly needed goodwill to farmers and townspeople and bring them together. Of the game birds, the grey partridge, compared to 30 years ago, is now quite rare but the Woodcock is still around and nearly always seen, when disturbed, in its favourite brook-side habitat.

Less conspicuous wildlife, invertebrates, fungi and lichens, no less important in terms of conservation, also take up lodgings in old orchards. Unfortunately, traditional orchards continue to be removed and replaced by more closely planted smaller trees with fewer varieties. These are the demands of commercial efficiency and the challenge ahead is surely to safeguard what habitat remains and hope that returning endangered species of all kinds are rediscovered. The *Gnorimus Noblis*, (Noble Chafer), a beautiful iridescent green beetle, rare in Britain for over a century, was thought to have disappeared from many English counties but it was recently rediscovered.

A survey of 26 orchards in Worcestershire funded by English Nature and the People's Trust for Endangered Species was carried out some years ago and the results were very encouraging. Evidence of the beetle has been found in sixteen orchards in the county and more finds are expected. This is a remarkable sign; earlier surveys were largely unsuccessful because the adult beetle is very hard to locate as it spends most of its two year life cycle inside the rotting trunks of old, neglected fruit trees and can often be overlooked.

Safe-guarding natural habits in the countryside can not only promote the restoration and sympathetic management of neglected orchards but it can also encourage people to seek out and buy the products from traditional orchards. Local environmental groups help raise the profile and heritage of the traditional English orchards scattered throughout the Teme Valley and the wildlife that depends on it. DEFRA has a conservation grant scheme called Higher Level Stewardship which has been encouraging landowners to restore and replant traditional orchards.

Farming

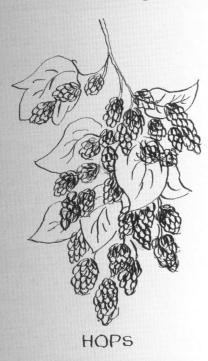

HOPS

CHANGES IN HOP GROWING SINCE 1850

Varieties of hops grown in the Teme Valley in the 1850s were Cooper's White, Canterbury White Bine and Mathons which is the only variety to have survived to the present time. Fuggles were introduced after 1875 and became the top variety grown until the late 1960s; varieties of Goldings - Early Bird, Mathons and Cobbs were also grown.

In the 1950s, the introduction of varieties like Northern Brewer and Bullion, were the first of the higher alpha/dual purpose hops which came into their own but by the 1960s, Northdown and Challenger were both widely grown in the Teme Valley until recent years. Since the revival of small micro breweries and real ale, there has been a strong swing back to Fuggles and Goldings.

In recent years, dwarf and low trellis hops like First Gold and Herald have been grown in the valley but have only seen limited success with the brewers. There are many advantages of growing in this style, for example, fully mechanised harvesting, easier training and lower establishment costs. When new varieties are developed to suit the brewers tastes, it's fair to say that this is the direction hop growing will take in the future.

In the mid nineteenth century the entire hop yard was dug with a three pronged fork, digging in farmyard manure or shoddy old rags. Plants were dressed in March – trimmed around the crown of the plant – and all hops were grown originally on pitched poles which were erected in April in readiness for training the young shoots in May which were then tied to the poles with raffia. Cultivation during the summer was carried out by a horse drawn nidgett – a form of wooden harrow to control weeds – and the plants were earthed in June using manual labour. The revolution in hop growing came in 1866 when Bomford of Evesham and Edwin Farmer of Kyrewood developed the first wirework systems, similar to that used today.

Following the turn of the 20th century hop farms became larger and the mechanisation of cultivations began. Hops were ploughed up in June and then ploughed down in the winter and in between, during the summer months, weed control was carried out by mechanical method. This was the style of weed control continued until the mid 1960s when chemical weed control became common practice.

First attempts to control mould (powdery mildew) were first brought in around the 1850s when the invention of a horse drawn powdering machine was introduced to apply flowers of sulphur.

Aphid control started some 15 years later. This was done by spraying hops with soft soap. Quassia extract was added a few years later but hop spraying did not become general practice until about 1883.

Soot and lime was also used for dusting plants or hills to protect plants and control plants from flea beetles in the 1860 when Red Spider was also spotted. Downy Mildew, referred to as spike, first appeared in 1920 and was eventually partly controlled by the use of copper dust. This was followed by the appearance of Verticillium wilt in 1924; this was thought to have been carried by troops returning from Belgium after the Great War as hops were grown near the front line on the Western Front.

Wilt spread to Herefordshire in 1967 and eventually arrived in the Teme Valley in 1985; it has now spread through out the valley with possibly only one farm not being affected. This soil born fungus is a killer for susceptible varieties like Fuggles, Goldings, North Down and Challenger.

Fish and company stink in three days.

The first air assisted spraying was invented around 1930 and the first systemic insecticide, translocated through the plant, was used in 1949 with great success against the scourge of hop growing, the hop damson aphid. The use of systemic insecticides also controlled many other insects and pests including red spider and caterpillar, but resistance has now developed to most of these early sprays which are being replaced with continually developing products. The use of these chemicals has resulted in more consistent quantities and quality.

The first American machine for picking hops was imported in 1927 but had little success in coping with the English crop. An English machine was developed at Martley in 1934, but production did not really start until 1948 when the Bruff and Hinds picking machines - both developed in Worcestershire - were introduced. It was in the 1950s that the big change to machine picking took over; this followed a series of walk outs and strikes by hand pickers although some hand picking survived until 1967 at Orleton Court. It was also around this time that the hop press was invented; prior to this hops had to be trodden into the hop pockets manually.

Most of the hop kilns in the valley date from the mid 19th century when big advances were made in design. Lateral draft was increased by building them higher, also hopper type flues were developed using two or more fire places in an inverted brick cone; a good example of this design still exists at Court Farm, Hanley Childe. After the turn of the century, fans were used and automatic coke stokers with cast iron heat exchangers and open flame oil burners were used. Open flame oil burners were used from the late 1930s onwards and nowadays, propane gas burners producing a much cleaner flame than oil are the latest innovations.

In 1734 a duty of 1 penny per pound of hops was introduced and this continued for 128 years. From then, hop acreage steadily grew to reach a peak of 71,789 acres (29,052 hectares) in 1878. Depending on the level of pest and disease, yields varied dramatically between 2 and 15 hundred weight per acre.

Acreage started to fall after 1885 as better husbandry and use of sulphur and soft soap became the norm resulting in more regular yields. The acreage dropped dramatically during the Great War due to government controls, not recovering again until the early 1920s.

The price for hops started to fall dramatically in 1924 and various efforts were made to try and form voluntary marketing co-operatives, but this was not

Hop Crib - 1948

successful and it took the Agricultural Marketing Act of 1931 to stabilize the market. A year later, The Hop Marketing Board was established and introduced quotas and production costing to give protection to the stable UK market. Following pressure from the European Community, the Board was disbanded in 1982 since when hop growing has been in steady decline with only 5618 hectares grown in 1983.

After the demise of the Hop Marketing Board, several producer groups were formed, English Hops being the largest, but sadly, with multi-desk selling, the prices gained for hops have declined.

A world surplus of hops, better utilisation by the brewers – palleting and isomerising hops – plus CO_2 extraction of the alpha acids which gives the bittering effect in beer, have been problematic. So have the large stocks of hops held by most brewers in the United Kingdom, all contributing to a decline in prices and the subsequent reduction in hectares grown.

In 2007 a crossroad was reached. The production of hops worldwide had dropped below quantities needed by the brewing industry and there was a welcome lift in prices. Spot market prices were up to 3 times higher than in 1996/97 and because of this, brewers were forced to nearly double future contracted prices to enable long term security for the industry and encourage present day hop growers to replant and produce the hops needed to meet demand. Fertiliser and fuel prices have more than doubled in the last 12 months and growing costs can expect to follow the same trends.

Many hop farms have disappeared from the valley in the last 50 years and questions are being asked about the future of hop growing in the Teme Valley over the next ten years. Despite the ups and downs, hops have been a way of life for many working families in the Teme Valley for many generations; only time will tell if there is still a profitable future.

Veronica Hipkiss hop picking

One hour's sleep before midnight worth two after.

HOPS WITHOUT BEER
The story of Miss Mildred Cooper

Despite spending a long and fruitful life working in the lush hop fields of Worcestershire, Mildred Cooper had never allowed beer to pass her lips.

Born in 1907 at Field Farm, Knighton-on-Teme, she was brought up and schooled in the village and appears to have lived a happy and contented life on the family hop farm. Believing that no man was good enough Mildred was never temped to marry, persuaded to move away or travel abroad and flatly refused to wear a pair of trousers. In a written record of her memories taken down when she was in her nineties and placed anonymously into Tenbury Museum some years ago, Mildred Cooper comes across as a delightful woman with a sharp clear memory and well able to look back on a life well spent with much detail and pleasure.

This, then, is her story, a story of a strong and hard working young woman with a remarkable knowledge of hop growing at all levels, her roots well dug into the domestic and agricultural life of the Teme Valley. Her reminiscences could have been lost in the past had she not agreed to tell it as it was with all its ups and down.

One of six brothers and two sisters, each born at Field Farm, all Mildred ever wanted was to be at home with her brothers and sisters and, like them, work on the family farm where the women folk were expected to wait upon the men. It was a big household to look after; a young girl was employed to help her mother keep house and a young boy and a man, living as part of the household, took care of the heavier domestic duties. Mr. Cooper employed about six other men to help work the land.

Daily food, milk, butter, cheese, flour, poultry and pigs, was mostly home produced, water came from the well and her mother made the clothes for all the family, including sailor suits for the smaller boys. Saturday night was bath night and usually taken in a tin bath in front of the fire; the family standard of living was just about average because, it appears, her father 'was always too busy helping other people to become rich.'

At first, the Coopers rented Field Farm as well before Mildred was born it was offered for sale at £2,000 and her father couldn't afford to buy it however eventually he did manage to raise the cash and became the owner. It was a remarkable achievement for a working man who had started out with virtually nothing except his own hard work. But good fortune didn't favour him because when his father Edwin Cooper, who also lived at the farm, died, the entire farm stock and contents of the house had to be sold and the proceeds shared among Mildred's father and his three married sisters.

From his share of the sale, her father bought a mirror valued at two shillings which Mildred, a great hoarder of memorabilia, always kept among her personal effects She also kept safe the catalogue and auctioneer's records from 1900 of the 'valuable effects' handled by the auctioneers, Griffiths and Boyce. These were listed as 58 well bred Hereford cattle, 9 powerful young carthorses and colts (well known as good workers), a brown mare, 15.2, rising five years, a good huntress, 68 Shropshire sheep, a five horse power portable steam engine, 5,000 gallons of prime cider in casks and two tons of eating potatoes.

Agricultural implements included a Swede scuffler, iron swing and wheel ploughs by Kell, Samuelson reaping and mowing machines, a winnowing

Picking hops at Coopers field, Bickley - 1928

One swallow does not make a summer.

Bank Farm - 1966

Hop bagging - 1993

machine, various sets of lanterns, a cow crib, oil cake crusher and a Dobbin cart. Mole traps, a root slicer and pulper, three barrels of soft soap, a couple of ferret boxes, a portable pig box, a bee house and 24 cider hairs added to the catalogue.

Many items connected with hop production also went under the hammer; these included 12 hop-picking cribs and crib cloths, 35 carrying sacks, 2 hop bushels, a hop breaker and kiln hair and a painted two wheel dog cart with a set of brass mounted harnesses.

The house contents hinted at an impressive and comfortable family home. Items ranging from a cottage pianoforte in a rosewood case built by Prowse of London, a Spanish mahogany 4-post bedstead, green damask furniture, a handsome 8-day grandfather clock manufactured by Rocke of Kidderminster, an antique carved oak chest with lock, key and drawer, a night chair and oval walnut loo table, and two stump bedsteads. There was also a combined Catelly barometer and thermometer, a nearly new Singer sewing machine, a double-barrel muzzle-loading gun, and a cheese press.

Mildred's wealthy uncle, William Skyrme was the biggest spender at the auction sale buying up most of the household effects. His remarkable spending power seems to have stemmed from his gift as a water diviner (dowser) and he was much in demand for his ability to find water for landowners. This was confirmed in a printed booklet belonging to Mildred containing some of the numerous testimonials her uncle had received from home and abroad. A Mr. W. Carne of Toll Fruit Farm, Ludlow wrote: 'We sunk a well at the spot you indicated and found a splendid spring of water at exactly the depth you stated – 30ft. We are now enjoying the benefit of it and appreciate it the more as before we were entirely without water'.

William Skyrme's son and grandson followed in his footsteps and made a good living from finding water for rich landowners but when Mildred tried dowsing she did not seem to have the gift. She wistfully recalled 'I didn't feel a thing even though I stood right over the well!'

It is clear from her notes that young Mildred had a leaning towards fauna and flora; she still had the book prize she was awarded for gathering the most wild flowers in Knighton-on-Teme, on the way to school. Occasionally she had to mind a pony and trap for somebody and she was not supposed to receive payment but when sometimes it was forced upon her, the sixpence she earned was taken to school to buy a First World War saving stamp. Although she worked hard in the home and in the hop fields, she received no regular allowance from her parents. She noted 'Dad said that we went to bed with our pocket money, meaning our food and clothing.'

Myths and superstitions featured largely in family life, both her grandfather and father were highly superstitious. She confirmed "There were a lot more swallows and house martins then making a lot of mess about the buildings but father wouldn't drive them away as he thought that would bring bad luck. Also, no female was allowed to come to the house on Christmas Day, except those already living there, so only boys would come to buy our milk. New mistletoe had to be hung up on Christmas Day while the old was not allowed out of the house again, but burnt inside. No horse was expected to be worked on Easter Day, Christmas Day and Good Friday'.

Another thing dad always said to do was to tell our bees when there was a death in the family. He once told me that when my brother died of the measles at the age of four the bees were not informed so they all died but, when my brother Fred died of a quinsy throat when he was twenty four we made sure we went down and tapped on the hive.

The Parish Church, Knighton-on-Teme

'At one time Dad had 25 horses, which was more than he had cows. He had two sets of threshing tackle and ran two other places as well as our own farm of well over 200 acres. Our horses never spent a night in – even in midwinter. Sometimes you'd see them rolling around in the snow. It was just as well they were used to it as we relied on horses to get round to the other animals in the deep drifts of 1947'.

Godliness and cleanliness formed the backbone of Mildred's family life. Her parents were strict and, without fail, the children had to bath on Sabbath eve and attend Sunday school between 10-11am staying on for morning service from 11am to noon. Later, mother went to church in the morning and the two sisters in the evening and the boys sang in the choir. Since her childhood Mildred has always stuck to mother's old-fashioned rule of never doing anything on a Sunday.

Back in the 19th century Mildred's grandfather was also regular church goer. Like most churches of the time the local church had high pews so you couldn't see anybody except the vicar in the pulpit.

"He used to tell us off for giggling when the collection bag, which was passed over the top of our pew on a stick, always hit him on the back of his bald head. After a while he said it had to stop and to avoid the hazards of the collection he chose to give the church a yearly sum of money. We were always brought up to behave properly and were never allowed to call adults by their Christian names, like the youngsters do now: I don't agree with that. We also had to wear clogs which constantly wore our stockings out but nothing was ever wasted in our home. Old stockings and trousers were dyed and cut into strips to make into rugs and mum and dad never allowed us girls to wear see through silk stockings or trousers, and haven't yet. We were very self-sufficient and always doctored ourselves by cooking up dandelions and nettles. Mother always believed in good, old-fashioned food, with plenty of soups and stews throughout the year, we enjoyed a roast goose at Christmas and Christmas puddings for birthdays as well as on 25th December. She was a very good cook and baked her own bread, cakes and tarts once a week in the old wall oven heated by burning about a wheelbarrow of old hop pole pieces. It was the job of us children to collect them with a warning from mother not to bring up any tarred bits – the pole bottoms were dipped to preserve them – as that would spoil the flavour of the food. Father always made a lot of cider for himself and the men. They more or less lived off it, each man would not only carry off a half gallon jar each day but would often return for several pints more. Dad loved to dip his toast in it and the doctor always had gingerbread with his, but I've never liked it".

When Mildred was 12½ years old her mother decided that there was no point in her staying at school any longer as she believed that there was nothing more for her daughter to learn and she left. One day, the local aristocracy called at the farm to ask for one of her two girls to go into service but Mrs Cooper wouldn't allow it saying there was plenty of work for them at home.

"And there was too" Mildred explained. "Everything from cleaning the house to milking cows, hatching turkeys under hens, rearing geese and ducks and collecting galeeny (guineas fowl) eggs, which were laid all over the place. We never got any pay and it was many years later before Dad put a bit in the bank for us children.

John Dingley stringing hops - 1997

One of my clearest memories of the animals is when we sold a sow and her piglets to a place at Lower Eastham, about five miles away. Wilfred Drew took them over in his lorry, but a week or ten days later the sow walked into her cot (sty) presumably after the piglets had been weaned. We were amazed at a pig walking so far and I said she must have made a careful note of all the road signs as she looked out the back of that lorry!' It was most unusual for a pig to walk so far on its own, but we often walked sheep and cattle the 4 ½ miles into Tenbury market. However, when a cow and her calf were taken in to market the calf went in the trailer while its mother walked behind".

Amazingly, all the Cooper children could recognise the particular trot of their parents' horse when they came home from market and according to Mildred, the dog could also tell them from the neighbours and would run down the road to meet them and ride back with them on the cart.

On top of her already heavy load of daily tasks Mildred soon became closely involved in the family's hop business. In those days most farms in her area each grew only about ten or a dozen pockets of hops, a pocket being an elongated, tightly packed sack containing about 1½ to 1¾ cwt of dried hops ready for market. However, the income derived must have been significant because when a controversial Government Budget effecting market trends was introduced the year before she was born (1907) it threatened a big decline in hop production. At the time, hop farmers from across the country were up in arms over the government's plans and Mildred's father and his friends travelled by train to London to join the 'Hop Saturday Monster London Demonstration' organised to save the English hop gardens and held in Trafalgar Square on 16th May 1906.

Mildred Cooper had a sound knowledge of hop growing and explained that although hops had grown wild in hedgerows since ancient times, in England they were not used for brewing on a large scale until the early 16th century. Before then the most popular drink was ale made from malt and clarified by ground ivy; beer was created when hops were used to impart flavour (hence 'bitter') and help it to keep longer. It is commonly known the hop has male and female plants but it is only the female flower that develops into the green-yellow cones covered in resinous glands, which are used in brewing. Different brewing varieties were gradually cultivated and improved and found to grow best in Kent, East Sussex, and Hampshire, parts of Surrey, Hereford and Worcester. At first the plants were simply grown up straight poles, but later various ways were introduced using the extra support of string and wire in hop fields. These were known as gardens in the south east and yards in the West Midlands.

Here Mildred clearly describes in her own words the old system used at her farm at Knighton-on-Teme.

"In November, a plough covered the roots over to protect against frost and in February the soil was ploughed down. The roots were trimmed to a crown and when they began to shoot, a wire peg was fixed either side of each to anchor the strings – made from coconut fibre, in Ireland – the overhead wires. A piece of ironwork called a monkey was used to reach and thread the string at the top'. When the shoots came a woman would thread two up one string and three up the other, so that each plant had five. In an average year each shoot should reach the top by 24th June and it was always said that the bines should be three weeks in burr and three weeks in hop before they are ready to pick The knack of knowing when was in the feel. Our best varieties at Field Farm were Fuggles and Northern Brewer, but we tried others such as Cob.

38

We always had to spray a lot against blight such as greenfly and we often used a powder with nicotine in but sometimes you had to wait hours for the wind to die down enough to blow the powder on. We used a machine with a fan, which was pulled by horses at first and later by a tractor and another problem was sparrows and finches feathering the hops to get the seed'.

For much of Mildred's life the sale of hops was strictly regulated by the Hops Marketing Board, established in 1931. Indeed, as Mildred recalled; 'someone might say – "Give me a pound of hops, I want to make some beer", but you daren't do that as they'd soon shop you."

Hop factors – dual agents of the Board and individual growers – undertook the grading, centralised storage, valuation and marketing of hops. Every pocket of hops was numbered and printed with the grower's name and every one was cut open in the middle and end and sampled by a factor.

The pickers who used to visit Mildred's farm numbered about 100 and included many from the Black Country as well as locals. Mildred remembers them well;

"They came by train to the local station at Newnham Bridge from where we collected them by horse and cart. But during the war there were no trains so we had to send a bus and lorry to the towns where they lived, some about 25 miles away. A woman organised it at their end and we had to give her enough money to give each picker a shilling to bind them to come. We had to clean out the cowsheds for them – sometimes whole families – and this was always known as "The Barracks". Each couple received a pair of white sheets, a blanket and a counterpane and they just bedded down on straw which was also used to stuff their pillow cases. These days those old sheds have been all done up with people living in them and it always makes me laugh to think that if our cows came back they'd know which bedroom to walk into".

On the night the pickers arrived they were given bread and cheese and every week each one was given 1lb of sugar and a quarter of tea. Otherwise they had to buy their own supplies from the local shop. Most of the pickers were fairly well behaved but had to be carefully watched once they started telling tales about each other; the children could also mean trouble.

Pickers used to pinch lots of our fruit to take back home with them; in the later years their cars were lined up on a Sunday, ready to cart the sacks way. As well as damsons, blackcurrants and pears Field Farm had orchards with all sorts of old apple varieties including Knot's Colonel which was the only apple Granny Cooper would put in her mincemeat.

Most of the cider apples were sold under contract to Bulmer's but enough were kept back to make lots of cider and perry for the family; by law they were allowed to sell off about 5½ gallons but most of the drink they made was given away. Mildred kept her father's old measuring stick; the one he used to put in the barrels to tell how much was left. It took the Cooper family years to build up those wonderful old orchards but now they have all but disappeared.

The fruit harvest and drink making fitted in well after hop-picking and before the main ploughing and corn sowing. The pickers liked a drink too, always getting off down the pub, especially on a Saturday night. They'd sing all the way back but that was more to comfort the townies who were afraid of the dark; sometimes they had parties on the farm and on occasions they were entertained by a magic lantern slide lecture given by a Methodist. The day to day health

Red sky at night shepherd's delight. Red sky in the morning shepherd's warning.

39

and welfare of the pickers and their families was generally well cared for and the local nurse would drop by to check up on the children.

Many of the pickers were gypsies; Mildred recalled them with mixed feelings:

"Some of them could be a damn nuisance and we were scared of them when we were kids and always treated them with caution. They'd collect basins of dripping from neighbours and if Dad went out he always told us to give the gypsies a pint of cider if they came round just in case they turned spiteful and set fire to the barn. Often a gypsy family would sit with a pan of food over an open fire but they dare not touch it till the father came back from the pub. Unfortunately he'd generally be half slewed and then kick the food over so nobody had anything".

'We had a couple of good camps here throughout the war; it kept a few of them out the army, but on the whole most of our lot were all right. Regulars like the Lock family had a van but their children slept in a place made of sticks with a sheet over, others slept under the stick shed. If a father or mother died on our farm it was custom for the family to set fire to their van on site.

'Dad always told the gypsies not to come to the house unless they were clean and tidy. Some of them did odd jobs such as pick fruit, pulling Swedes and mucking out the cowsheds. They did swear quite a lot and one lady used to excuse herself by saying "Gaffer – don't you mind if I cuss a bit".

The hop bines were pulled and cut down and the pickers sat on stools and boxes to strip them into the cribs (called "bins" in Kent), sacking containers supported by poles and put together by the local carpenter. The young children used to sit on the ground and fill umbrellas with hops which they tipped into the cribs when full. Sometimes a whole crib would be taken by a family, but others would have partings across for individuals to protect their pickings. At least twice a day – just before dinner (lunch) and in the evening – the busheller ("tally man" elsewhere), generally one of the Cooper brothers, would go round to measure the amount of hops picked. At each measure the hops were carted off in sacks of about eight bushel each, to prevent the cribs overflowing. The amount picked was entered into each picker's account book as well as the busheller's record sheet.

Ideally, the hops were picked green, dried and pressed straightaway to maintain their quality which rapidly deteriorates when they go brown. To facilitate this, drying has to take place round the clock as Mildred describes:

'For many years much of this was done by an old man called George Meredith, who had a big white beard like Father Christmas and was like a grandad to us children. He worked in a square kiln (oast-house in Kent) which had only one door and sometimes he hardly ever came out. The fire was in a raised up iron grate fuelled by anthracite; wood and ordinary coal were too smelly and sparky and would have set the whole place on fire. Wooden steps led up to a closely raftered floor about 10-12 feet above the fire and there the hops were laid out on sheets with rings attached to the wall so that they could be lifted out easily.

They were then put in layers about 2-3 feet deep because a decent weight was needed to keep the heat in, drying took about 10-12 hours and the hops needed to be turned by hand every so often; when electric fans came in they dried much quicker. In the mid- 1950's our farm was the last in the district to get power; we needed a three-phase motor for the hop work and it was expensive to install. We also used to buy bars of sulphur in sacks and put so many pounds in a long-handled frying pan under the fire. This was supposed to bleach the hops and keep them a nice golden colour but it was awful if you were up top as you'd gasp for breath and think you were going to die'.

It was not surprising that the old hop-driers like George Meredith slept so well.

Not only did they work very long hours but also endured the slightly narcotic effect of the hops in confined spaces. Indeed, it is the soporific effect of dried hops as well as their fragrance which has made them popular for stuffing pillows today.

When dry, the hops were set aside to cool for a couple of hours and then a mechanical press was used to pack them tightly into a pocket suspended under the floor with an iron ring to keep the neck open.

In the old days Mildred's father took the pockets to a special hop market at Worcester where bargains would be struck, but later the family dealt through factors and merchants, mostly Percy Henley from Kent. These agents would also visit the farm to inspect the growing hops to get a good idea of what they were buying.

Although hop-growing slowly declined in the late 20th century, lately more productive varieties of English hops have been introduced and recently some growing areas have experienced a revival. In the 1960s lager suddenly became very popular and to make this brewers required continental varieties of hop unlike the old English ones which impart a bitter flavour. However, in more recent years there has been renewed interest in 'real ales' and the number of bitters has increased sharply as smaller breweries have been encouraged into production. This looks good for the future prospects of hop growers and, as a result, there have been substantial new plantings in the delightful, hilly countryside near Mildred's former home at Field Farm.

When Mildred's beloved Field Farm was finally sold and split up in 1974 she had a bungalow built near by. "It broke my heart to leave" she said.

Since then most of her relatives have passed away and only six of the old parishioners at Knighton-on-Teme remained in the hamlet; she clearly missed the days when 'if you went out of a Sunday there'd be two carloads of people waiting when you got back. Everyone helped each other much more then'.

Sustained by her memories, an unusually large collection of old family photographs and a wonderful sense of humour, at the end of her long and productive life, friends say she had a twinkle in her eye when she commented 'I must have been the same age for a long time and I never tasted a drop of beer.'

HOPS

FROM THE HOP TO THE BOTTLE

Much has been written in the story of English hops and history confirms that it all began in the 15th century. Hop brewing was first introduced into England by the weavers of Flanders, who, enticed by the prosperous wool-trade in Britain, sailed across the English Channel, settled in Kent and introduced their brewing techniques to the locals.

However, many years had passed before hops were finally accepted for brewing; beer was effectively outlawed by Henry VIII in preference to ale, a strong, sweet brew of barley flavoured with herbs, spices and tree bark. After the death of his son, Edward VI reversed the laws and passed special legislation permitting the use of hops again and in the 1700s duty was imposed and smuggling of hops became a valuable occupation. It was also around this time that an act was passed requiring hop pockets, the sacks that contain the dried hops, to be printed with the grower's name.

At the start of the 20th century hops were being grown in 53 counties in the UK including Wales and Scotland, producing 72,000 acres of hops and none more so than the Teme Valley, the northerly hop-yards in Europe. Many new varieties came onto the market, including the most celebrated Fuggle and a Hop Marketing Board was set up in London with statuary powers to control and ensure a sheltered, if unrealistic market for hop-growers. Fifty years later it was disbanded by the European Economic Community rules and in recent years, Herefordshire (1000 hectares) Worcestershire (350 hectares) have become the largest hop growing areas in the country.

The Latin name for the hop is 'Humulas lupulas' and it is a tall climbing plant distantly related to cannabis. It is a dioecious plant, which means that the males and females flower on separate bines but it is the females that bear the hop cones, and the perennial plants are produced from cuttings and have a productive life span of up to 20 years. Twiddling the sticks - winding the stems around the strings - commences around April, flowering occurs in July and with the support of string and poles the stems grow to a height of 16 feet with roots down to a depth of 12 feet.

Harvesting takes place in September when the bines, with the important yellowish cones, are cut down to about 3 feet. These contain the lupulin, a tacky, oily substance of very complicated chemistry which provides the aromatic oils needed to balance and flavour the beer. Careful handling is needed during the separation of the tender hop cones from the leaves and stems; they are then dried in a kiln or oast house to the moisture content to about 8-9%. After the drying process, the hops are pressed into hop pockets, a sack approximately six feet long, and stored ready to be delivered to the brewers.

Every year hop-pickers came by any means of transport, into the hop growing areas and it was generally a good natured and social time for all the family. Pickers were accommodated in 'Tin Towns' - clusters of fabricated buildings set around the around the farmhouse and fed by the farmer's wife who also kept large stocks of food on site for pickers' families to buy. Most farmers treated their pickers well and kept them fed, watered, and warm by providing ample fuel for the 'hop devils', the local name for the large, and metal fire braziers. Pay day for the pickers was Saturday, but they were not use to the strong local beer and cider and what started as good natured singing often ended in fisticuffs and the local constable was called on to sort it with no questions asked.

42

Hours sleep - six for a man, seven for a woman, eight for a fool.

Once the harvest was gathered in, pickers and farmers came together for a
final concert, bags were packed and everyone headed home, usually to the West
Midlands. The end of this colourful era came in the 1960s when the invention
of the hop-picking machine was introduced and the advance of mechanisation
was under way.

But back in the old days when the Teme Valley virtually over-flowed with
hop yards, it was all so very different then; what better way to tell it as it was
than through the memories of Miss Mildred Cooper, a pioneering female hop-
grower, from Knight-on-Teme, who, despite spending a long and fruitful life
working in the lush hop fields of Worcestershire, had never allowed beer to pass
her lips. Her story appears earlier in the book.

The pickers came from the Black Country by train usually to Newnham
Bridge and Tenbury and were taken to the various farms, but during the war
there were no trains and they travelled by bus and lorry. They were generally
well looked after by the employers, particularly the children.

Straw shows which way the wind blows.

Hop pickers going to Newnham Bridge station from White House Barracks, Eardiston - 1902

In the hop kiln, a huge fire fuelled by coal in an iron grate was used to dry out the hops were laid out on sheets with rings attached to the wall about 10-12 feet above the fire. Drying took about 10-12 hours and the hops needed to be turned by hand every so often, but when electric fans came in they dried much quicker.

At one time there were 280 acres of hops growing in the Teme Valley divided between six growers, today there are just 50 growers in the entire country.

44

KEEPING THE HOP KILNS BURNING

Looking around the lush green countryside bordering Shropshire and Worcestershire, it's hard to believe that a fifty square mile coal field lies below the surface and for hundreds of years black gold, needed for industrial and domestic use, was mined by local men.

Documented evidence dating back to 1565 confirms that the Worcester Corporation leased the Pensax mine specifically to supply fuel for the city and by the early 17th century working mines were established in every parish in the coal field. The larger ones employed around fifty men who used sophisticated pumping equipment and a wooden railway to move the coal to the River Severn. Over the years there has been little change in the scale and operation of this mining method and the Tudor technology was used in some local coal mines until the 20th century.

Since the 16th century, locally mined coal at Mamble, Bayton, Pensax and Abberley was used for household fuel, brick making, iron smelting and, more importantly hop drying; its high sulphur content was especially good for yellowing and preserving hops. The coming of the railway brought in a more competitive market for coal and the mine owners found themselves up against bigger mining companies, including Clee Hill, for a bigger slice of the fuel market.

The early mines were typically bell-pits where the miners would dig a hole down several feet to the coal seam and then work the coal surrounding the hole until imminent collapse prevented further digging. Remains of these pits can still be seen in the fields around Mamble in the form of a raised spoil heap with a circular hollow in the middle for the tramways which would have taken the coal down to the canal at Southnett. The canal was used from 1794-1859.

Canal use was further encouraged by the opening of the new Leominster and Kington canal favoured by mines owned and operated by the Blount family and their links to the Tenbury and Leominster Canal Company. This didn't auger well for the future of the local, smaller mines.

Farmers, nearly all being hop growers in the district, had through these early times, carted their own coal, (except those near the canal), sending their teams and wagons to collect coal directly from the pit. The old wagoners of the early 1900s told of seeing the miners getting the coal some 20 to 30 feet down in the basin shaped pit and all the coal was brought to the surface by a hand turned windlass. Hop growers were dependant on the local coal for drying hops and, because of the availability, nearly every farm in the area grew hops at one time and hop farmers in the district sent their own teams and wagons to collect supplies directly from the pit.

Hop farmers from the Bromyard area with no local coalmines to depend on always hauled their coal with teams of horses and wagons, travelling over Bromyard Downs, through Sapey, on to Stanford Bridge and Stockton to Pensax pits. The Baiting House Inn at Sapey is said to have got its name from being used regularly by wagoners with their teams of horses who would call in for food for the men and also for the team.

For a farmer living west of Bromyard, sending his wagoner with his team for a load of coal from Pensax would mean starting very early to complete the return journey in a day. It was very important that the wagoner took plenty of cider, not only for his own consumption but for the miners who would load him up quickly if he could promise them a good drink afterwards.

Mamble & Buckets Leasow
Collieries receipt - 1870s

The smoke of a man's own house is better than the fire of another's.

The return journey, fully laden, was long and hard for the horses, especially up the hill from Stanford to Sapey; it would necessitate several stops for the horses to get their wind back. It is said that the farmer would send a boy along with the team; his job was to stop local people stealing coal from the wagon while the team was resting and he would carry a long swishy stick to thrash the hands of any intending thief. No doubt by the time the team had reached the Baiting House, a break for man and beast was very welcome.

The last forty years or so have seen a swift decline in the mining for local coal and it's hard to believe that about ten years ago 500,000 tonnes of top quality domestic coal was taken out of the Titterstone, Bell and Watsall mines on Clee Hill. It was recovered when quarrying for Basalt stone.

Nevertheless, old mine sites leave their mark on the land. Aerial photographs show old pit shafts, and a few artefacts like a tool or two found in the old mining grounds are kept in museums to ensure a place in rural industrial history, an important legacy to the memory of the coal miners who dug deep to keep the hop kilns burning in this delightful corner of England.

Martin Powell helping Philip Spilsbury
with the hops - 2007

Opposite:
Soup Kitchen at Moor Farm, Eardiston

47

Farming

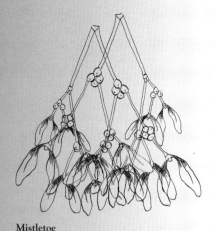

Mistletoe

Inland Post 1/2 pence

THE KISS AND GO PLANT

For hundreds of years holly and mistletoe have been the familiar, seasonal trappings of Christmas, the red and white berries providing the traditional colours seen in decorative garlands and displays across the world. Picked fresh from the apple bough or the hedgerows, they are fertile, living plants that have lasted since time immemorial. But it is for mistletoe that Tenbury is better known.

Mistletoe grows in the Teme Valley almost unnoticed for most of the year, peaking during the late autumn and for hundreds of years the sight of apple and fruit orchards blessed with great balls of mistletoe has added to nature's wonderful, seasonal display. On a clear day, the only plant with a pure white berry and green foliage is painted onto a bright blue sky and it's no small wonder it catches the eye leaving little doubt that this prolific harvest of the magical, mystical English plant is worthy of its place in the agricultural history of Tenbury Wells.

Worshiped over the centuries by the Druids for its healing and aphrodisiac powers it has also been used as a folk remedy for a variety of ailments including blood pressure, heart problems and epilepsy. But beware, taken in large quantities, the waxy white berries are said to be toxic.

Viscum Alba, to give it its Latin name, has a unique and precarious lifestyle and history; Pagans consider it a sacred plant noted for having magical and mystical elements. These days it is more often referred to as a plant of pleasure, cupid's gift to lovers and the 'kiss and go' plant attracting stolen kisses at Christmastide.

Mistletoe is a parasite which happily grows on a host tree, the female plant being the most valuable. It relies on the mistle thrush for propagation, the bird either wiping the sticky glutinous berries on a suitable bough or eating the berry. This passes through the digestive system of the bird and is deposited on a suitable bough where it quickly roots into the sap system of the mother tree taking out most, but not all of its nutrients. It is a semi-parasite and not a full parasite plant which can be grafted onto a tree and can also be grown from seed, but not successfully making the bird the professional planter and man the amateur.

English mistletoe grows well in the Teme Valley and thrives in the warm, wet climate where many deciduous trees, like apple and most types of fruit tree are plentiful; it also grows on some evergreen trees and it has even been seen growing on a holly tree and once on cotoneaster. Unfortunately, these days many of the old orchards in the valley have been ripped out in favour of more profitable crops leaving little room for mistletoe growth.

Interestingly, mistletoe rarely grows on oak trees although it is said it once appeared on a farm local to Tenbury and the oak tree it grew on was rented out for £80.

During the Winter Solstice the mistletoe was cut by druids using gold shears, dropped onto pure white sheets held out by maidens and carried away on ox carts to the music of trumpets and drums. A few years ago this ancient ceremony was re-enacted in the Tenbury area for the BBC 2 Tracks programme.

As well as Worcestershire, mistletoe grows in about five counties in England, nearby Herefordshire and Shropshire, Gloucestershire and Somerset. It has a foothold in some other counties too but does not thrive; it also grows a bit in the northern regions, including Edinburgh. It is the county plant of

Many a slip twixt cup and lip.

neighbouring Herefordshire where it grows very vigorously. However, mistletoe is not a hybrid. There is only one variety which, through the centuries, has remained in its pure, original form to become not only a true plant of pleasure but through its medicinal possibilities, the plant of hope. Mistletoe features strongly in superstition and it is said that for every kiss taken under a bunch of mistletoe, a berry must be removed, but beware, a man should never kiss a girl with the same colour hair as his girlfriend or wife! In times gone by, women wore a bracelet of mistletoe on their wrist to ensure that they had a large family and it was often used to make a love potion. This was considered to be dangerous as mistletoe is also very poisonous.

Legends associated with mistletoe are many, particularly in the Nordic races. It is said that the Nordic God 'Baldar the Beautiful One' was killed by the evil Godone Loki who made a poisoned arrow from a woody stem of mistletoe. His mother Friga took it from him and flung it high into a tall tree and that, they say, is why we now see big bunches growing in very tall trees. Travelling people who collect and bundle up mistletoe for sale at the markets are very professional and to get at the big bundles in the tops of trees they are supposed to take a 'pot shot' with a 12 bore shot gun to bring it down. It was never allowed into churches, only York Minster can display mistletoe, mainly because of its Nordic connections and it hardly ever appears on wood or stone carvings in this country.

Since Victorian times, Tenbury has been the centre for holly and mistletoe sales; these have been held in the town, year in year out and such

A tall order

Picture: CHARLOTTE WINN

Adel Evans, aged seven, offers a kiss under the mistletoe to Pc Chris Pearson at a sale of Christmas trees, holly and mistletoe.

Pc Pearson was on duty at the sale at Tenbury Wells, Hereford and Worcester and Adel travelled from Warrington where her father, Mr Dimond Evans, runs a market garden.

Price trends were set yesterday at Tenbury, the first of the season's big holly and mistletoe sales.

Buyers were bidding keenly for an entry which was smaller than expected. Mistletoe is becoming scarce because cider orchards, where it grows as a parasite, have become unprofitable and are being ploughed up.

Happy Noel!

TENBURY farmer Noel Butcher, found himself under the mistletoe when pretty Sandra Clark welcomed him to the Tenbury holly and mistletoe sale. The annual sale was conducted by auctioneers Russell, Baldwin and Bright where Sandra is employed. See "Holly prices rise" — Page 5. Picture: JOHN PRATT.

Under water famine, under snow bread.

Holly wreaths at the annual market

Auctioning holly and mistletoe

is the quality of Teme Valley mistletoe it is sent to Stonehenge for the winter solstice celebration and used to decorate marquees and halls for winter weddings.

Buyers from top notch department stores in major cities, garden centres and country houses travel to Tenbury for the three days of sales held in late November and early December boosting trade and the local economy, but this almost came to a sad end in 2003.

The former livestock market in Teme Street was eventually sold with little public information on future plans for the traditional holly and mistletoe or indeed, the economic wellbeing of Tenbury Wells and the Teme Valley. Distressed and angered by the decision, the community rallied round to find ways of keeping the sales in town, and a Mistletoes Festival, complete with a first ever Mistletoe Queen was organised. Actress Lorraine Chase, star of long running soap TV 'Emmerdale', based on a farming town community, is a great fan of mistletoe and came to Tenbury to crown the Mistletoe Queen and help raise the profile of the town.

A year later, Jen Green, a founder and principle organiser of the first Tenbury Mistletoe Festival, persuaded Tenbury Member of Parliament, Bill Wiggin, to put down an 'Early Day Motion' in the House of Commons declaring that "The first day of December should always be known as National Mistletoe Day and Tenbury Wells the Town of English Mistletoe". This attracted considerable local and national attention as to the future of the traditional Holly and Mistletoe sales and its place in the town, should they be forced out of the Teme Street market site.

Permission for the sales to remain on the traditional site was granted by new owners Tyrell's Potato Chips, but due to unforeseen circumstances, in 2007 the sales were moved out of town to an excellent site at Little Hereford which, all things considered, proved to be a highly successful venue. The high profile and popular event was featured on television and radio and the holly and mistletoe sales were beamed across this country and abroad and Teme Valley mistletoe continues to go world wide proving that Tenbury Mistletoe is definitely 'a kiss or two above the rest'.

Tenbury's first Mistletoe Queen Chloe Eliding, Town Mayor Maureen Pardoe and queen's attendant Molly Cree - December 2004

What is bred in the bone comes out in the flesh.

BRITAIN'S MISTLETOE AMBASSADOR

Holly and mistletoe may be the familiar trappings of Christmas but the smiling face of popular country man and traditional mistletoe farmer K. Stanley Yapp can tell a story or two when it comes to national and world-wide publicity for Tenbury's romantic plant. What he doesn't know about this magical, mystical plant could be written on a single, creamy white berry.

Stan Yapp is among the last of the traditional mistletoe farmers in the United Kingdom dedicated to avoiding modern farming methods in his apple orchards high up on the Herefordshire/Worcestershire border and he definitely knows his stuff.

One of nature's rural gentlemen, for years he has been a committed, active and supportive member of the Tenbury Agricultural Society, his expert knowledge of the plant dubbing him 'Britain's Mistletoe Ambassador'. Constantly called upon by world-wide media for interviews on radio and television, they seek him here or seek him there, but, when it comes to mistletoe stories and glories, Tenbury's popular Mr. Mistletoe is first port of call. To prove the point, in 2003 Royal Mail chose his mistletoe for the 2003 Christmas postage stamps.

For hundreds of years, the romantic kiss-and-go plant has been recognised as a potent folk remedy for a variety of ailments but taken in large quantities the waxy white berries are said to be toxic.

Stan loves to chat to anyone keen to listen about this much loved plant. "It is a wonderful plant but has had a most precarious existence. Mine still grows in a pure original form passed down through the centuries as a wild British plant. In these times of modern farming, mistletoe is fighting a losing battle but, because I have a great love for it, it's only cranks like me that stick to the old methods."

You can't buy mistletoe seeds to grow in the garden. Its very existence relies entirely on the mistle thrush to propagate it. The bird feeds off the berries and the seeds; these are covered in a sticky substance and later wiped off the bird's bill onto the branches of the host tree where it grows into large clumps.

Stan Yapp at the mistletoe sales with young lamma from Red Barn farm - 2004

You can't catch an old bird with chaff.

51

A HAPPY CHRISTMAS.

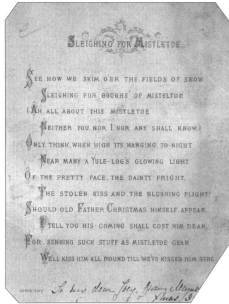

SLEIGHING FOR MISTLETOE.

SEE HOW WE SKIM O'ER THE FIELDS OF SNOW
SLEIGHING FOR BOUGHS OF MISTLETOE
(AH, ALL ABOUT THIS MISTLETOE
NEITHER YOU, NOR I, NOR ANY SHALL KNOW.)
ONLY THINK, WHEN HIGH ITS HANGING TO-NIGHT
NEAR MANY A YULE-LOG'S GLOWING LIGHT
OF THE PRETTY FACE, THE DAINTY FRIGHT,
THE STOLEN KISS AND THE BLUSHING FLIGHT!
SHOULD OLD FATHER CHRISTMAS HIMSELF APPEAR
I TELL YOU HIS COMING SHALL COST HIM DEAR,
FOR SENDING SUCH STUFF AS MISTLETOE GEAR
WE'LL KISS HIM ALL ROUND TILL WE'VE KISSED HIM SERE

"To my dear Ivy" - 1890

Sadly, these days, many old orchards normally associated with the Teme Valley have been ripped out in favour of more profitable crops. But Stan Yapp is a great believer in planting for the future and he has planted four orchards on his land with high hopes that his mistletoe will continue to survive.

Rich green holly grows wild in the countryside and in the garden; the trees and hedgerows and trees bursting with berries the colour of blood in late autumn. Cut down into large bunches it is teamed up with mistletoe and taken to the wholesale market in Tenbury Wells for the annual November and December auctions where Stan has been a regular punter for many years.

"This is the biggest sale of its kind and dates back to well over 100 years. The market employees lay it out in tidy, colourful rows ready to go under the hammer of auctioneer Nick Champion. With buyers and sellers regularly travelling from across the country to our small market town there are many people to catch up with from days gone by and it becomes a bit of a social gathering."

Popularity for the plant is big on the continent and in the USA, but only as a decoration and in cosmetic and pharmaceutical products, but Stan believes its greatest role is yet to come, particularly in the field of medicine. The mistletoe berry contains an element of lectin, believed to be beneficial in the treatment of life-threatening illness. Recent trials in hospitals at home and abroad have shown positive results and it is Stan Yapp's opinion mistletoe is now a plant of hope as well as pleasure.

Two years ago The BBC invited Stan to take part in a Christmas special of 'The Weakest Link' fronted by Anne Robinson. They tested his memory, quizzed him on general knowledge and filmed an interview to see how he would come across on television. The show attracts a big audience but Stan was ready for the challenge.

He recalled "This was a once in a life time moment. I wasn't worried about the questions, or Anne Robinson; it was a 'dog eat dog' situation with the other contestants, the better you were the more others ganged up to vote you off but I was determined to do my best."

In 2003, he put his own stamp on the Christmas post. Encouraged by Stan's world-wide connections, Royal Mail launched a series of Christmas stamps featuring mistletoe from his orchards at Leysters. But it doesn't end there.

If all goes well, his face is destined for the famous National Portrait Gallery in London housing works of art by celebrated artists going back hundreds of years. Last year he was approached by Oxfordshire based artist, Paul Saville, to ask if he could paint his portrait and enter it for the renowned BP portrait award featuring people who have jobs that are dying out. Stan was naturally thrilled to be chosen and should the already short-listed portrait be the winner, Tenbury's Mistletoe Man will sit happily among the faces of the greats.

For a country man who believes 'Always leave the world in the state it was in when you arrived' it pays off in the end.

Opposite:
Portrait of K. Stanley Yapp
by Paul Saville

Young men think old men fools. Old men know young men are.

53

Farming

HEREFORD COW + CALF

SHOWING OFF THE HEREFORDS

The National Show of Hereford Cattle, held each year in conjunction with the Tenbury Agricultural Society's Countryside Show at Tenbury Wells, is firmly established as a major event in the Hereford Breed's summer Show calendar. The Show, which is strictly for the horned strain of cattle, is registered in the Herd Book of Hereford Cattle and is now organised by John Wright, the Secretary of the National Hereford Show Club. The Show is self-financing and with an annual budget of over £6,000 the Club relies very heavily on sponsorship and donations; it is well supported by the Hereford Cattle Society and their marquee close to the judging ring provides all-day catering for members and guests and is a popular meeting place for Hereford breeders, stockmen and other enthusiasts.

The Club also provides a forum for the exchange of ideas and information about the cattle and each year in June a visit to one of the major herds is arranged. Whilst the membership of the Club predominantly comprises breeders, the club is always pleased to welcome anyone, regardless of age, with an interest in horned Herefords, whether or not they breed cattle. A point of clarification is required concerning use of the term 'horned'; this refers to the fact that this strain of cattle, which can be directly traced to the animals registered in the first volume of the Hereford Herd Book published in 1862, all carry the genetic instruction to produce horns. However, it is not common practice these days to keep horns on the cattle and most breeders de-horn them as calves; de-horning of cattle is favoured on grounds of practicality and safety.

The Club exists to support and promote the horned strain of Herefords, principally through staging the National Show at Tenbury but also by visits to prominent herds around the British Isles.

The inaugural Show was held in August 1983 on the former Tenbury Show site at Palmers Meadow and was an unqualified success. The Champion bull, Wabash Superior 111L, was imported from Canada by his exhibitors, Messrs HG Smith & W Milner Ltd. In contrast, the Female Champion Westwood Laura 180th travelled but a few miles with her breeder Mr R.T (Ray) Davies and his son Clive from Westwood Farm at Mamble. The Show was judged by world renowned breeder Walter Romay from Uruguay and this set a distinct trend in the appointment of internally recognised judges each year; the second Show, in August 1984, was recorded as having had the largest entry of Hereford cattle at any Show in the UK that year, and from 1984, it was agreed that it shall be known as the National Hereford Show Club, which would assume responsibility for organising the National Show of Hereford Cattle each year on the Tenbury Show Ground on the edge of town. The current secretary/treasurer is John Wright and he has been organising the National Show since 2002.

Many folk from the Tenbury area will recall Ray Davies, one of the founders of the National Hereford Show. Ray was a long-standing member of the Tenbury Agricultural Society and was largely instrumental in arranging for the National Hereford Show to be held in conjunction with the Tenbury Show, an arrangement which endures to this day.

The show takes place on the first Saturday of August each year and approximately 125 cattle from 35 to 40 exhibitors from across the United Kingdom enter for the competitions. The cattle arrive on the day before the show and are housed in designated standings in two large marquees; facilities are provided for washing and preparing the cattle for competition.

If you want a job done, ask a busy person.

The Hereford Show is claimed to be the biggest one-day showing of any single breed of cattle on the UK summer show calendar; according to gender and date of birth there are sixteen classes for individual animals and four classes for groups, ranging from pairs to groups of five. Prizes, prize cards and rosettes are awarded to 5th place and classes are grouped according to age. After judging the classes, the Judge determines the Champions and Reserve Champions for both males and females in each age section, then the overall Grand Female and Grand Male Champions and finally the overall Supreme Champion and Reserve Supreme Champion. This is followed by a Grand Parade into the main ring where the prize-giving ceremony in the Hereford ring takes place. Some 26 trophies and cups are displayed and presented; two trophies in particular are of significance to Members of the Tenbury Agricultural Society - The Sir Archer Baldwin Cup and the T.E Smart Cup Memorial Cup.

Over the years, there have been some truly outstanding examples among the champions, particularly the contemporary type of the Hereford breed and all aspects of cattle preparation and showing techniques are provided by experienced stockmen and women. Since its beginnings, the National Hereford Cattle Show has always been strongly supported by all of the progressive and well known local breeders of horned Herefords and it shows in the results from all the classes leading to home-bred male and female Grand Champions.

The coming together of the National Hereford Show Club and the Tenbury Agricultural Society Countryside Show has been a positive move forward for both parties and long may it continue to the benefit of both organizations.

Supreme Champion at Tenbury Show.
Sara Band and Emma 37th.
Exhibitors Pam Nuel and
Robert Snelling - 2002

Westwood Target at Tenbury Show.
Bred and exhibited by Clive Davies - 2003

Ray Davies with champion
Hereford at a Christmas show

March winds and April showers bring forth flowers.

FARMING STOCK - BEEF CATTLE

Hereford cattle most likely descended from the early oxen of this area that were used to plough and work the arable land, they were, the most numerous by far in the 1850s. This was a time of change in farming, pastures were being improved and heavier crops of grain and roots were grown and cattle numbers increased. Most of the animals were out wintered, apart from the younger and fattening cattle.

It was usual to plan for the cows to calve in late winter or early spring so that best advantage could be taken for the calf to be strong enough to cope with the milk, helped by the flush of grass in the warmer weather.

Records show that around 1880, some 800-1000 cattle were sold at Tenbury markets, the main sales being the April and October Fairs and a fortnightly sale of around 150 head (fat store) nearly all Herefords but with a few shorthorn and Hereford cross shorthorn as well. This did not change much until the 1930s when Friesian, Ayrshire and Channel Island cows were introduced into the expanding dairy herds. The Hereford was still the main beef bull used through until the late 1950s but with the introduction of A.I. (Bromsgrove Avoncroft and sub centre at Bromyard) some dairy farmers started to use Charolais and later Limousin, Blonde D'Aquataine, Simmental, Belgian Blue and other beef breeds.

With the increase of British Friesians crossed with the Hereford Bull in the 1950s and 1960s, the offspring, black with white face, were an excellent beef animal. At this time at least half the cattle in local markets would have been Hereford Friesian crosses, the heifers of this cross were very popular as single suckled cows all over the country.

In recent years, most single suckler cows were crossed with a continental bull, some for several generations, leaving some superb beef animals, often winners at the primestock shows.

There is a move by some supermarkets to offer a premium for Hereford beef and this is proving quite popular with farmers and the public. Rare breeds such as Longhorn, Highland and others, which in the 1950s came close to extinction, have now gained in numbers and the meat is readily sold at specialist outlets.

Arnold and Thomas Rogers

56

BILL SINNETT - ONE OF THE BEST

Bill Sinnett, probably the best 20th century stockman for cattle, sheep and horses in the Tenbury district, was born near Bromyard and educated at the Grammar School. He then went to work on his father's farm at Edwin Ralph and while working at home he also rented land around the district and claimed he owned enough animals to stock his first farm. In 1940, Bill moved to Weston Farm, Bockleton where he bred Clun Forest sheep and Hereford Cattle (some pedigree) and also kept a flock of Welsh ewes. Crossing the Welsh ewes with a Clun ram he produced an excellent hardy, prolific ewe with plenty of milk which proved to be ideal for crossing with a Suffolk or Down ram.

Besides being very busy with his farming, Bill always found time to take an active part in the local National Farmers Union and Tenbury Young Farmers Club. For many years he was Club President and leader and was always ready to give advice and give talks on livestock, help the Young Farmers at judging practice and holding the club's annual shearing competition at his farm.

Bill's grandfather moved from Pembrokeshire about 1890, bringing his implements and livestock by train to Hardwycke Mill Farm, just north of Bromyard. He delivered milk around the town by pony and float and sold it by measure, pint or half pint, and poured it directly into the housewife's own jug. Grandfather's milk was in such demand that he needed to produce more; maybe it was lack of buildings or acreage that prevented him from keeping more cows but he decided to milk his existing cows three times a day and feed them according to yield. The cows were housed undercover most of the time and led out daily along the road for exercise with a rug over them to keep them warm on cold days.

This practice of increased milk production was at least fifty years before the farm college's did serious research work (* Robert Boutflour around 1950), on this subject and it was soon evident that the genes of his forward looking grandfather had been passed on to his grandson, Bill.

When he was young, Bill's ambition was to breed Clun Forest sheep and Hereford cattle and to grow hops. Although he had improved the cattle and sheep while farming Weston Farm, he achieved his ambition when he bought Stockton Court in the late 1950s and was able to grow hops. After a few years he had improved his Cluns to a very high standard and, with the aid of his son John, he was winning major show awards including Royal Show champions.

However, Herefords were losing their popularity and after taking part in experiments to breed the horns off them he decided to give up breeding. Soon after, despite all the success with the Cluns, it was decided to disperse the flock and go into Suffolks, and apart from advising on the original purchases for the Suffolk flock, Bill left the decisions and breeding policy to John.

By careful selection for breeding, the name of W.H. Sinnett and Sons is among the top flocks in the British Isles and they have won many of the major awards in the show ring and the flock competition on several occassions. With over-production, hops became unprofitable and it was decided to cease growing hops and use the land for grain and potatoes.

By then, the Sinnett goal had been reached; he had achieved his ambition to succcessfully breed the finest Cluns and Herefords and grown hops. But the changing scenes and times of the farming pattern in the Teme Valley have seen them phased out and Bill has long given up the everyday decisions on the farm.

On May 1st 2008 Bill Sinnett celebrated his 98th birthday and, well looked after by his lovely wife Mary, he has lived to a great age.

Professor Robert (Bobby) Boutflour was Principal of the Royal Agricultural College, Cirencester 1931-1958

57

Farming

SHROPSHIRE SHEEP.

FARMING STOCK – SHEEP

Shropshire and Ryeland (Herefordshire) sheep were the two main breeds in the Tenbury district in the 1850s. Both breeds had been noted for their high quality wool for several hundred years, before the import of cotton, which completely changed the clothing industry.

Shropshire and Ryelands (the wool was known as Leominster Ore) were exported to many countries particularly in the newly emerging developed commonwealth. By 1900 the Merino became the recognised wool producing breed of very fine quality. Whereas the value of the fleece of our British breeds would have more than paid the cost of keeping a sheep for the year, gradually in the last 50 years the worth of wool has gone down and down and by 2000 the fleece value hardly covered the cost of shearing.

For both our two local breeds the change of emphasis from being a chiefly wool breed to a dual purpose wool and meat animal brought about changes, mainly in body conformation.

By the 1890s, the Clun Forest and Kerry Hill breeds (both bred from Welsh border stock) were emerging and slowly took the place of the Ryeland and Shropshire. By the mid 1930s they were the main breeding ewe for lamb production on most farms in this area. With the emphasis on meat production, the popularity of the Shropshire as a terminal sire decreased and was taken over by Oxford Down, Hampshire Down and Suffolk rams. The Suffolk ram became the most popular, being bred to mainly Clun and Kerry ewes for fat lamb production.

By the 1960s, the Welsh half-bred ewe (border Leicester ram on a Welsh ewe) with plenty of milk and great mothering ability, became very popular in the Tenbury District and usually crossed with a Suffolk ram, produced superb prime lambs. Although the Welsh half-bred ewe is probably one of the best lamb producers, their popularity waned when scrapie started to appear in unacceptable numbers: this is thought to have been introduced from the border Leicester breed, where, on the Scottish borders, scrapie had been known to exist 300 years ago. In fairness to the Welsh half-bred breeders, great efforts have been made to eliminate this disease and the present day Welsh half-bred ewes can be bought with every confidence.

By the 1980s the Welsh mule (blue faced Leicester ram on a Welsh or Beulah ewe), the north country mule (blue faced Leicester ram on a Swaledale ewe) and a Scottish mule (blue faced Leicester ram on a Scottish black faced ewe) had become equally popular. These three breeds are now the main breeding ewes throughout the country. With hybrid vigour from crossbreeding, they are prolific with good mothering ability and adequate milk to rear two lambs; they are ideal mothers. Put to a Suffolk, Texel or Charolais ram they produce quality lambs. The export of lamb carcasses is very important as one in five lamb carcasses is exported, most going to France, where they particularly favour the compact, slightly lighter lean Texel-cross lamb.

Liver fluke and worms have always been a scourge amongst sheep, but with the draining of boggy land where the fluke snails breed and with the modern anthelmintic drenches, sheep keeping, even at high stocking densities can be practised safely.

Sheep scab (a small parasite in the wool and skin) has been known for generations and old remedies were made up by the local chemist. Since about 1870, dipping has been compulsory from time to time to try and eradicate

February - As the days grow longer the cold grows stronger.

this pest. Some lethal ingredients such as arsenic, D.D.T. aldrin and organo-phosphorous dips have been used. With the properly timed use and care, modern dips are very effective and safe and also serve as a deterrent against flystrike (maggots) and ticks.

Today's shepherd has all the aids and remedies and, if used at the right time, they are very safe and effective for the welfare of the sheep.

In the last 50 years, with the great improvement in the quality of pastures, it has become necessary to vaccinate all sheep, ewes and lambs against clostridial diseases.

Foot rot, difficult to treat in the past, is now reasonably easy to keep under control with timely paring of the feet and putting the flock regularly through a foot bath containing an antibacterial solution.

Mr Barwise 1892 washing sheep at Lowertown Farm, Berrington. Up until about 1950 all were washed about a week before shearing

Set sage in May and it will grow away.

SHEEP DIPPING

The first Tenbury Advertiser we have from 1874 has an advertisement for J. Slade, Chemist, Tenbury who offers for sale – Slades Fly Powder, prevents the fly strike, probably a powder to put in the wool to keep the flies away.

In 1880, liver rot or fluke caused great losses, this was always worse in a wet year when the fluke snails were abundant and was only controlled years later with the advent of a reliable drench and the draining of the very wet land that harboured the snails.

By 1883 Mr. Morris, Chemist, Teme Street, Tenbury was still selling Slades powder and Coopers sheep dip and lending a dipping apparatus to the farmers. This is probably the first dipping operation, not only for fly strike and maggots but for sheep scab which was very widespread at this time. A report in the local paper of a sheep scab outbreak at Luston, Leominster said that out of a flock of 273, 96 were affected.

In 1907, Colonel Wheeler, Newnham Court, a forward thinking agriculturalist, installed probably the first swim bath dip in this district. He not only had his own sheep dipped but made it available to all the local farmers at a cost of a penny a sheep using a Board of Agriculture approved dip. Later Mr. McCoy, Chemist, in Teme Street, Tenbury sold several brands of approved dip and lent a wooden bath big enough to hold one sheep at a time. This operation was very hard work with two men, one either side of the bath, having to lift the sheep in, immerse and soak it for one minute, lift it out and hold it on its back on the draining board for about half a minute before releasing it.

This dipping was so necessary to control maggots and sheep scab and was compulsory; for many years it was overseen by the local policeman who would take his watch out of his waistcoat pocket and check the sheep were kept in for a full minute. For many years all sheep going to store markets had to have a licence to say they had been dipped.

Of dips used to control maggots and scab, Arsenic, D.D.T., Dieldrin and Organo-Phosphorous have been used but most have now been taken off the market for being too dangerous to the operator.

Shearing with hand clippers, Eardiston - 1920

Opposite Top: **Cattle Market Teme Street,** circa 1900

Opposite Bottom: **Nick Champion's** new Greenfield sale site on the Worcester road

Farming

MOVEMENT OF ANIMALS

For hundreds of years animals of all descriptions have been walked to market; sheep and cattle would walk 15 to 20 miles a day comfortably if allowed to browse the grass verges occasionally. There was a time when drovers would walk stock from Wales or Scotland to London markets, arranging resting and grazing for overnight stops. At our local Tenbury market, most of the cattle, sheep and pigs were walked by farmers and their workers. Some sheep and pigs would be taken in carts or light spring drays. A young calf was usually put in a float or cart and the cow would follow closely behind for miles.

The animals would graze the roadside verges as they walked at a speed of about two miles an hour, so anyone living some distance away would have to make an early start to be in time for the 11.00am sale.

The drovers or farm hands would usually be accompanied by a dog who occasionally had to fetch them from a field or if they had taken a wrong turn and as long as the livestock were walked at a leisurely pace, the animals were happy enough despite the occasional hazard like an over-friendly bull grazing in a roadside field who caught the eye of the passing females. It was down to the dog to hurry them past the field; an old dog knew just about every trick on the walk, he had seen it all before and it was up to the herdsman to wave the big stick to make sure the bull did not try to jump out and follow the ladies down the road.

This walking of livestock was easy until the increase in motor vehicles in the 1930s, but the majority were still walked up until the middle 1950s, however with more traffic the last animals walked into Tenbury market in about 1965.

The first livestock lorries in this area were 2-3 ton capacity with high wooden sides and a tarpaulin for a roof in the early 1930s. In 1939 at Tenbury there is a record that 1574 cattle were sold at the April Fair. By the 1940s the stock lorries doubled in size and most had two decks to carry extra sheep and pigs.

By the end of the 20th century large livestock transporters had two decks for cattle and three or four decks for sheep and were capable of carrying up to 500 sheep or 70 cattle with animals lifted on hydraulic platforms to load and unload.

When the numbers of sheep in the Tenbury district increased after the Second World War, the capacity of the Teme Street sale-yard was not enough and special sheep sales were held on the Palmers Meadow where the swimming pool and car park are now located. At their peak in the 1960s and 1970s as many as 12,000 sheep were sold in a day.

Some of the local stock transporters were Wilfred Drew, Billy Morris (Puddleford), Neaths (Pensax), Bill Davies, Bill Faulkner (Brimfield), Don Bristow, Marshal Hill, Harold Drew, Raymond& Charlie Jones (Upper Sapey), Bernard Birch, A.E. Jones and Norman Lloyd both from Ludlow and J. Yarnold & Sons.

By the end of the 20th century most farmers had a four wheel drive vehicle and a stock trailer for transporting their livestock and produce to market.

Fingers were made before forks.

THE DROVERS

For centuries drovers have played a vital part in moving animals and goods from one area to another but it wasn't until medieval times that the status of the drover became more prominent in the farming communities. Cloth-makers from Europe spotted the potential and quality of the English wool trade and as the market grew and wealth increased on the backs of the 'wandering ewes', local market routes, particularly across the Marches of England and Wales, became extended to cope with the longer distances resulting in a network of tracks between villages, towns and cities being opened up across the countryside. Drovers may well have started out as robbers or rustlers, but in Elizabethan times they had to be licensed by three Justices of the Peace and had to be married householders of good character and outstanding skill, not less than thirty years of age.

The custom of droving was something of a mystery to ordinary folk more used to living their lives in small farming settlements but respect for their worth and vocation continued to grow.

In the mid-1800s, stock needed to arrive at the fair or market in prime condition thus the handling of livestock was of critical importance to the farmer and a drover acting in a cruel manner, especially by use of a pointed stick, could be imprisoned.

Drovers carried their own food, which usually consisted of oatmeal, a couple of onions and a rams horn filled with whisky. The oatmeal mixed with water made a porridge more known as 'crowdie' which was a feed for hens and when added to onions and cattle blood produced a type of black pudding. Strangely, it was not unusual to find drovers knitting as they travelled which eventually became a pastime-cum-industry for all the family, male and female alike, which added to the income of the household.

Wayside resting places along the routes became overnight, sheltered accommodation earning names like the Black Bull, the Slaughtered Lamb and the Drovers Rest, later becoming village inns and public houses.

In many cases a horseman would ride ahead of the herd when nearing a settlement and sound a horn to warn the locals to gather up their small herds to avoid them getting mixed up with the visiting sheep and cattle.

Health and Safety of sorts kicked in by Royal Proclamation when outbreaks of foot and mouth, TB, sheep pox and scab and other parasitic diseases had to be recorded; drovers were legally required by law to report to the Church Warden of the parish any sick animals in transit.

Harold Drew cattle lorry. Seen around markets at Tenbury, Ludlow, Craven Arms, Kidderminster, Leominster and Ludlow - 1970

However, there were no laws relating to the risky way of life of the drover or indeed the wellbeing of the drover family because records concerned with the droving scene are very few; people generally considered them to be of no great consequence with little or no writing or reading skills.

Nevertheless they were generally reliable, honest and trusted, often carrying large quantities of cash after sales and were also used to collect taxes, but they earned little for themselves despite being away from home for months on end. They also carried letters for delivery and were the news-gatherers bringing the latest news and gossip to villages and towns.

When the crescent moon is upside down it will catch the rain.

Man with hook thought to be Black Jack the drover

BLACK JACK THE DROVER

"Don't underestimate the drovers of old", warns Francis Gough. She recalled one such local character from the early thirties and tells it as it was.

Drovers moved stock from market to farm long before the stock lorries came on the scene and one such was Black Jack. " *I presume his name was Jack and no doubt the prefix came from his being dirty; dirty and drunk he may have been but he was so reliable. I remembered him from the early thirties when I was small and to me he appeared to be very old – because of his ragged clothes I expect.*

Bromyard market was held on a Friday; my father and two of his neighbours used to attend and as our farm was near Craven Arms, the two venues must have been 27 to 28 miles apart, quite a journey for farmers in those days, not to mention the drover. But following the market at Bromyard on Friday, Black Jack would arrive at dinnertime on Sunday with the precise number of livestock that had been bought, having dropped off stock at the farms of the two neighbours before setting off to Medley Park, where I was born and where Tom Howard from Dean Park farmed before us. I don't remember a dog, but I do remember seeing Black Jack drunk in a ditch – cider no doubt."

My brother tells of a sheep being lost between market and farm and Black Jack arrived the next day with the missing sheep on a sack-truck. Drovers were amazing men – no SAT NAV in those days. Had they not been reliable they would not have been paid!"

Nick Champion selling lambs in front of transporters

Livestock Auction, Teme Street market

65

Farming

Thatched Rick.

CULTIVATING AND PLANTING CEREALS AND ROOT CROPS

Throughout its long history, the Tenbury Agricultural Society has experienced huge changes in the cultivations of the land. Tractors replaced horses, the number of staff required was reduced and the farmyard probably became a 'quieter' place as one man could get on a tractor and drive off after the preparation of his implements. Previously, staff got up early to feed and water the horses to prepare them for their hard day's work and there would be all round chatter and cheerfulness - even if it was only talking to the horses! During both wars, land that had never been ploughed was ploughed up, for example Old Wood Common. Fields had a rotation and often one field was left fallow. The growing corn was cut a little earlier than it is nowadays and the stooks would be left out in the field to ripen and mature before being carted to the barns or ricks. It is said that oat stooks should hear the church bells ring 3 times. It was considered to be quite a skilled craft building either ricks or bays. The heads were always placed inwardly and the middle kept full to tie it all in. Most of the ricks would be thatched against the weather. People would come and follow the binder as it was cutting and have great fun chasing rabbits, or the occasional fox, as they fled from the corn. Rabbits made a good cheap meal during the war years and farm labourers were pleased to have them to add to their other 'perks' of milk, wood and a tied cottage with a pigsty to keep a pig for killing.

During the winter months a contractor would come round with a threshing box, and sometimes a straw tyer or stationary baler to bundle the boltins or bale up the straw; wire was used to tie up the straw on the bale. The introduction of the threshing box must have been a godsend. It was usually driven by a steam engine fuelled by coal and water for the boiler but this was before the tractor became more popular. A considerable amount of labour was needed for threshing and it was custom for neighbours to help each other which made it a friendly and cheerful time. Efficient management of the labour force was vital; the set-up called for two or three men on the bays or ricks using pitchforks to put the sheaves on to the threshing box where two more were waiting to cut the strings on the sheaves before dropping them into the rotary drum. A couple more would put the grain into huge hired Gopsil brown sacks and carry them up the steps or stairs into the granary. The bags were too heavy to lift directly from the floor below so a hand operated sacklift was used to raise the sacks high enough for the man to get them on his shoulders to carry them to the granary.

Two or three more labourers would be managing the baler and stacking the bales up and another would carry the chaff away. The chaff would be mixed with treacle and fed to cattle and horses; the men were usually fed by the farmer's wife, along with plenty of cider.

Many years later, during the 1940s to early 1950s, the Combine Harvester was introduced and the harvesting was carried out in one operation. At first a man rode on the combine filling bags with corn and pushing them down a chute to the cornfield; a couple of men picked them up and loaded the bags on a trailer and transported them to the farm. As time progressed there was only one man, the driver, on the combine. The corn went into a big bin on the combine which in turn sent it straight into a trailer from where it was taken to the farm to be tipped into a suitable store. They say it was a lonely life for the combine operator.

Varieties of cereals have changed and improved over the years giving better yields, vigour and quality; nowadays some varieties change annually and there is

He who shears his sheep before St. Saviours Day loves his wool more than his sheep.

so much choice it's become almost like choosing wallpaper. Some of the old wheat varieties were Bersee, Cappelle, Holdfast, Square Head Master; oat varieties included Maris Quest, Peniarth and barley Maris Otter. With MINTIL (minimal cultivation of the soil) becoming the fashion for the planting of cereals, has the circle completely turned? Many years ago farmers ploughed just 4" deep and 6" wide and scattered the seed directly on the furrows by hand and used a harrow to surface and bury the seed. It is debatable today why it is necessary to turn over such big furrows with heavy tractors to get the same results.

Today, modern agriculture is characterised by the widespread use of tools and machines to cultivate the ground, sow the seeds and harvest the crops. Ploughs, harrows, seed drills and other implements, at one time pulled by oxen or horses, are now tractor driven. Just as the use of machines has vastly increased agricultural output per worker, so the use of scientific methods has transformed crop yield per acre. Three factors have been responsible for this transformation; the greater use of artificial fertilisers, chemical control of pests, diseases and weeds, insecticides, fungicides and herbicides, and the development of improved strains of plants. The 'fiddle' gave a more even spread of the seed than by seed hopper or hand.

It was before the TAS existed in 1701 that an English farmer, Jethro Tull, devised the 'Seed Drill', which carried out drilling and sowing mechanically. This machine put the seeds in straight rows at a more accurate seed rate, and made weeding easier; Tull's wheeled seed-drill was followed by his invention of a horse drawn mechanical hoe; this required someone to ride on the back of the horse drawn seed drill to put it in and out of gear on the headlands. Next came the combine drill which not only planted the corn but placed the fertiliser by the seed; this proved to be very beneficial if the ground was not in very good heart. Nowadays most corn is planted by a combination drill with the drill mounted on the cultivator and the planting is carried out all in one pass. Years ago the use of tramlines was unheard of but today they are a necessity to allow the tractor and sprayer to go through the growing corn to kill off the weeds and protect the corn without trampling it down.

George Watkins outfit - 1993

Crops extract minerals from the soil to aid their growth. In time the soil becomes deficient in the elements required for natural growth, notably potassium, nitrogen and phosphorus. To some extent, crop rotation - the successive planting of different crops in a field - renews these elements and allows the soil to recover; for example, legumes such as peas and beans restore nitrogen in the soil. However, on some modern farms, cereal crops are grown on the same land year after year, and in this case essential elements have to be replaced by fertilisers. Since the amount of natural fertiliser, such as manure, is insufficient for today's needs, artificial fertilisers have to be added. Crop rotation, which first won wide acceptance in Britain in the late 18th century, was developed not only to allow the soil to recover, but also to control pests, diseases and weeds.

Primarily roots, whether mangolds, swedes, turnips and the like, were grown for folding (eating) in the field for stock to graze but when animals became more abundant and it was necessary to house them in winter, a different format took place.

Mangolds and sugar beet were grown in rows on ridges like potatoes and not only did they grow better, but were easier to harvest by hand. They produce many seeds in a cluster from which, when planted, a good many seedlings emerged making it necessary to single and cut out any excess. In the old days, it was quite common to see men and women staggered across a root field 'hoeing'; nowadays the seed is rubbed and graded before planting so that only one plant emerges from one seed. Hand hoeing was carried out to eliminate weeds, but when the 'steerage hoe' was invented this disturbed and cut out the weeds between rows; this has now been replaced by automated crop spraying.

Root crops had their green tops cut off by hand and roots carted away and put in a clamp. Sugar beet was put close to the road ready for collection and once a permit had been issued, it was taken to the sugar beet factory in Kidderminster; in early times it would have travelled by train from Tenbury Railway Station. The other roots were put in to tumps and covered by leaves to protect them from the frosts. Once they had been carted off the field, usually by November 5th, they were piled into one big tump or 'bury' near to the farm buildings and straw, hedge trimmings or fern was placed over them for protection or they were taken to the farm store.

Nowadays sugar beet is planted and harvested six rows at a time and a huge machine harvests the sugar beet which is then transfered to trailers and taken to the farm store.

The sugar beet factory at Kidderminster was closed to allow developing countries access to sugar so local sugar beet had to be transported to Allscott, but the end was soon in sight for the factory and it was finally closed in January 2007. It was no longer economicaly viable to transport the sugar beet all the way to Newark in Nottinghamshire and this meant yet another huge change to the farming pattern in the Teme Valley.

42 tons to the acre at Kyre

Opposite:
Farm Labourers at work C.1900

A bird in the hand is worth two in the bush.

69

The Great Estates

ESTATES

Back in the 1850s nearly all the land in this area (a ten mile radius of Tenbury) was owned by estates, mostly 3 to 5 thousand acres in size and most had been owned by the same family for several hundred years. Some of the landlords were leading agriculturists, breeding pedigree Hereford cattle and Shropshire sheep, often exported to many countries around the world, as well as growing fruit, hops and arable crops. The rest of the estate was let out to tenant farmers, often for several generations. Even if the estate owner did not farm himself he would have been a major employer of labour to serve in his big house and maintain the gardens and grounds, as well as craftsmen of all trades to repair or renew the farm houses and buildings to a high standard.

Besides the everyday work of running his estate, the owner usually served as a magistrate or on the district council as well as serving on committees for the workhouse, hospital, church or hunt, in fact just about everything that concerned the town or district; very important people.

It seems farming in the first half of the 19th century was thriving, most of the farm houses and buildings were modernised and many new hop kilns were built at this time. The value of farms sold in the 1850s and 1860s was high due to farm produce finding a ready market, but farming gradually entered a long depression commencing in the 1870s. Five very wet years at harvest time ruined a lot of farmers, especially on the heavy soils. Liver rot (fluke) decimated the sheep flocks; sheep numbers dropped by 50% between 1874 and 1914.

From 1878 to 1888, the estates had to accept greatly reduced rents (30 to 50% less); to keep their tenants in business (many tenants gave up in this period) the press stated that within a few miles radius of Great Witley, thousands of acres of land was tenantless. To make matters worse for farmers, cheap grain was coming here from America and Australia, and the first frozen meat; in 1884 27,000 tons of meat from America and 5,000 tons from Australia. It was recognised that this increased quantity of imported meat would affect the U.K. farmers' income by lowering the price of meat to the public.

Landowners were hit by the fall in income, due to the reduction in rent and some estates, or portions of, were sold to prosperous businessmen. Some estates had to take over semi-derelict farms because no tenant could be found. The only saleable asset, which helped estates to survive, was large quantities of growing timber (oak, ash and larch), and this went on into the 1930s. Unfortunately, very little of this felled woodland was replanted.

In 1888 Lady Northwick of Burford (whose husband had died a year earlier), instructed the agents of her estates in Shropshire, Worcestershire, Somerset and Middlesex, that her tenants were not to be charged for the next half year's rent and to forego all claims against tenants in arrears. Lady Northwick wished this gift to be regarded by the tenants as a memorial to her late husband.

In the same year it is recorded in Gaut's History of Worcestershire Agriculture that there was general gloom left by the depression and a remarkable decline in arable farming. Again in 1888, Mr. J.J. Jones of Abberley Hall died; his father had been a mill owner from Oldham in Lancashire and had bought several estates in the area some years earlier, namely, Elmley Castle, Abberley Hall, Pensax Court and Astley, in all 8,050 acres extending from Stanford and Stockton to the Severn at Shrawley.

Don't count your chickens before they are hatched.

The local papers carried adverts for years telling where growing timber was for sale on just about every estate; the only saleable asset.

By the start of the 20th century, estates, in part or whole, were put up for sale and this carried on until the start of the First World War.

The war years, with the need for extra food to be grown, helped to restore farming temporarily and after the de-control in 1920, prices rose sharply, by more than 50%. As well as livestock fetching high prices, fruit sold well during the war and extensive plantings were made from 1920 to 1922. As a result prosperity, unequalled for more than a century, was experienced.

A large number of ex-servicemen, unused to the soil but attracted by the bright outlook, acquired land by purchase or renting and settled down to earn their living as farmers, fruit growers or poultry keepers.

The slump began in 1922, with increased costs and lower market prices, agriculture drifted along the downward path, prices falling to below pre-war levels. There was one ray of hope, Parliament withdrew the duty on home produced sugar and in 1925 the sugar beet factory opened at Foley Park, Kidderminster. By the mid 1930s, Parliament set up marketing boards for milk, pigs, bacon, hops and potatoes and brought some stability to farming. In the meantime, most of the estates in this area were partly or wholly sold. The farming recession from the late 1870s, a period of over 50 years, had crippled them financially. A lot of farms were sold to the tenants at rock bottom prices (£10 to £30 per acre, including house and buildings).

COURT OF HILL

The mansion and lands known as Court of Hill, previously owned by Captain A.N.V. Hill Lowe, is an original Jacobean residence approximately 7 miles from Ludlow and 3 miles from Tenbury Wells. This outstanding oak building, complete with oak paneling, handsome carving and a very fine old staircase, was erected by Andrew Hill in 1683 on the Shropshire and Worcestershire border and the family have remained in the parish of Burford since the 14th century.

A reasonably spacious house surrounded by a 350 acres of park, Court of Hill is approached by a winding, graveled carriage drive through an avenue of mature oak and beech trees leading to the front of the south facing house. Its magnificent position, about 650 feet above sea level, offers sweeping, panoramic views over south Shropshire and neighboring counties; a panorama of the countryside unfolds to the south and west. With the Ludlow, North Hereford and Clifton-on-Teme hunts close by, the property comes with excellent hunting ground, good rough shooting and fishing in the near by River Teme. There is also valuable growing timber on the estate.

According to old sales particulars, the house itself has an excellent drawing room, a library with an Adam ceiling and a large, heated conservatory; domestic offices on the ground floor include a butler's pantry, house keeper's room and servants' hall, plus a large, light airy kitchen, scullery larder and dairy. A Jacobean staircase leads to the first floor paneled state bedroom complete with dressing room, two further bedrooms, a nursery and bathroom and, on the second floor, a further good sized bedroom, night nursery and six servants' bedrooms. It is much the same layout today.

The outside courtyard has stabling with saddle and harness rooms, two loose boxes and garaging for three cars. The south facing garden is used for tennis and croquet and there is a walled kitchen garden and an avenue of fine chestnut trees.

A stitch in time saves nine.

The whole estate extends to 349 acres of excellent parkland pasture, orchards, paddock and arable land with forestry, including larch and ash plantations, a home farmhouse, farm buildings, entrance lodge and seven cottages some with gardens and a smallholding.

EASTON COURT ESTATE, LITTLE HEREFORD

Since 1775, some land holdings lying north of the Teme at Little Hereford have been known as The Easton Court Estate. The estate has been owned by only three families or more accurately bloodlines, two of the three related by marriage. First the Collins' who eventually changed their name back to Dansey - their forebears - to ensure their Norman inheritance through the female line and all three families' family lived in Little Hereford and at Bleathwood for an unbroken 700 years. They were followed by the Bailey family, who bought the Estate from the Danseys in 1840, then in 1908, via an intermediary, sold it to Col. Richard Wingfield Cardiff, grandfather of the present owner, Lady (Jennifer) Lloyd. The Colonel was President of The Tenbury Agricultural Show for one year in 1911.

It all began for the estate in the 12th century when the Norman family of Delamere settled at Little Hereford and lived in a fortified house with a moat just north of the present footbridge over the Teme. The family are thought to have built the west end of the church nave in about 1200, although the font appears to be 100 years older. The tower was added a little later, probably financed by the family.

The Delameres received a grant of lands from King Stephen who took his army over the Teme in 1139 on his way to fight his disloyal cousin Princess Matilda, (also known as Maud.) Little Hereford literally means "little ford of the army" and the lands involved in the grant were those forfeited by The Earl of Hereford who by them had become rebellious and joined the Princess. The actual acreage at the time is unknown but the manorial rights attaching to the Easton Court Estate eventually stretched over 3,500 acres and this may provide a clue.

In 1316 a Delamere was made "Lord of the Township of Little Hereford", a township said to have stretched along five miles of the Teme and, if so, was much larger than the present parish and it's fair to conclude that even then the Delameres might have owned more than 3,500 acres.

It would be surprising if Temple Farm, in the tenancy of the Hodges family since 1940, was not within the Delemere's portfolio of lands; the mediaeval farmhouse is mentioned in Doomsday Book and has been part of the Estate for as long as estate records have existed. In the early days the village or township was centred on the Delemere's fortified house and there is known to have been a millrace right round the church with up to seven mills along it, plus a few mill cottages. The vicarage was down there too, beside the church, in the Glebe field which has been tenanted for at least 100 years by the Stevens family.

In the Delamere period the flooding was sometimes so bad that it probably caused the "rood altar" in the Church to be constructed on top of what would, before the Reformation, have been a rood screen to allow the congregation to take communion upstairs, out of the wet. By the beginning of the 16th century the whole village seems to have been dispersed from the Glebe field to higher ground, probably because of flooding.

A rolling stone gathers no moss.

In 1516, Sybel - (the spelling is from her tombstone) the last of the Delameres - married Christopher Dansey, owner of Brinsop Court Estate near Hereford. She was also known as Joanna and after the marriage the couple built Bleathwood Manor. The manorial rights were transferred from the Motte and Bailey building near the Church and they moved into their handsome Tudor house. Recently handsomely restored, it was for a time after Col. Wingfield Cardiff's death, in first the tenancy and then the ownership of Harry Hyde, the father of Nick and Robert Hyde who are still tenants of part of the Easton Court Estate.

Records show that the Danseys owned some 7,500 acres at Brinsop and Little Hereford taken together and did so until the executors of the builder of Easton Court, Richard Dansey, were forced to sell off the Brinsop Estate, following his death in 1813. Some years later, in 1837, the trustees or mortgagees had to sell off the Easton Court Estate as well.

It is easy to speculate that the building of Easton Court had been a bridge too far for Richard Dansey's finances and at the time of writing his will he described how his Easton Court Estate also included land at Huntington, north of Bleathwood and at Ashford Carbonel; it was a considerable property portfolio. Evidence in his will shows that it was not only the long shadow of his debts which had brought Dansey down; he also left money to children of two families in Bleathwood confirming rumours that he may have been "playing away from home". At the time, he had apparently fallen out with the vicar, stipulating in his will that he did not wish to be buried at Little Hereford if the burial was conducted by "the present incumbent" the Rev. Herbert Hill. Perhaps the feeling was mutual as the vicar may have known something of Richard Dansey's domestic habits. As a result he was buried at Brinsop.

Anecdotal evidence speaks of the Baileys having a very large estate based on Easton Court. The mansion itself was enlarged to more than double its Dansey size with the addition of an art gallery and a library and the first occupant to enjoy the refurbished building was Joseph Bailey, the M.P. for Herefordshire in the mid 19th century; his widow, Elizabeth Mary Bailey, continued to live there for some time after his death. During her time there she produced an illustrated manuscript book about Little Hereford with watercolour sketches of many of the houses and cottages in and around Little Hereford and Bleathwood. This is now kept at Glanusk, originally the seat of her son Sir Joseph Bailey Bt, later elevated to the Peerage as Lord Glanusk. Eventually his mother unexpectedly remarried, forfeiting her tenure of Easton Court Bailey and the Court itself was thereafter let to tenants, latterly a Col. Creighton Browne, whose lease expired in 1908 when the sale of the property to the Cardiffs happened.

Towards the end of the Baileys', ownership the estate was again extended and an iron foot bridge, marked Easton Court Estate, was erected across the Ledwyche Brook. Although unmapped, it was placed there in 1895 and lies at the bottom of a field, now owned and farmed by Phil Bedford, to provide a crossing point for the otter hounds, which hunted in the area until after World War Two.

By 1908 some of the Baileys' property had been sold out of the Estate; in particular Easton Farm, now called Easton Court Farm and in the tenancy of the Morgan family. Before then it was in the ownership of a Mr Smith.

In order to facilitate the estate's transfer to the Cardiffs, a solicitor from Worcester and Tenbury, Mr Percy Giles Holder, gradually over several years, parcelled up all the Baileys' past and present holdings - amounting to just over

2,000 acres - into his own name and re-conveyed them piecemeal to Col. Wingfield Cardiff. Most of this was completed by 1914 but some conveyances had to wait until the end of the First World War; one of the last parcels was the shooting rights over Easton Farm. Evidence shows that Col. Wingfield Cardiff took out a very considerable mortgage to purchase the Estate.

After the Colonel's death in 1945 there was clear evidence that death duties meant serious downsizing at Easton. Over several years, the trustees of his eldest son, Brigadier Ereld Cardiff, offered over half the estate for sale and more than 1,000 acres went under the hammer. Properties sold off included Bleathwood Manor and much of its farm, Bleathwood Coppice, Halfway House, Upper House Farm, Middleton Farm, Lower House farm and some of New House Farm, as well as Wood gate Cottage and the Old Rectory Cottages; some of the surrounding land was sold for development in Little Hereford itself.

When Mrs Peggy Cardiff, the Brigadier's widow, died in 1999, inheritance tax raised its head again and four more houses and 5 acres of land had to be sold.

Today, Easton Court Estate survives in the ownership of Lady (Jennifer) Lloyd as a relatively small agricultural estate of under 1,000 acres complete with four farm tenancies, each mentioned in this little history, and four let houses.

By coincidence, Sir Richard Lloyd's great grandfather, Sir Richard Dansey Green-Price, Bt, and Member of Parliament for Radnorshire from 1880 to 85, was the son of Frances Milborough- Dansey, who, at the time of her marriage in 1837, lived at Easton Court. A first cousin of Sir Richard is Norman Dansey Green-Price who lives near Knighton, Powys. Through this connection, the Christian name Dansey is still recognised in the Green-Price family of which Richard's nephew, Sir Robert Green-Price, Bt. is the family head. Today it survives as a surname in New Zealand to where many of the Easton Court Danseys emigrated in the 19th Century.

Many years ago it was customary for family members to be buried in the church vault at Little Hereford but in 1886 flooding and silt prevented this and the vaults were filled in. Monuments commemorating the Delamere, Dansey and Bailey families are a proud feature in Little Hereford Church.

GODSON ESTATE

The Court House Tenbury was demolished in the 1960s and it is believed to have come from a vicar of Burford bought by the Godson family with surrounding lands when he died. They also had a large number of farms, accommodation lands and urban property in the Tenbury area as well as land in Kidderminster and London with several large houses. The late Mr G. Godson resided in later years at the Court at Tenbury, always being in town for the local Tenbury Show. He always had the Union Jack flag put up on the roof of the Court on show day and he wore a rose picked out of the Court garden to the show. He used to attend the cattle sales in Tenbury Market and local fruit shows. He was chairman of the magistrates for many years.

The estate farms stretched along the Kyre Valley and Kyrewood, and also in to the parishes of Leysters and Middleton-on-the-Hill and Pudleston in Herefordshire. There were farms at Pencombe and a lot around Kidderminster and up the Severn Valley. Mr G. Godson owned several pubs, a house in London and another in Worthing.

When Mr G. Godson died in 1962 some of his estate was sold straightaway and the rest a few years later. He left many bequests including money to buy

You can't make an omelette without breaking eggs.

hunting gates to three local hunts and a donation to Shrewsbury Horticultural Society to build a summer house at The Quarry, Shrewsbury which became the home of the famous flower show.

GREETE

The Greete Estate lies about 3 miles from Tenbury Wells and is sited on land considered to be the most productive and fertile soil in the valley. The estate was once noted for having delivered the largest amount of agricultural produce ever transported by rail from Tenbury Wells - or any other town in the area. On many occasions the estate's tenant farmers have won prizes for being the best farms in the district, having excellent farm house accommodation and a wide range of farm buildings with good, quiet roads for access. Because the estate was intersected by two good trout streams, fishing was a popular sport along with good mixed shooting and hunting with the Ludlow and South Shropshire Hunts.

The entire site, 6 capital farms, 4 small holdings, cottages and enclosures of land or accommodation land, was sold, complete with sporting rights, on behalf of Miss Hope-Edwards, at the Royal Oak Hotel, Tenbury Wells, on Tuesday August 26th 1919.

LORD NORTHWICK'S BURFORD ESTATE

The once very extensive and prestigious Burford Estate, which also included the Manor of Oakwood, was once owned by Lord Northwick. It also included a number of farms within the Burford area, the 462 acre Dean Park, 132 acres at Dean Lodge, Harpfields and Whatmore Court, Nash.

The Northwick/ Rushout family home was Northwick Park, a splendid mansion at Blockley, on the eastern outskirts of Worcestershire but almost entirely detached from the county. Records in Noake's Worcestershire confirm that it was surrounded by the counties of Warwickshire and Gloucestershire and more aligned with the Cotswold towns of Chipping Campden and Morton-in-Marsh; the estate also enjoyed town houses in Cheltenham and possibly London. A generous man, in 1860, Lord Northwick presented an organ to Blockley church.

But it is Northwick's connection with Burford and the Tenbury Agricultural Society that is of most interest. He provided the first permanent site for the show at Castle Tump, opposite Castle Mead for the annual show before which, for about forty years, had been travelling event with ploughing matches in the Teme and Kyre valleys.

Following his marriage to Miss Bateman from nearby Shobdon Court, just over the border in Herefordshire, Lord Northwick and his wife returned to Burford by carriage to attend a celebratory ox roast held in their honour in Castle Tump. In a personal address to all the people in Tenbury and Burford he announced that from then on he would devote a greater proportion of his time to improving the area. He also warned them on the dangers of over-doing the cider.

After his death in 1887 the estate was greatly reduced in size and in his memory the tenantry presented a lych-gate to Burford Church; with his passing the estate was inherited by his cousin Sir Charles Rushout who reduced the Burford estate even further after the Great War. When Rushout died in 1931, Whatmore Court was sold and the estate passed to the Honorable Mrs Francis Whitbread, daughter of the then Lord Studley, and in 1952 she finally sold

Don't put all your eggs in one basket.

Burford House to the Treasure family bringing the final curtain down on Lord Northwick's splendid estate.

During his lifetime Lord Northwick played a major part in the social development and well-being of Burford and Tenbury Wells. In 1864, backed and supported by local solicitor William Norris, Secretary of the Tenbury Show, he became a driving force in bringing the railway into Tenbury Wells via Wooferton and later extending it through Teme Valley. This came about through the purchase of the defunct and bankrupt old canal route and using it by laying a railway track through Newnham Bridge and into Kidderminster. At the time Lord Northwick was Chairman of the Oxford, Worcester and Wolverhampton Railway Company; this gave him the knowledge and experience needed to provide a rail for Tenbury.

Seven years after his death his widow, Lady Northwick, introduced a pension scheme for all staff over 65 years old. It amounted to six shillings per week for 40 years' service, five shillings for 30 years and four shillings for 20 years. She also granted a pension of 12 shillings a week plus a rent free house and garden to Mr E. Heath, Night Watchman at Burford House for the past 28 years. It is the first recording of a pension in the Tenbury district.

Today the house remains in the Treasure family and Oxford based Burford Garden Company own the on-site Garden Centre.

NEWNHAM COURT

Newnham Court was a very extensive estate of farms and properties, stretching through the centre of the Teme Valley to Tenbury and on to St. Michaels and Berrington. Over the years some of the farms were sold off, particularly on the borders of the estate such as Mamble, but most of the farms bordering the River Teme were retained until quite recently by Mrs Batley, the daughter of Col. Wheeler. Her father had owned the estate and for many years farmed Newnham Court Farm until he retired in 1931.

The Wheeler family had been leading agriculturalists specialising in hops and fruit growing and they also bred Hereford cattle and Shropshire sheep (many of them exported to the Americas and Commonwealth countries); for most of his life he was a leading figure in the Tenbury Agricultural Society.

Col. Wheeler also owned Palmers Meadow, previously used as the Tenbury show ground until it moved back to Burford. This decision was taken to try and accommodate the ever increasing number of motor cars and lorries stemming from the bigger event incorporating not only the national Hereford show but much more livestock. However the Newnham Estate's many hop yards and orchards once a wonderful feature of the Teme Valley are now sadly depleted. In the hey-days of the hop picking season, it was a grand sight to see and hear great numbers of pickers descending on the Teme Valley in special trains. They were usually housed in farm buildings or special barracks for the entire season, many staying on to pick the vast quantities of fruit grown on the estate. When the picking season was over, special trains returned to take them home to various parts of the West Midlands. Milk from the estate's farms was also delivered to the railway station for transportation by train to the industrial Midlands and later replaced by the lorries which collected the milk churns from farm gates.

Newnham Court Farm is now owned by Lupo Fresh – a German firm who grow and market 170 acres of their own hops making the company the biggest growers in the area and the second biggest in the UK.

A watched pot never boils.

THE STANFORD ESTATE

The Stanford Estate still exists today and although much depleted it had been owned by the Winnington family for several generations. The Winningtons date back many centuries and prior, to World War Two, the family owned over 5,000 acres which included most of the village of Clifton-on-Teme, the Shelsleys and several farms near Broadway in Worcestershire. However, since then there has been a steady reduction in the acreage of the estate but it continues to retain a number of farms and a substantial amount of excellent woodlands ideal for sporting shoots.

The church holds the graves of the Winnington family

Since 1904 the estate has been the meeting place for the Shelsley Walsh Hill climb, the oldest motor sport venue in the world. It is still held on its original course and is considered by the sport as the Monaco of hill climbs and enthusiasts have streamed into the area throughout the years. Motor sport icons Sir Malcolm Campbell, Stirling Moss, Peter Collins and John Surtees are among a long list of world champions who have appeared at Shelsley.

After the death of his uncle, the Baronetcy was passed to Sir Edward Winnington and the family has connections through marriage to the Spencer-Churchills and some members of the family are buried at Stanford Church.

THE KYRE ESTATE

The Pytts family bought the Kyre estate in the 16th Century in a rundown state. They renovated the house and parkland, all the bricks were made on the estate, and timber, mainly oak, cut from the woodland and only best facing stone was obtained elsewhere. In 1586 the great pool, 20 acres surface area, was created; this was within the deer park, at that time extending to 500 acres. Later the deer park was reduced in size to 200 acres, with about 150 fallow deer, the fencing was of cleaved oak palings on a post and rail frame. Part of this fence was still in place up to the start of the Second World War, when the park was ploughed and cropped.

Perhaps, because of the general conditions, the needs of the poor and the responsibility of the parish began to be addressed. The 1601 Act said that each parish was to look after its own poor, levy a rate to provide cottages for pauper widows, set the able poor to work and provide apprenticeships for children. Kyre complied and built 8 cottages for pauper widows. The Almshouses, known as Pytts Cottages, still exist as low rent accommodation. There are now five houses and they can be used by couples.

By 1651, agricultural labourers' wages were one shilling a day and stayed at this level until the end of the 18th century.

The Kyre estate was gradually enlarged by several generations of the Pytts family, and at one time was around 5,000 acres bordered by the Wolferlow, Bockleton, Hanley William, Saltmarsh Castle and Bredenbury estates.

In 1767, Kyre common, within the estate, was settled illegally by some of the locals also looking to have places of their own and they had to pay an annual fine or knock the house down. Today there are just 3 cottages remaining of the original 14 that were built.

During the late 18th century there was much agricultural improvement on the estate, as drainage of the land and crop rotation was practiced which provided extra winter feed for cattle. By the 1850s there was over a thousand acres of orchards on the estate as well as hops and corn. The oak trees in the

Two wrongs don't make a right.

77

woodlands were in great demand for their exceptional height and girth, said to be as good or better than anywhere in England.

The Pytts family were related to the Childe family who owned the Kinlet estate and in time one of the Childes inherited the Kyre estate. The last owners of the Kyre estate were the Rev. E.G. Baldwyn-Childe and his wife; before inheriting the estate he had been vicar of Kinlet and Cleobury Mortimer. When they moved to Kyre House in 1880, extensive renovations were carried out and they also brought some of their servants and families with them. The Rev. Baldwyn-Childe became Rector of Kyre and he also farmed the Grove Farm, with a bailiff in charge, who lived in the farmhouse. When he gave up farming in 1891, he sold a herd of 135 pedigree Hereford cattle. He died in 1898 and the estate was carried on by his wife, who had farmed the Perry Farm for some years, with a bailiff in charge, breeding Hereford cattle and Shropshire sheep. She gave up farming in 1904, no doubt due to her many commitments on the estate and serving as church warden, school governor, guardian of the Tenbury workhouse and many others.

Her nephew and heir, an army officer, was killed in 1915 in the First World War and in 1917 about half the estate was sold off. Mrs Baldwyn-Childe, a much respected person, who managed her estate well and served the local community in many ways, died in 1930 aged 97 and was still church warden. She left £111,000 in her will.

She left her estate to her great nephew, who within a few weeks of her death, started to sell off the contents of Kyre House. The silver and more valuable paintings were taken to the London Auction Sales.

In July 1930, a five day sale of fine old English furniture, with important pieces from 16th, 17th and 18th century, including Elizabethan tables, Jacobean chests and chairs, arquebuse, crossbows, a pair of Cromwellian stirrups, choice sets of Hepplewhite, Chippendale and Adam chairs, grandfather and bracket clocks, Adam mirrors, a Sheraton toilet table, Pembroke and sofa tables, chests of drawers, Turkish and Indian carpets, embroidery and linen.

The contents of 25 bedrooms, were sold along with Hepplewhite and Georgian poster beds, Sheffield plate and old English pewter, choice selection of original drawings and paintings by, or attributed to, old Italian and other Masters – this being the whole of the "Kyre Park Collection" formed by Jonathan Pytts Esq. who died in 1781, and some of the items made over 1,000 guineas and went to museums and private collectors.

Kyre House and the estate of about 2,000 acres was sold privately, reputed to be for £60,000 to George Heath, a garage owner from Birmingham. He stripped the house of anything saleable, such as fireplaces, stairs, oak panelling and the drive gates. All this was sold in 1931 with quite a few items bought to go to America.

George Heath called another sale in 1935 to sell any remaining furniture, garden ornaments and the contents of the estate yard. In 1936 he put up for sale the agricultural property, 15 farms, smallholdings, cottages and land, in all 1,962 acres. Some lots were sold at the auction but it took another two years to sell all the property. Farms made from £10 to £30 per acre including the house, and buildings and cottages £70 to £150. Kyre House and grounds was sold and was briefly used as a mink farm, the feral mink are still in the area. It was then bought by the Earl of Clarendon who aimed to restore it but war intervened and it was used as a convalescent hospital for servicemen from 1940.

After the war the house and grounds were sold to the City of Birmingham for use as a children's T.B. Sanatorium. The hospital took 70 children with most of its staff being recruited locally, and trained staff were sent from Yardley Green Hospital in Birmingham. Treatment for tuberculosis at that time consisted of fresh air, good food and plenty of sunlight. In 1961 the hospital was closed as the development of T.B. drugs treatment meant that the hospital was no longer required. The building was then purchased by the then Spastics Society and made into a home for adults suffering from cerebral palsy and used until 1988. Since that time the house has reverted to private occupation.

THE RISE AND FALL OF THE GREAT ESTATES

Throughout the centuries, farm lettings were a natural, productive and friendly way of life for rural communities and when an estate let out a farm to a new tenant, usually at the death of the former tenant, many of the neighboring farmers would rally round and help the new tenant settle in and set him up in the first year of renting. They would group together and send in a team of horses and implements needed to plant the first crop on the new tenant's land, lend him the things he needed to get started and help him get his first rent together. Families would also leave pieces of furniture and bedding at the farm house door. Furniture usually let with the farm would perhaps be a grandfather clock, polished table and a babies cradle! When he eventually gave up the farm tenancy, the cradle was expected to stay as part of the farm chattles.

Rent agreements often insisted on the way certain fields were to be used and designated, for example, kept as arable with a patch of roots, usually swedes or mangolds, grown to keep the game for the annual shoots held and arranged by the landlords who also ensured that shoot beaters had proper coats, in some cases white with red collars and cuffs. Special staff looked after the gun dogs, loaders and the people to carry the prized pheasants, snipe or woodcock. The final shoot always finished shooting about 3.30pm.

It is thought that the decline of the estates in and around Tenbury and Burford set in about 1880. Many had a very large staff to maintain the big house plus a full compliment of gardeners, builders, and carpenters to maintain the farm buildings, estate cottages and grounds as well as gamekeepers and farm laborers. However, many never returned from the battlefields of France, either killed or severely injured, and this, coupled with the changing world order, led to depression across the land resulting in the breakup and sale of the farms to tenants. Death duties on estates when owners died also brought problems as did the new challenges facing agriculture, particularly when children who had previously attended village and town schools moved away to take up jobs. Soldiers who had fought in the war were given a free passage to most places in the British Empire, as were groups of suitable children.

Twenty-one years on Britain was plunged into the Second World War which had further, disastrous repercussions for the estates and there was no stopping the sad and slow decline of the great estates.

Like two peas in a pod.

World Wars

THE LOST GENERATION

When the 'call to arms' came in 1914 for men to fight in the Great War, the men and boys of Tenbury Wells and the surrounding villages willingly signed up for the King's shilling. They needed little persuading from recruiting officers; it was their duty and they queued up to exchange working clothes for khaki uniforms and farm implements and tools for rifles and gas masks. Escorted by regimental officers and military bands they marched off with a wave and smile to God knows where. Most ended up on the battlefields of France up to their eyes in the mud, barbed wire and filth of trench warfare waiting to be gassed, shot or blown away, without a hope in hell of a "promised land fit for heroes". Today they lie in the peacefulness of the war cemeteries in France and Belgium, their young lives so suddenly brought to an end.

Like many other towns and villages across the United Kingdom, Tenbury and the Teme Valley has its share of war memorials highlighting those who gave their lives for their country. Many 'old comrades' have faded away with time but memories still linger, some recorded in the annals of Tenbury history.

In the Teme Valley the recruiting of local men effectively reduced farm labour and, as well as manpower, horses were also recruited to drive the gun carriages, field ambulances and food wagons. Although some people in authority took the danger of invasion seriously, it wasn't until enemy airships, U-boats and bombers were brought into the action that the realisation of an invasion dawned on the powers that be. Nevertheless it was still some time before central government initiated home defence plans on what to do if the Germans landed. Every town and village in the UK was ordered to keep watch and look out for spies.

Tenbury rightly took the situation seriously enough for the Tenbury Advertiser to carry the following Special Notice;

Opposite:
Recruiting begins in Tenbury Wells

"IN CASE OF A ZEPPLIN AIR RAID."

The authorities wish to announce that in case of an air raid the warning will be the fire gong through the streets of the town. When this warning is received it is imperative that all the light be immediately extinguished and that the public remain indoors - taking the best care they can". A test was held but not everyone heard it and there is no record of a spy being caught or a Zeppelin spotted in the skies above the Teme Valley.

It was a desperate war fought on land, sea and in the air and for rural communities it was also fought in the fields and food growing areas, and forests; it was the war to change everything. So much so that the Government was eventually forced to agree that 'women could work as well and as responsibly as men' and they went off to work on the land and in the factories.

By the end of hostilities in 1918, 750,000 servicemen had been killed, most of them young men between 18 and 25 years old; hundreds of thousands more were injured and maimed. Their deaths were great tragedies for so many families. Children grew up without fathers, widows grew old alone and young unmarried women went childless. A lost generation with so many talents and skills forever remembered in a two minutes of silence on Armistice Day. Not many of their old comrades are left, but 'we will remember them.'

Maureen Kendrick with her photo of John Wall

SHOT AT DAWN

When men from Tenbury responded to the call to arms in 1914, they were expected to do their duty for King and Country and fight to the death even when facing mortal danger. They were also warned that the execution of troops for desertion was as much a deterrent as punishment and it was also made clear by the British and Commonwealth Army that they could not carry cowards and traitors; those making a run for freedom could expect to be shot for bringing shame on their country.

Commemorated on a plaque in Bockleton Church, John Thomas Wall, son of Harriet and William Wall, is one of five villagers who died on active service in the Great War. What it doesn't say is that at the age of 22 he was taken out, blindfolded, tied to a stake and shot by his own side. More than 300 British soldiers met the same end.

The tragic story unfolded when John Wall, Jack to his friends, joined the army in 1912 and served as a Lance Corporal with the 3rd Battalion The Worcestershire Regiment, earning his Sergeant's stripes after three years exemplary service on the Western Front. He was Second Sergeant with Six Platoon when he was ordered to advance at Bellewaerde, Ypres, on August 10th 1917. What appeared to happen next is debatable. According to his court marshal, the young soldier, instead of moving forward some 700 metres to join up with his battalion, chose to take cover in a dugout with two junior men. In his defence he explained that the ground was fully exposed to the enemy and under constant artillery attack and any attempt to move up would be suicide for his men. His Company Sergeant Major agreed with him but insisted that Wall should have at least attempted to go forward and he was found guilty of desertion and sentenced to be shot at dawn for cowardice.

When his cousin Maureen Kendrick, maiden name Wall, from Dark Orchard in Tenbury Wells, first heard the details a few years ago, she said "I could not make it out".

John was her father's 'never spoken about' first cousin and she was shocked when she was finally told that John was shot for cowardice so she set about finding out if there had been a miscarriage of justice. After all, she had been led to believe he was shell shocked and caught heading for home in a boat, but after visiting military museums, the public record offices and chasing reluctant relatives for more information, doubt crept in.

Brought up and schooled in the rural environment of the Teme Valley, it was clear from his service record that Sgt. Wall was a serious young man, exemplary, disciplined and with a very good character, but having thoroughly investigated the circumstances of his court martial and subsequent execution Maureen Kendrick was left with a disturbing feeling that a miscarriage of justice had taken place. Records show that it was usual for the sentence to be carried out by a firing squad from another battalion but in John Wall's case he was shot by men drawn from his own company. This was confirmed in a written entry found in the pocket book of a comrade in the trenches stating "Sgt. Wall 'B' Company shot by order FGMC for cowardice in the face of the enemy" and in 2003 she helped launch a campaign for a pardon for him and any other soldiers treated in the same way.

In her determination to push the issue forward her attention was drawn to Private Peaceful, a book by author and children's Laureate Michael Morpurgo which he had set in the battlefields of Belgium during the First World War. It

Lightening never strikes twice in the same place.

tells the story of how a young soldier and his friend, born and brought up in the rural countryside, became caught up in the shambles of an appalling and horrific war and were eventually executed for cowardice in 1917. Michael Morpurgo had found the name Private Peaceful on a grave of an unknown soldier buried at Bedford cemetery near Ypres and in an interview with the Tenbury Advertiser in November 2003 he agreed that John Wall was behind his inspiration for his book.

For Maureen Kendrick came the hope that Private Peaceful could help the campaign for her cousin and the other 300 or so soldiers executed for cowardice or striking an officer to get the pardon they deserve. Many of them were just boys, shell shocked by the carnage in the trenches; today it would be referred to as Post Traumatic Stress Syndrome.

Maureen and other members of her family pressed on with clearing their cousin's name. Success came when government legislation introduced in August 2006 cleared the name of the boy from Bockleton, along with the other British soldiers shot at dawn, and he was officially pardoned. Despite all her efforts, Maureen Kendrick thought it might never happen but thankfully it did. For ninety years her cousin had been legally branded a coward and a traitor; now he can rest in peace.

John Thomas Wall

an Entry in the Army War Records of Deaths 1914–1921		CERTIFIED COPY OF		AN ENTRY OF DEATH				
						Application Number	$\ell_2 \mathcal{R}$ Y 2902	

Registration of Births, Deaths and Marriages (Special Provisions) Act 1957

Return of Warrant Officers, Non-Commissioned Officers and Men of the Worcestershire Regiment
Killed in Action or who have died whilst on Service Abroad in the War of 1914 – 1921

Rgtl. No	Rank	Name in Full (Surname First)	Age	Country of Birth	Date of Death	Place of Death	Cause of Death
13216	Private (3)	WALL Jack	23	England	6.9.17	France	Shot for desertion

An Entry relating to the death of Jack Wall

THE FOUR LEGGED HEROES

When the war broke out in Western Europe in August 1914, the men and boys of Tenbury Wells willingly answered the call to arms, but so did the horse owners. Ten million fighting men were killed during Word War One, almost 800,000 were British; less known is the fact that around a million horses were sent to battlefields in France but only 62,000 returned. While generals regularly listed the loss of men, guns and ammunition, few cared less about the brave animals killed, maimed or left to starve without so much as a kindly bullet to put them out of their misery.

In the past senior military personnel believed in the supremacy of the cavalry attack and after defeating the French at Waterloo, Wellington cared enough to make sure the surviving horses were cared for. Not so in the Great War. Horses, particularly from the rural and farming communities, just like soldiers, were conscripted and shipped to France and Belgium where they faced unimaginable sufferings on the Western Front. As well as cavalry charges, horses, donkeys and mules dragged gun carriages, ambulances and food wagons under fire, but it was the out of date cavalry charge that did for most of them.

It was generally agreed by the War Office that trench warfare made such charges not only impractical but impossible and despite official warnings some did take place. In spring 1918, the British army launched a final cavalry charge. Out of 150 horses used in the charge only 4 survived, the rest were cut down by German machine gun fire, gassed or ripped to pieces on the barbed wire.

Horses were still needed on the battlefield, predominately as a way of transporting materials to the front line. Mechanised military vehicles were relatively new and prone to problems and it was agreed that horses and mules, were more reliable compared to a lorry, and needed very little upkeep. Many of the cavalry officers were less than sympathetic to the plight of their four legged friends and some even believed that keeping them was a hindrance rather than a necessity on the battlefield. They needed to be regularly fed and watered and

Horses used to pull gun carriages - 1914

84

the British Army was having to ship around one million tonnes of fodder across the English Channel, causing the generals to complain that ammunition was more important than feeding the horses. Nevertheless supplies were not enough and when the fodder ran out many were left to die. British farmers were brought in to advise on feeding the animals. They needed to be fed three times a day, never before heavy work and given water when needed; unfortunately due to the inexperienced riders instructions went unheeded. The horses were often overloaded causing saddle sores, their mounts were generally inconsiderate and careless.

Between 1916 and the Armistice in November 1918, the death toll on horses on the Somme battlefield was over 58,000 killed and 77,500 wounded by gunfire, poison gas, and aerial bombs. The carnage was so great that British farmers and stable owners could not keep up with demand; horses were still needed at home to work the farms and as transport, so more were shipped across the Atlantic from the USA and Canada and others were transported from Australia. At the end of the war very few horses were ever returned to their owners, many of them ending up on French dinner plates.

The same scenario could have happened again in World War Two but thankfully mechanisation intervened and tanks, landing craft and armoured vehicles came into their own.

In 1945 Brooke Animal Hospital, a charity, was set up to protect horses from life's cruelties; today it remains the British tribute to the brave animals who gave their lives for their country.

Mustering the horses before taking them to the station - 1914

85

PEACE IN OUR TIME

The gap between the Great War and World War Two lasted two decades. In autumn 1938, the last year of the peace, the British Prime Minister, Neville Chamberlain went on a 'Peace in Our Time' mission to Munich and returned with a document signed by the German Chancellor Adolf Hitler. It had been a wasted journey; the so called peace agreement wasn't worth the paper it was written on. Meanwhile, back in Tenbury Wells the chat was of unrest in Europe but life went on as usual or did it? While all appeared normal, behind the rural scene preparations for war were in hand.

Air Raid Warden chief, Mr. K. Briggs, was already finalising plans for turning part of the council officers into the Air Raid Precaution base, thirty women had volunteered for duties and safety trenches were on schedule for Palmers Meadow and along the Bromyard Road. War finally broke out on September 3rd 1939 and on the following day the evacuees, mainly children, began to arrive. They were met by Leonard Ashley the Evacuation Officer and Reverend J.A. Chesterton the Billeting Officer and taken to the parishes by bus. Seeing all the children with gas masks hanging round their necks affected the community; they had come from Birmingham and looked so sad and lost. Entire schools came together and the parish hall had to be divided up into classrooms to cope with them all. The vicarage garden made a delightful playground and the city children were amused at having to grow vegetables on the allotments at the back of Pembroke Mead.

With the war came school dinners and a canteen, managed by Miss Brotheridge, was built along the Bromyard Road; as well as supplying the schools in the town, meals were also distributed to schools across the Teme Valley. At the same time many factories were transferred to Tenbury including Richard Lloyd, detonator manufacturers Strong's, Bedford Dials, Spencer's and Earls Plastics.

Most of the farming communities had already volunteered for the armed forces and others were conscripted so the Land Army girls arrived to take over the work on the farms. It soon became clear that the British system of farming in 1939 would not do for wartime. County War Agricultural Committees were set up across the country to co-ordinate and monitor the farming industry. This was necessary because of the problems stemming from the inter war depression and the build up to World War Two. An emergency food programme came into force which required greater communication between the farming communities and central government. The county committees became the channel for enforcing war time farming policies at local level and the go-betweens for the distribution and use of farm machinery, allocating land use for crops etc. and co-ordinating POW labour.

Ration books were handed out for just about everything, including petrol. Every person had them and when it came to food, free range rabbits and home grown vegetables helped stretch the family budget. Clothing was something else; sixty clothing coupons per person had to last for over a year and didn't go very far. Regardless of need or fashion, a pair of shoes took five coupons but a good needle woman could run up a nice little number for the saturday night dance. National Identity cards were issued and in 1942 the Pump Rooms became a gas cleansing station - just in case!

Homes and businesses blacked out windows with lined curtains after dark and all vehicles, including cycles, were required to have dim lighting which caused a

Look after the pennies and the pounds will take care of themselves.

COUNTY OF............HEREFORD............WAR AGRICULTURAL EXECUTIVE COMMITTEE

DEFENCE REGULATIONS, 1939.

THE CULTIVATION OF LANDS ORDERS, 1939.

To   T. G. Hodges Esq.   of Temple Farm,
                                   Little Hereford,
      (incoming tenant)   Ludlow.

in the County of............Hereford

or other the occupier of the land described in the Schedule hereto

THE............HEREFORDSHIRE............WAR AGRICULTURAL EXECUTIVE COMMITTEE being the body authorised to exercise on behalf of the Minister of Agriculture and Fisheries within the administrative County of............Hereford............the powers in that behalf conferred by Regulation 62 (1) of the Defence Regulations, 1939, hereby direct you to carry out in respect of the land described in the Schedule hereto the works of cultivation specified in the said Schedule.

Failure to comply with this direction or any part thereof is an offence under the Defence Regulations.

Dated....19th February, 1940.

                                 By Order of the Committee

(Address)   WAR AGRICULTURAL OFFICE,
               4, ST. JOHN STREET,
                     HEREFORD.

                                     Chairman   Strike o
                                     Secretary   words
                                     Executive Officer   inapplica

SCHEDULE.

District	Parish	Ordnance Map—No. and Edition	Area	Description	Required Cultivation
Leominster & Wigmore	Little Hereford	(1904) 507	Acres 6.460	Pasture	To plough as soon as pos but not later than 31st M 1940, then cultivate and in a husbandlike manne the harvest of 1940 wit of the following crops :- Wheat ; potatoes ; b oats ; sugar-beet ; mixed beans ; peas ; or rye.

W.A.C. 100   P 85.   (2997) Wt 30813/1013 500x BPL 1

Your eyes are too big for your tummy.

good few accidents. The following November until January the town was snowed up, roads were closed and the only way to move in and out of Tenbury was by rail.

By 1940, the Home Guard, volunteer Air Raid Precaution wardens and fire watchers had been recruited, anti-gas gas instructors and first aid workers trained up; gas masks came into being and the air raid warning sirens tested. Dotted about town and valley the search light and anti aircraft batteries were made ready to spot enemy invaders. Bombs were being dropped around the area. The army spent two weeks on military manoeuvres at Eastham, a German Junkers 88 was brought down in flames at Brown Clee Hill and, oh yes, the YANKS arrived in town. It was possibly the first time the community had seen a black person, but everyone was made welcome, particularly by the children, who liked to gather round the field kitchens to watch the food being cooked hopeful of a few tasters.

In 1941, Kyre Park became a Red Cross and St. John convalescent home for other ranks, Puddleston Court more or less went the same way and Rochford House was turned into a Red Cross Centre. In 1944 the Women's Voluntary Service arranged for Tenbury to adopt West Ham in London's East End where heavy bombing by enemy aircraft had wiped out many homes; the district rallied round and sent off 1500 domestic gifts, including beds and furniture to help them through hard times. The stalwarts of the Women's Institute also rallied round to cope with evacuees.

At home or abroad it was everyone's war and when victory in Europe was announced by Winston Churchill, the then Prime Minister, in 1945, Tenbury celebrated, put the flags out, and according to some, painted the town red; a Welcome Home Committee greeted the return of the men folk. Rationing continued until 1954 and it was some time before farming got into its stride again.

Never put off until tomorrow what you can do today.

"BAREHANDS" BATES

Harold Raymond Kingsmill Bates was a pupil at St. Michael's College from a very early age. Born on November 3, 1916, his father, the Rector of Horsington in Lincolnshire, sent him to Tenbury's famous Choir School for an academic and spiritual education. The young boy turned out to be academically very bright, particularly in practical sciences and by the time he was 10 years old he had built himself a crystal radio receiver in his rooms at the Choir School. His interest in all things radio grew, resulting in what was to become one of the most heroic acts in Second World War naval history. Encouraged by his father, Harold became a Choral Scholar at Magdalene College, Oxford, where he studied music before joining the Merchant Navy.

At the onset of the Second World War he transferred to the Royal Navy and was soon in at the deep end of the Battle for the Atlantic. He served as Electrical Officer on board HMS Duke of York on escort duty in the Mediterranean protecting troopships during the North African Landings, when his electrical skills and extraordinary bravery clicked in on Boxing Day 1940. The German battle cruiser Scharnhorst had left Norway for an attack on a Russian convoy just off the North Cape and HMS Duke of York, flagship of Admiral Sir Bruce Fraser was under orders to radar track, give chase and intercept the enemy. The weather conditions were atrocious and the ship was facing a full on, force 8 gale; Bates and two radar operators were positioned high up the swinging tripod mast reporting on echoes from Scharnhorst. A German bomb whistled beneath his feet causing shockwaves and all three men were thrown onto the deck. He was puzzled by the lack of any further echoes and, looking upwards, he noticed that the radar antenna was out of alignment and in the dark and bitter cold, he climbed back up the mast and using a small torch, repaired the radar by holding two 'live' electrical cables together with his bare hands, he was able to reset the stabilisers. It did the trick, the radar was up and running, the chase continued and Scharnhorst was sunk.

At the time, the importance of radar was a bit of a mystery for the general public but when the announcement came that for his extraordinary act of bravery Lt. Bates was to be awarded the Distinguished Service Cross, he was a hero. The British press got hold of the story, told it as it was and he was immediately nicknamed 'Barehands Bates' but he wasn't best pleased to see himself portrayed in cartoons, comics and on the backs of cereal boxes, holding the highly dangerous electrical wires together. His career at sea forged ahead; he landed a raiding party of Commandos behind German lines to find prisoner of war camps and release the prisoners and in 1945 he was on the Quarterdeck of HMS King George V for the Japanese surrender in Tokyo Bay. After the war, his promotions included a transfer to shore duties specialising in the radar control of guns and missiles, later in the development and testing of the Medium Range System (MRS3), an automatic radar control system for ships' guns. He was eventually promoted to Captain RN and appointed Assistant Director of Royal Navy Intelligence and later served as Deputy Director of the Admiralty Underwater Weapons Establishment at Portland.

After 30 years' service in the Royal Navy, he retired in 1969. Encouraged by a passion for fast cars, usually Jaguars, he bought a filling station in Trowbridge, Wiltshire, and settled into civilian life driving one of the first Mini Coopers. He eventually returned to his native Lincolnshire and died aged 89 on May 9th 2006. Inspired by his school days and daily worship at St. Michael's, throughout his long life Harold Bates' love of church music brought him many happy memories of his early years in Tenbury Wells.

Too many cooks spoil the broth.

Gladys Hoskings - 1939

Gladys with her medal - 2007

DIGGING FOR VICTORY

The Land Army fights in the fields.
It is the fields of Britain that the most critical of the present war may well be fought and won.

The words of Lady Denman – founder of the Women's Land Army.

They wore squeaky cord trousers, dark green jumpers and red and green arm bands; the Land Army girls were in town. It was 1939, the United Kingdom was at war with Germany for the second time in twenty five years and, within a year, the convoys bringing supplies across the North Atlantic were under constant attack from enemy U-Boats. There was just enough food in the country to last two weeks. It was a desperate situation demanding swift action from the Government and the War Cabinet, who, realising that a huge population of soldiers and factory workers had to be fed, decided that something must be done and called for a regiment of women to take up arms - pitchforks, spades, forks, rakes and any other agricultural implements to help feed a nation at war. The response was phenomenal.

City women joined their country cousins to enlist in the Land Army, but when it came to country life they turned out to be more green than the grass they found there. Nevertheless, no matter the weather, in snow, rain, wind or sun, women all over the country battled tirelessly to produce enough food as the Women's Land Army fought in the fields of rural Britain, where one of the most critical battles of the Second World War may well have been won.

Around fifty young women were billeted in Tenbury at the Land Army hostel on the Bromyard Road; one of them is still alive and kicking in the town to this very day. Now in her mid-eighties she recalled the day she was called up.

Gladys Hoskins was conscripted into the Land Army when she was just 20, she recalled "Winston Churchill was dead against us women working for the war effort but the gravity of the situation at the time forced him to change his mind. We had the choice of working in munitions or on the land; if you had any sense you chose the outdoor life."

Born and brought up in Homefirth, the Yorkshire setting for the current TV series 'The Last of the Summer Wine', Gladys worked in the local mill, then a reserved occupation, and when the call to join up came, she went to Huddersfield to start a journey that would take her to North Herefordshire and the Teme Valley.

"They gave me a package containing my uniform and my posting came through for Derbyshire, not too far from home but a few days later I was told to report to Worcester. Bags packed, and brand new uniform made up of corduroy breeches that squeaked when you walked and a thick green jumper all badged up, I was whisked off by train to meet up with the group to be transported to Worcester. It was a bit scary".

They were all leaving home for the very first time to be dispersed to farms across the county and Gladys found herself in Tenbury Wells, "The blossom was everywhere and it was quite the most beautiful place I had ever seen", she said.

Home was a hostel on the Bromyard Road, opposite where the primary school stands today; the girls lived four to a cubicle, up at 6am and off to work by 8am. "It was a very happy place with a nice Warden and her assistant, a kindly Scottish woman with very red hair, who warned us "always keep your legs crossed gals", before we left for work.

Once bitten, twice shy.

From stringing hops, feeding cattle and ploughing to cabbage planting and rat-catching it was tough going, particularly for the city girls, but it was harvest time and it was threshing that did for Gladys and most of the other girls. She recalls "It was filthy work leaving our hands torn and bleeding. The day's work done and tired out, the best moment was when the gum boots came off." Hop picking was always a jolly time for the land girls; families came on holiday to do the picking and the staff at Tenbury Cottage Hospital had their own crib for collecting hops to raise much needed funds.

The Yorkshire lass settled in well and on one occasion she enthusiastically volunteered to go threshing. She claims "At the time I didn't have a clue what threshing was but being a good Yorkshire lass I put my hand up because it paid an extra bob a week. What a revelation it turned out to be. I was assigned to cut the bands; this was done by climbing up a ladder to the top of the threshing machine while it was grinding away, cutting the bands and feeding the sheaves into the machine."

Out in the fields packed lunches consisted of two slices of bread, a small piece of cheese and, if you were lucky, on a good day a nice slice of cake – not much for labouring from sunrise to sunset. There were some rewards. Most farms had milk and fruit to cook, with plenty over for us to eat as we liked; I could even send fruit home to my mother in Yorkshire. I remember one kindly farmer's wife who regularly called us into the kitchen to feed us up and for a special treat we would find a huge bowl of cream and a big, homemade apple pie."

After three years working the land Gladys became very ill, the dust from the threshing sheds had collected in her lungs and she was off work for a couple of weeks. The forewoman called to see her at the hostel and offered her a change of scenery; it appeared that the vicar of Lindridge needed temporary cover for a privately employed land girl who had to go to hospital in Birmingham.

"It was suggested by the forewoman that it would be a nice little job for me and help ease me back into work again", Gladys recalled. " I was very keen to give it a try and the first thing the vicar had to do was show me how to milk the cow; there was also a pig and a huge garden to tend to. The vicar had a great sense of humour and one day I was working with him in the garden when he was due to officiate at a funeral. As the hearse came up the drive he dashed through the back door coming out at the front with his robes on, still wearing his work boots. When he came back he called out to me "That's another one planted".

It turned out working for the vicar was to be a good move. Having learned to milk cows put her in good stead when a farmer from Berrington called at the hostel needing someone able to take on milking duties at his farm. Gladys was the only one competent to do it and she ended up working full time on a dairy farm.

Weekend socialising more than made up for the hard work. Harvest suppers and barn dances provided opportunities to meet the local families and, although most of the young men had gone to war, the land army girls were soon swept off their feet and romanced at the village hall dances by the farmers. Gladys Hoskins married a local chap, had four daughters and has spent most of her long life in Tenbury Wells.

Looking back with pride, Gladys Hoskins sees her vital role in the war as an experience well worth recording. All things considered, conditions in the hostel were good, something between the army and boarding school and, like the

armed services, land army girls were given a personal number and expected to go wherever ordered.

Gladys explained "I had joined the army after working in the mill; it was a reserved occupation making the cloth for all the uniforms. I would liked to have enlisted earlier and have had more choice, but by the time I was released from the mill in 1943 the only choice to be made was the Land Army or working in dangerous conditions in factories underground filling shells with explosives where at the end of a shift you come out with yellow stained hair and skin."

It was exciting to be in Tenbury on VE Day; people had cleaned out the entire cattle market for a big get together for the whole town. There was dancing and singing and it was a great moment after years of black-out when all the town lights were switched on again.

At the turn of the 21st century Gladys was one of only three former Land Army girls invited to add their personal stories to the Imperial War Museum sound archive and today she delights in showing off her treasured war medal kept safe along side her distinctive green and red arm band in a memory box at home. In 2007 the Government announced that a medal would be struck for all former Land Army women; it's come a bit too late for some of them. Gladys is delighted, not only for herself but for her comrades in arms who dug deep for victory but never lived long enough to receive their own medal.

"I'm no war hero" she said, "Just a grandmother, a non-military woman called upon to help her country in its hour of need. When I look back I realise I have never worked harder in all my life but I will never, ever forget the kindness of the people of Tenbury and Teme Valley who took us in and cared for us when we were so far from home."

Opposite:
The young Gladys on her milk round
in Bromyard Road

The farther the sight the nearer the rain.

PRISONERS OF WAR

Like many other farming areas across the United Kingdom, prisoners of war were detailed to work on the land and the Teme Valley was no exception. German and Italian prisoners were transported to local farms on a lorry with a tarpaulin cover stretched over a frame to shelter them from the weather.

Prisoners were always accompanied by an armed guard, usually a British civilian who carried a rifle. When the prisoners jumped off the lorry the guard handed his rifle to a prisoner while he climbed down - there were no steps; they were so happy to be out of the war they were unlikely to attempt to escape.

David Powell from Bank Farm, Rochford, was but a lad when prisoners of war were employed at the family farm, but he remembers them well. He recalls German prisoners of war coming to work at the Bank Farm around 1946; some prisoners were stationed at Ludlow near to the present cattle market, others were based at Leominster. However those working at Bank Farm were from the hostel sited opposite the supermarket on Bromyard Road by the Crescent. David can still remember them coming to work on bikes, but felt they were humiliated by having to wear tunics with a big round circle - like the sun - displayed on the back, for identification purposes. Milestones were removed from the verges so that the prisoners did not know which way to go to escape. Later on, Italian POWs came to work at the farm; it seemed as though they had better food provided for them but did less work.

Two particular Germans, 17-year-old Reinhold Mullecker and Henry Miller, who was much older, spent a long time at Bank Farm but in David's opinion Reinhold was a star. Despite being very, very strong and fearless, he admitted he was very scared of the war and was relieved to have been captured early. "Both men were a great help to us although we had about a dozen other men working for us.

It was at this time that my father decided to restart hop growing; hop poles were bought - 18' long x 4" top inner poles, 24' x 6" top end poles and the corner post would be at least 12" in diameter and 24' in length. All the poles had to be peeled and creosoted to preserve them and Reinhold and Henry did most of it.

The creosote tank was hired at Newnham Farm and while the creosote was bubbling away in the tank, Reinhold, for some unknown reason, took the damper out of the chimney and threw it away into the pile of poles. This caused a greater draught and the creosote bubbled right to the top of the tank, luckily our chaps recovered the damper and replaced it just in time to save the creosote from boiling over into the fire below. Had that happened the consequences could have been devastating.

They worked hard at hand digging most of the anchor holes round the outside of the new hop yard - there were not many mechanical diggers about then - and Reinhold carved his name on a tree trunk in the hop yard by the edge of the River Teme and it is still distinguishable today."

At the time, David's father had a lot of young, unbroken horses and Reinhold would be in his element jumping on their backs without a bridle or anything; they also had some very tall perry pear trees at Bank Farm, some reaching 40-50 feet high. Reinhold would scale them without a ladder and shake the pears off.

David remembers that throughout their time at Bank Farm, Reinhold and Henry were always very good to him; he believes that came about because his mother was very kind and caring towards them and making sure they were

The oak before the ash we get a splash. The ash before the oak surely get a soak.

properly fed even though their ration allowance was the very minimum.

He still has the toys, a ship in a bottle and the violin they made for him, and he vividly remembers an incident when Henry really told Reinhold off.

"Sometimes I would walk up the drive with them on their way 'home' and on this one occasion Reinhold got on his bike, caught hold of my hand and went faster and faster. My little legs were going like pistons and when they wouldn't go any faster just dragged. Henry was not amused."

After the war ended, and the prisoners returned to Germany, the Powell family lost contact with Henry but have stayed in touch with Reinhold. When he returned to Germany, he found that his house was wrecked in the war and he has since built a new home, mostly surrounded by forests in Birkenhordt, for himself and his family. Reinhold and his wife have been back to Rochford and David and Don Potter, who also worked at the farm, have visited Reinhold and his family in Germany. He is still quite fluent with the English language and they correspond at Christmas and telephone each other on Christmas Day. Now in his 80s Reinhold enjoys good health, and remains a true friend to David Powell and his family.

Prisoners of war were also drafted in to work for the Hodges at Temple Farm, Little Hereford, particularly at busy times of the year like the harvest, planting and hoeing. The War Agricultural Committee would send out as many prisoners as needed some perhaps more keen than others like Walter, a hard working German who liked being at Temple Farm. As well as working for the family they also taught him English, including a few 'naughty' words which often got him into trouble. He was supposed to be watched over and he was quite happy with that and although he should not have been fed, he was given breakfast, dinner and some food to take back to the camp. They also gave him cider which made him even happier. Prisoners had to work hard until the war ended and for two years after to help get Britain back on its feet but Walter stayed on for another year because there was no work for him in Germany. Even after the war they stayed in the camps and still had to wear brown and green trousers and a coat with a sun on the back. There was no going to the pub but they went to the dances in Leominster where the English girls taught them to dance; they had to be back in camp by ten o'clock at night.

The prisoners would make money cutting up old beds from the camp to make jewellery and toys for local children. When Walter eventually went back to Germany, he was given a suit and wages of £25 (600 German marks) which he said was quite good money but when he got back he was unfairly treated for working for the English. He always said that he had made new friends and enjoyed his time in England and that prisoners had helped feed Britain and get agriculture back to normality.

The Strength of the Community

EARLY CHILDHOOD EDUCATION

In and around the Teme Valley local children started school at around five years old at either a Church, Board or charity school. They received a basic education in reading, writing, arithmetic plus religion in church schools; it was compulsory for girls to do needlework, darning, knitting and some cooking. During the Boer War and the Great War, lady visitors came to the schools to encourage the girls to do their bit and knit socks for soldiers. Prayers were the order of the day in most schools.

The school building was usually a couple of cold, over crowded rooms where discipline ruled, pupils did as they were told and left as soon as it was legally possible. Girls and boys were separated into two departments; the girls were taught by unmarried, lower middle-class women but when rules preventing married women from working were introduced, many a teaching career came to an end. Parents paid a penny a week for school fees and this was among many reasons for irregular attendance. Others included poverty, illness, bad weather competitive sporting events, seasonal work like hop-picking when it was acceptable for pupils were taken out of school; children with head lice, sores, infectious diseases, and poor footwear and clothing were often excluded from school. Corporal punishment by cane was regularly dished out for bad behaviour. School uniforms were very rare, nevertheless pupils presented in a tidy, clean manner, except the workhouse children who stood out like a sore thumb. As well as teaching duties, head teachers also had to train pupil teachers on site. They learnt to complete the daily log book, carry out inspections, prepare for examinations and exercise safety regulations. In 1912 they were paid an annual salary of between £100 and £200 pounds; teaching assistants earned £30 to £50 and pupil teachers were taken on to help keep the property tax low. In the late 19th century children could leave school at ten years old and could earn more than a sixteen-year-old pupil teacher.

For most pupils childhood was short; after school the girls had to do their share of household duties like fetching and carrying water, washing and ironing clothes and occasional cooking. This was considered good practice for going into domestic service, usually at 13 years old, although some were pushed into service even younger. The boys humped bags of coal and logs to keep the house warm and before they went to school had to scrub and clean the yard.

In the early 1800s The National Society for Promoting the Education of the Poor was established by the Church of England and The British and Foreign School Society was working its way around the area setting up schools. In Tenbury, Edward Goff, a self-educated and selfmade wealthy coal merchant from London, came onto the education scene. Born in North Herefordshire, Goff was a deeply religious man with Calvinist leanings and when he retired from his business wanted to ensure that poor children should not miss out on education. After his death in 1813, he left substantial funds enough to found free schools in his native county; one of them in Tenbury Wells. Although not of the Baptist faith, Goff respected them enough to place them among his trustees and amid fears of indoctrination the Baptist Church founded Goff's school at The Steps House next to the Bell Inn, Market Street.

When the owner died the school almost died with him; his executors gave the Baptists notice to quit the premises but with help from the trustees a temporary school house and meeting place was found. Eventually the Goff's School site in Market Street was purchased.

God made the country, man made the town.

Faces & Places

TENBURY IN PICTURES THROUGH THE YEARS

A 10 MILE RADIUS OF TENBURY

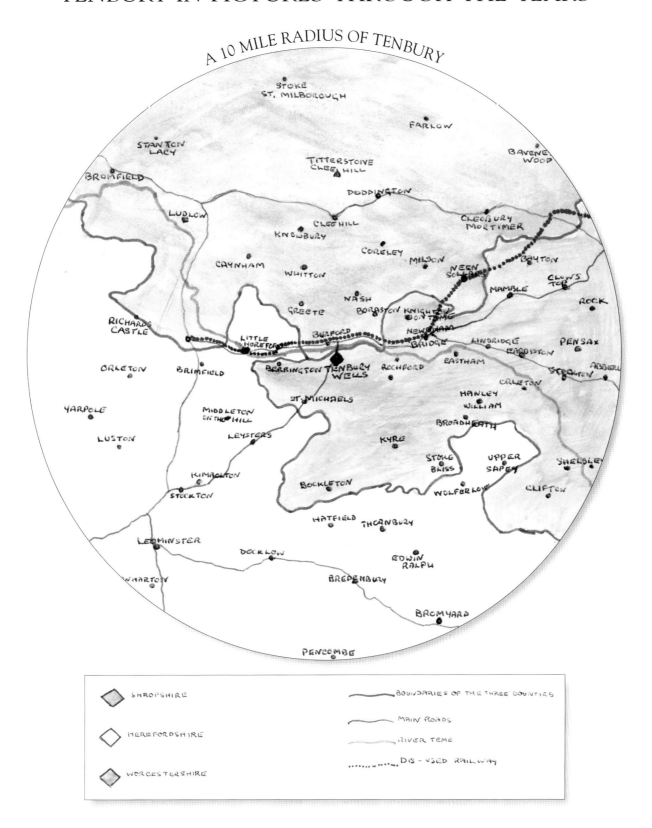

SHROPSHIRE		BOUNDARIES OF THE THREE COUNTIES
HEREFORDSHIRE		MAIN ROADS
WORCESTERSHIRE		RIVER TEME
		DIS-USED RAILWAY

The late John Wilding always had a good eye for
livestock. A great supporter of Tenbury show, he
bred and showed his Shire horses which gave him
a lot of pleasure.
John was a great character and enjoyed the
company of 'like minded' folk, he had a wicked
sense of humour and his fun loving character
rubbed off on others too.

iii

Top Left:
Portrait of K. Stanley Yapp by Paul Saville

Top Centre:
Andrew Wright, Nick Dunne & daughter Stephanie

Top Right:
A Tenbury Apple a Day for M.P. Bill Wiggin

Centre Left:
Gladys Hoskins showing medal

Centre :
Mrs Ronnie Hipkiss

Above:
M.P.s in Banfields

Bottom Left:
Town Mayor Maureen Pardoe with Mistletoe Queen
Chloe Eliding and attendant Molly Cree - 2004

Far Top Left: **John Dingley** stringing hops
Far Left: **Tenbury's famous mistletoe**
Centre Left: **Millennium Orchard**
Centre: **George Watkins' outfit**
Centre Right: **Football** on Palmers Meadow
Centre Bottom: **Tenbury Fire Appliance**
Centre Bottom Right: **Early Titan Tractor**
Bottom: **TAS Centenary Dinner Menu** - 1858-1957

Entertainment

ERIC WILLIAMS
(Member of the Inner Magic Circle)
Assisted by "MA"
in COMEDY MAGIC

o

DORIS & RAY
in SONGS FROM THE SHOWS
(Solos & Duets)

o

THE "ORACLES"
(Members of The Magic Circle)
in "THOUGHT TRANSFERENCE"

SHORT FILM OF THE CENTENARY SHOW
Presented by Dr. J. E. BLUNDELL-WILLIAMS

1858—1957

TENBURY
AGRICULTURAL SOCIETY

Centenary Dinner

FRIDAY 7th MARCH, 1958
ROYAL OAK HOTEL

1957
Tenbury
J. B. NALDER, Esq.

President 1949
E. NANAURO, Esq. M.C.

CHANNAK, Esq.

H. B. MORGAN, Esq. F.A.I.

Menu

MUSHROOM SOUP
GRAPEFRUIT JUICE

SEVERN SALMON & MAYONNAISE SAUCE
FRESH GARDEN PEAS
BUTTERED NEW POTATOES

COLD ROAST TURKEY & YORK HAM
ASSORTED GREEN SALADS

BROWN BREAD & BUTTER

HONEYCOMB MOULD & PEACHES

FRUIT SALAD & FRESH CREAM

CHEESE: STILTON, CAMEMBERT, CHEDDAR

BISCUITS

COFFEE

Toasts

H.M. THE QUEEN
The President

THE PRESIDENT
Dr. J. E. Blundell-Williams
Reply, T. E. Sweet, Esq.

AGRICULTURE
Dr. D. H. Robinson, B.Sc. (Agric.), Ph.D., N.D.A.
Reply, A. E. Baldwin, Esq., M.P., M.C.

TENBURY AGRICULTURAL SOCIETY
Capt. B. E. Wallace, M.F.H.
Reply, J. Nott, Esq., M.B.E.

OUR GUESTS
Proposed by H. B. Morgan, Esq., F.A.I.
Response by C. V. Hancock, Esq., M.A.

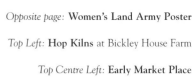

Cattle Market, Tenbury.

vi

After three years of hostilities between community and church, a public meeting was called and in May 1816 it was agreed that a National School backed by the Church of England should be set up in opposition. Thereafter it was referred to as The Tenbury National Madras School funded by a voluntary subscription, legacies and fee paying parents. Premises were rented and adapted into one large school room, writing materials, books and furnishings were donated by local benefactors and traders. Benjamin Home from the National Society Central School in London was engaged to introduce and explain the Madras system of teaching. This was based on a teaching method first seen at a Military Male Orphanage for the illegitimate sons, (no mention of the girls) of native women and British Soldiers, near Madras. It was brought back to England by churchman and educator Dr. Andrew Bell following a promotional trip to India in the 19th century. On a visit to the orphanage he discovered younger boys learning how to read and write the alphabet by sitting in a circle around the teacher who scratched the letters with sticks into the sand in a rather haphazard way. Sometimes the older boys tried to help the 'teacher' so Dr. Bell stayed on to run the orphanage, developing new teaching methods. To do this he encouraged and trained the older boys to assist with the teaching. When he eventually returned to England he published a paper explaining his 'peer group' method of teaching and it was eventually adopted by national schools across the country. It was later changed to the Monitoring System of Education and proved to be a cheaper way of making primary education more inclusive with bigger class sizes.

At the time, Tenbury National School was a large room with a schoolmaster in charge to discipline child progress and testing them for knowledge; he also trained up the brightest, older children into monitors to supervise pupils learning in small groups. The master was responsible for accessing pupils and promoting the bright children to a higher level and demoting the less bright; the system generally worked out well. The school committee was naturally delighted with both the educational and financial success of the new method; the reduction in financial outgoings gained by reducing teaching staff was a bonus, pupil numbers steadily increased and learning, even for the slower children, improved. With the increase in new admissions came the need for larger premises and by 1829 the trustees had raised enough private and voluntary donations to build a school capable of coping with some 150 boys and 50 girls. Eleven years later, a Pupil Teacher programme was initiated which encouraged young people over thirteen years to take up unpaid apprenticeships. They were trained by the headmaster and examined annually by Her Majesty's Inspectorate and each examination passed was rewarded with a small stipend. At the end of the apprenticeship they became teachers, received a payment from the Government and given the opportunity to try for a Queen's Scholarship and place at a Teacher Training College.

The school's educational success brought demands for even larger premises. Government grants became available to help relieve financial management problems and in 1885 the trustees agreed to invite the then virtually unknown Birmingham based architect, James Cranston to design and construct a purpose built school building on Bromyard Road; the budget was just under £1,000. Following good reports of excellent improvement in infant education, school inspectors recommended a further substantial grant towards future funding for primary places and, by the end of the 19th century, a new Infant School was erected on the opposite side of the Bromyard Road. It is now known as Tenbury Church of England Primary School and over the years further buildings were added.

Today, Tenbury also has a High School which is a mixed comprehensive school specialising in Science and Mathematics with 450 mixed pupils between the ages of 11-16. It has recently opened a state of the art sports complex, a new Learning Resource Centre, modern Science laboratories and computer suites. In 2005 the school was judged to be 'outstanding' by OFSTED and again in 2006 for its Extended Services. Over the years it has collected many other awards including Investment in People, and the Eco-schools 'Green Flag'.

More important, under Head teacher Stuart Cooke and his staff, Tenbury High School provides a happy, caring, and well ordered environment in which academic skills, self-discipline, consideration for others, and presentable appearance is vital. After school clubs flourish, booster classes support the curriculum and a wide range of community activities for children and the local community are offered within the school's Extended Services programme. Stuart Cooke believes that programming projects that are educational and fun, like arts and music events in the community, can bring a knock-on effect on motivation which often leads pupils to do better. Tenbury High School is now well established at its Oldwood site and is well and truly an integral part of the Tenbury and Teme Valley community.

Clifton on Teme
primary school pupils - 1915

Years 1 & 2 pose infront of the school to match photo above - c.2004

Neglect your belly and you're soon on your back.

GOOD WOMEN WHO DO GOOD THINGS

When Arabella Prescott from Bockleton, the widow of a London banker, splashed out £2,678 on Park Villa in Burford, little did she realise then the impact her generosity would have on the future health and wellbeing of the local community. In 1871 she leased it out free of charge, initially for a 12 month period to be used as a hospital, not knowing where the road would lead. A committee of local worthies was appointed to run it, St. Mary's Cottage Hospital was born and Arabella became the 'Lady President', taking on all the day to day expenses. Although she had donated the building, equipment, furnishings and fittings and garden, she was not keen to take on day to day running of the hospital. Many of the patients came from the farming environment and in the first instance the hospital was staffed by a single nurse supported by a servant; local doctors freely gave their time and some patients also helped out with nursing and domestic duties.

Arabella Prescott

A year later Mrs Prescott put the property up for sale for around £2,000 but only local landowner Lord Northwick showed any serious interest eventually offering £1,750, almost £1,000 less than Arabella had paid for it. Having proved its value to the community, Northwick leased the hospital to the committee at a shilling per year and a public appeal went out for funds to finance the hospital by private subscriptions and church collections.

Extensions were added to the main building, including an open-air veranda to help patients suffering from tuberculosis, and finances were on the wane, that is until Queen Victoria's Diamond Jubilee in 1897. To commemorate the event the committee launched an appeal for funds to buy the building and £350 was collected through hop-picking, flag days and concerts; some of the money was also spent on bringing vital mains water into the hospital. To further help with running costs Lady Northwick gave £100 to help clear up debts.

Further development continued and in 1912 the Elizabeth Wing, four 10 - bedded wards, two bathrooms and lavatories plus a light, roomy operating

The Cottage Hospital. Tenbury.

theatre were built. Following a donation of £300 from W.E. Davies, given specifically to help accommodate more staff, two bedrooms, a bathroom, a lavatory and a large scullery were also added.

In 1928, rising costs in patient care forced the hospital to close its doors and a public meeting was called; opinion was varied and forthright ranging from "What would the founder think?" when it was made clear in some quarters that the poor would suffer support poured in from all the parishes in the district and it was reopened in 1930 by the Arch Deacon of Ludlow. Sister Proctor and a staff nurse were employed at the hospital with two Queen's nurses to cover the district.

It wasn't until the 1930s that the first major rebuilding work began. Colonel W.R. Prescott, great-grandson of Arabella, continued to support the hospital and as Chairman of the Committee stayed onboard to see to the work, the wards of today plus two private wards, an operating theatre and driveways - to completion. He remained Chairman until 1939 when he was called into active service.

Further fundraising provided for two more bedrooms and conveniences plus a further extension containing a male and female ward, a well equipped operating theatre was added to the Elizabeth wing. Memorial gates and an ambulance were donated and in 1937 radio was available in the wards.

At the onset of the National Health Service (1948) St Mary's was handed over to The Mid Worcestershire Hospital Management Board and the Hospital League of Friends, with representatives from seven surrounding parishes. Since then the determination, commitment and sheer affection for the old building has guided the hospital into the new century to become a vital asset for the care and well-being of the community.

Since the hospital was taken into the National Health Scheme, the hospital matrons have been Miss Giles, Miss Margaret Morris and Mrs Jean Grosvenor each one setting a standard of responsibility and duty second to none and leaving their mark not only on the hospital but also a grateful Tenbury community. Today they are a hard act to follow for modern matron, Mrs Ginny Snape who has carried the mantle of the past into the future with equal professionalism. Undeterred by threats of closure, lack of funds, and staff shortages, her reassuring presence eases the way for patients with dignity and care and making sure staff are sent for up-to-date training.

Today, support for the hospital continues to be wide ranging and generous; the list of donors over the years is far too long to mention. Practically every local club, association, school and parish, as well as private donations, have funded the cause and the response to the League of Friends £800,000 Millennium Project has been phenomenal.

Arabella Prescott died in 1886 and was buried in the church at Bockleton in a coffin made from wood from her own estate. Her legacy, the gift of a hospital to Tenbury Wells, is said to be the memorial to her son who died aged 21, from a fever caught while tending his dying gamekeeper, four years before she bought Park Villa.

Whichever way you look at it, her vision continues through so many people, none more so than the Tenbury League of Friends who for many years have been dedicated to upholding the memory of a few good women who did so many good things.

A creaking gate hangs a long time.

HATS OFF TO THE LEAGUE OF FRIENDS

Tenbury Hospital League of Friends is sixty years old in 2008. Since its early beginnings in 1948 this dedicated band of indomitable volunteers lead by a trio of former Matrons have pulled out all the stops to ensure that the Tenbury community has access to a well equipped and comfortable local hospital. From day one, this required considerable sums of cash for capital funding and day to day running costs but the farming community and a small market town with a very big heart backed them to the hilt.

With the promise of a National Health Service for all in 1948, the idea for a volunteer group of local people grew into a League for Friends following an Inaugural Meeting held in October 1948. Representatives from seven local parishes were co-opted, a Ladies Committee was set up to run the League and from then on it was fund raising. A year later local clergy organised an annual Good Friday egg collection which brought in up to 6000 eggs. Donations and legacies came in from all quarters and by order of the local magistrates, Sunday takings from the Regal Cinema were donated for many years. In the first instance, the income was used to supply daily papers and magazines to the wards and to help with convalescence and care for older people, including the nursing and other staff at the hospital. It was an impressive start for the League resulting in an invitation to be represented on The Mid-Worcestershire Management Committee who ran the hospital at the time.

Although the League had been primarily set up to care for patients , nurses and staff, during the 1950s substantial funds were raised to improve facilities in the operating theatre, bring radio and television and other electrical goods into the wards and provide a greenhouse and shrubs for the hospital garden.

In 1966 Hilda Giles retired as hospital Matron and was replaced by Margaret Morris and over the next five years the Friends paid for major refurbishment of the casualty and out patients departments and, in 1971, the Hospital Centenary Committee purchased a plot of land on the eastern side of the hospital. This

A ewe full of life is better than one full of teeth.

was initially used as a car park and set aside for future expansion to the main building of the hospital; it proved to be a good investment by the committee.

The following year Mrs Watts became the League's Secretary, Dr. Blundell-Williams was appointed Chairman and new equipment included an ambulift, sluicing machine, adjustable beds, an X-ray film drying cabinet and an automatic washing machine; piped gas and air suction was also installed in wards and the car park completed. Despite the heavy expenditure, at the end of the decade, the League had almost £5,000 in hand.

The 1980s brought many changes and challenges for both the hospital and the League of Friends. A new X-ray department was built at cost of £35,400, with the League contributing £20,000. The new department was officially opened on May 9th 1981 by Dr. Blundell-Williams and former Matron Hilda Giles. The land around it was landscaped and paid for from the balance of the Hospital Centenary Fund.

Two years later Dr. J.A. Burnett became Chairman, Philip Bull Treasurer and Mary Thorpe the Secretary, a position she still holds today. After 30 years of devoted service Matron Margaret Morris retired and Jean Grosvenor was appointed to replace her; she later took the title of Manager of the Hospital.

Changing times and shortages in the National Health Service raised the pace of much needed fund raising; £54K was needed for a contribution towards a major extension housing Outpatient, Physiotherapy and Ophthalmic departments; the Tenbury community raising an incredible £32K in 17 months. It was opened in September 1985 by Margaret Morris.

The Health Authority came up with funds for much needed telephone, computer and nurses' call systems. Later, the League became a Charity and joined the National Association of Leagues' of Friends and the Revd. Duncan

Tenbury Hospital present day

It's a poor prospect for a parish when the dogs outnumber the sheep.

Dormer was appointed Hospital Chaplain. The Voluntary Ambulance Service was replaced by professionals and relocated to the hospital site, Betty Boffey was appointed Membership Secretary and remains in office today and Muriel Lanman launched her 'Christmas at the Hospital Fund' for patients hospitalised over the festive season. Incredibly, by the end of the 1980s, the League's bank balance stood at £67k. But the big push was still to come.

To mark the forty-ninth anniversary of the NHS the Health Authority upgraded the hospital kitchen and flooring and the League gave £160K towards the upgrading of the operating theatre and once again Tenbury did its bit and raised £25k in record time. Further changes were made to the committee and in 1995 Margaret Morris became the popular Chairman.

Bill Wiggins in the League of Friends Charity Shop

Muriel Lanman's Robin lapel badges raised £4,000 for the Christmas fund, an Education Fund to help staff to improve their qualifications was set up and in 1996 Jean Grosvenor and her staff were awarded a Government Charter Mark for excellence. As it headed for a secure and healthy future for town and valley, the League of Friends completed the successful purchase of land behind the hospital from South Shropshire District Council for £80K; from then it was something of a roller-coaster ride.

In 1997 an appeal for funding to increase the Day Care and Palliative Care units was about to be launched when the future of the Kidderminster Health Care Trust was put in jeopardy. This forced the League to abandon the detailed plans submitted by Hospital Manager Jean Grosvenor; she eventually retired but continued as a member of the League's committee and has since seen her plans developed. Her retirement saw the end of an era; there would no longer be a Matron at Tenbury Hospital; the duties shared between Nursing Manager Jenny Hinton and Marketing Manager Jane Beckett, Deputy Director of Operations at Kidderminster Hospital.

But the glory days of the League of Friends came in April 2003 when contracts were signed and the first sod was cut for the second stage of the £800,000 Millennium Project. The ground was broken by a delighted Margaret Morris, clad in white safety helmet, accompanied by Project Manager Jean Grosvenor, Mary Thorpe, the Leagues long serving Secretary and Michael Ridley, the Chief Executive of South Worcestershire NHS Trust. The Trust had injected £80K into the project. The Evison Trust and Jordan Foundation also chipped in with grants of £25,000 each and, more important, guided and cajoled by the League of Friends, the Tenbury community funded the remaining £670k.

It was a mighty effort from a unique group of people, leaving current Modern Matron, Ginni Snape with a community hospital definitely fit for purpose.

In November 2007, Chairman Margaret Morris passed the baton into the safe hands of Jean Grosvenor; there is still much to be done to keep the hospital in uptodate equipment and the patients in a comfortable environment.

With sixty years of success behind them it's 'hats off' to the amazing Tenbury League of Friends and long may they reign.

THE STORY OF A MIDWIFE

My great grandmother, Emma Cox, born February 11th, 1840, was sent from her home in Staffordshire to help her aunt who kept a pub in Highwood, Eastham, near Tenbury Wells. She was just a child; she was not sent to school and was never able to read or write. Nevertheless, she became a midwife, working with the local doctor.

My aunts told me she would go out on her cases carrying her basket covered with a piece of white linen and wearing her long white starched linen apron. In her basket with her instruments she might put her nightie and provisions for herself and the family she was visiting. They were often too poor to pay her. Her fee for a delivery and after-care was half a sovereign. Sometimes she got nothing, sometimes she was given the clock; my cousin Harold remembers her returning one day with a suckling pig in her arms.

I remember the clocks. In her tiny cottage, one room up, one down, every wall, every shelf was covered with them. They ticked, they struck, they chimed, I was too young to notice if they told the right time but my aunts remembered the ritual of winding keys and pulling on pendulums and nights noisy with the constant ticking, striking and chiming.

When, in 1902, midwives had to be trained and certificated, Emma received exemption in view of her record of competence. She, my grandmother and my aunts were very proud of her certificate of exemption on fine parchment.

I have seen her diary of deliveries from 1911 to 1913, written of course for her by her daughter, my grandmother. It records the births of many babies including three of my cousins and Gordon, my half brother.

Eventually she had to hand over to her niece, Nellie Ralph. Nellie was trained, wore a uniform and was very different from great-granny. She would not work without payment so great-granny still delivered the babies of the poor and destitute.

In January 1927, when Emma Cox was nearly 88, my uncle Bill was sent by my grandmother to break the news of my grandfather's death to her. It was 11 o'clock at night, bitterly cold, the snow a foot deep, and Uncle had to push his bike most of the way. When he arrived, the cottage was empty. He called on the village policeman nearby. He guessed where she would be: a young girl, unmarried, was due to give birth. Nellie Ralph had refused to attend her.

Uncle Bill followed her footsteps in the snow; from time to time she had fallen – the imprint of her basket was clear. When he arrived at the girl's cottage there was candlelight upstairs. He called and great-granny opened the window to tell him to wait. At last he heard the cry of the newborn baby and after a while great-granny came to the door with a twist of newspaper for a light. She had carried coal and firewood as well as food, at the age of 88.

Her grandchildren loved her visits. She lived in Highwood; they lived in Tedstone Wafre, a walk of 16 miles there and back.

I was nearly five when she died in January 1929 aged 90. I remember her as tiny but forceful even then. I remember her clocks, the steep staircase to her bedroom and her purgatory grate; a deep hole under the fire basket which held the ashes. We carried bucket after leaky bucket of ashes to a heap up the garden near the well.

The well reminds me of another story about great-granny. Her older son, Tom, returned home badly scarred from ghastly experiences in war (in South Africa). Every night he walked in his sleep and every night she followed him, summer and winter, up the garden, round the well, and back to the house. He was a gamekeeper and he shot himself long before I was born. When great-granny died, she left her house to her remaining son, William, also a gamekeeper, and her 'bag of gold' to my grandmother. I think the half-sovereign uncle George gave me may have come from it. I don't know how much money the bag of gold represented. Great uncle Bill sold the house (called Snale's Park) in 1930 for £50.

THE TENBURY UNION WORKHOUSE

TENBURY WORKHOUSE

The Tenbury Poor Law Union was set up in 1836 to cover 26 parishes mainly in Worcestershire, the rest spilled over into Shropshire and Herefordshire. A number of possible sites were considered before the Tenbury site was chosen and a year later George Wilkinson, a leading workhouse architect, was commissioned to build a workhouse with a double courtyard, something of a rarity in workhouse design. The number of residents was set at 70 but the inmates numbered well below this figure. The total cost of £1,365, a considerable sum of money in those days, included all the furnishings and fittings and most of the costs came from public appeals and loans. The land was donated by Mr. George Rushout Bowles (Lord Northwick) to highlight the social importance of a workhouse. In 1871 he put his hand in his pocket again and came up with money for an infirmary on the same site. But he wasn't the only benefactor, in the late 1800s Francesca Baldwin-Child of Kyre Park provided a small, green corrugated iron building for use as an isolation hospital.

For almost every family the thought of ending their days in the workhouse was the most feared thing that could happen to them. If the breadwinner of the family died and there were no relations to offer a home, his wife and children would go to the workhouse as would old people, single or married couples who were destitute; men, women and children were segregated.

In 1894 when the government of the day first discussed the granting of an old age pension, it was said that a lot of men who had worked up to the age of 65 and had never cost the country anything, in old age very often finished up in the workhouse. When the pension was eventually granted in 1907 it was worth five shillings a week; at the time it cost eight shillings to keep a person in the workhouse.

Besides the inmates, usually 40 to 50 men, women and children were dependant on money raised through the parish poor rate; vagrants, also known as travellers or tramps were entitled to a night's lodging and food, usually 6 ounces of bread and a pint of oat gruel. Able-bodied inmates were expected to work at various duties in the workhouse or the infirmary. The vagrants, after a nights lodging spent sleeping on the bare boards, were also given a meal but before leaving were expected to work. This usually involved breaking about 13 hundredweight of large lumps of Clee Hill stone tipped in the workhouse yard; using a sledgehammer they had to break it down to a size suitable for repairing the roads. One vagrant who left without doing his allotted work was arrested by the police and sentenced to 7 days in prison. Another sad story is of a tramp who refused to break up the stone and wanted a pair of eye shields because his sight was so bad. The Workhouse Manager sent for the police and a local doctor was sent to examine him; he explained that the man was almost blind and was excused work.

A peck of March dust is worth a king's ransom.

The Isolation Ward

Vagrants were only allowed to stay over for one night and then moved on to another workhouse or got work on farms in the Tenbury district to do seasonal work root hoeing, haymaking, fruit picking, harvesting or hop-picking for a few days. Country folk were very sympathetic to unfortunate travelers and the vagrants were usually allowed to sleep in the farm buildings. If there were no seasonal jobs to do, they would be given a meal, even if it was only bread and cheese. In return the travelers did a bit of gardening or chopped a few sticks for the fire.

Sadly, in the 1920s and 1930s many of the so called vagrants and tramps were ex-soldiers from the Boer War and the first World War who were shell shocked, gassed or had lost limbs or maybe their marriages had broken up, but whatever the reason, because of the war they were unable to settle down to a regular job.

Shortly before the start of World War Two the workhouse was finally closed and became council offices and one end of the building converted into the fire station. It is now a listed building. The old infirmary was once used as offices for the now closed livestock market and the little green corrugated iron isolation shed, until recently a café for buyers and sellers, was unceremoniously demolished at the behest of the new site owner.

The workhouse bell can still be seen if you look hard enough and it is said that there is still a World War Two air raid siren in the top of the old fire station section of the building.

Ground Floor Plan of isolation ward

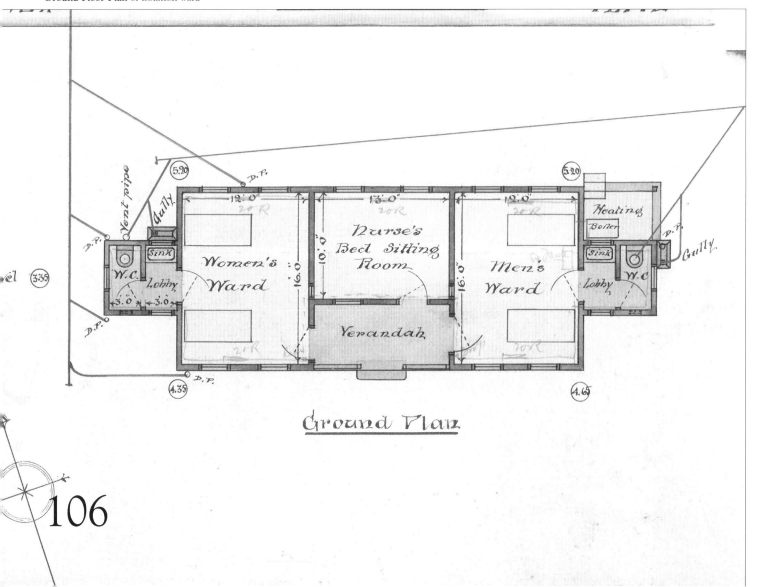

Ground Plan

THE MOVEMENT OF PEOPLE

The movement of people in and out of the area has been a common factor in the changing face of Tenbury and the Teme Valley. Since at least the 1870s people from the Tenbury area have immigrated to far flung places across the world, particularly to the Empire and Commonwealth countries such as Canada, Australia and New Zealand. The Tenbury newspaper from this period carried advertisements most weeks, usually from J. Bevan of Cross Street, who was offering passages from Liverpool to America and Canada from £15 to £20 as well as from Glasgow to Australia and New Zealand.

Records show that some local people went out at the time of the gold rush, including the two sons of farmer Mr Clarke from The Terrills. They travelled the long sea journey to Western Australia and landed at Freemantle and from there, pushed a wheelbarrow loaded with tools and belongings, stopping off to prospect for gold at various sites along the way before finally reaching Kalgoorlie, 250 miles inland. The one brother later started a successful gold assay business in that area but the other brother came back to Tenbury to take over the family dairy farm which he ran untill the 1950s.

When Mrs.J.G.Banfield died aged 91 in 1933, her obituary in the Tenbury Advertiser recorded that as a bride she went to Australia at the time of the gold rush returning home to Tenbury in 1869.

In the 1884, people keen on emigrating to North West Canada were tempted by offers of 160 acres of virgin soil free, however there was a catch, they needed £60 to £200 to start off a farm and live until the first crop.

Persuasive offers came fast and furious with the building of the railroad. The Canadian Pacific Railway, was given land 25 miles either side of the track right across the prairies and they then set out to encourage European farmers to become settlers, bringing in more business for the company especially by carrying grain for export.

In 1907, the Tenbury Advertiser advertised a similar offer of 160 acres free in Canada. The aim was to encourage even more farmers to emigrate, set up their own farm, stop paying rent, make a happy home and enjoy a healthy, bracing climate. This was offered under the old flag of cheap fares and comfortable, speedy travel and promised that work could always be found on farms for experienced men, domestic servants, carters and all types of willing workers. This is why so many Englishmen and their families were tempted to go to Canada.

With a considerable number of young people, mainly from farming families, going abroad and a gripping recession in agriculture in Britain, the estates were finding it hard to find suitable tenants for their farms. To fill this void, farmers mainly from central Wales, started to move into the Tenbury area. In the 50 year period from 1890 to 1940 probably one in five of all farmers in this district had come from Wales. Also in the 1880s, six farming families came from Cumberland and settled at Berrington and St. Michaels.

The next big change could arrive this year (2008) with the recession in farming, many farmers' sons and daughters are leaving agriculture for some other venture and one wonders where the next generation of farmers will come from.

In celebrating 150 years of Tenbury Agricultural Society, let us remember those early agriculturalists who founded it and express a fervent hope that the Society, and farming, will continue to thrive.

Driving through flood water

Pumping out

THE GREAT FLOODS

Since time immemorial Tenbury has been hit by serious flooding. Much has been recorded for posterity; however this short piece covers the 150 years of the Agricultural Society taken from newspaper reports in the style of the day and from personal memories.

The 1886 flood was the worst since 1772 when part of Tenbury church had to be rebuilt. The whole valley seemed to have turned into a roaring torrent which brought down with it trunks of trees, the bodies of dead animals and wreckage of all sorts in indescribable confusion. So irresistible was the force of the current that every bridge upon it received damage more or less serious, whilst several were destroyed. Amongst these was the wooden bridge at Little Hereford which was carried away.

The water was so deep and the current so strong that garden walls near Tenbury church and Church Alley loosed a wall of water into Teme Street, bringing with it all movable things in adjacent gardens and yards, such as tubs, cucumber frames, wheelbarrows, beehives, poultry and pigs.

The force was so great that it broke shop windows and doors down, releasing buckets, hampers, cases of wine, groceries, casks and bales of carpets. William Jones, a tailor, was drowned in his house in Church Street. Hundreds of cheeses, pickles, tinned goods and groceries were seen floating down Teme Street after torrents of water smashed the windows of Mr. Goodall's shop next to the Vaults. It is said that the noise of the water as it tore down the street made a sound so loud as for it to be impossible for people to hear their neighbours shouting from the other side of the street. Plenty of people were confined to their upstairs rooms for two days without any food. The flood water was at least five feet deep in the principal streets and over three feet deep in the knave of the church. The iron railings in front of the Union Workhouse were broken down and the garden crops washed away. The inmates who slept on the ground floor were for sometime in jeopardy, but Mr Higgins, the Master, waded through the water and carried them to safety upstairs. The wall dividing the Advertiser premises and Mr Winton's new sale yard was washed down and Onibury railway bridge was washed away as a coal train was passing over; the locomotive got over safely but the trucks were washed into the river.

The 1924 Great June Flood

The late Mrs Ida Brooks who lived at the Boat House Farm, Eastham, said the river rose so fast overnight that farmers had no chance to get their animals to higher ground. She remembered seeing the flood rushing past their farm, debris of all description and lots of animals, some dead, some alive, being washed down by the torrent of water. Cattle belonging to Mr W.H.Bowkett, the butcher, were washed from the Little Palmers meadow, four miles downstream to near Eastham Church, where they got caught up on a hedge bank; two local farmers, Mr Bert Froggatt and Mr H.J.Spilsbury, swam their horses to the stranded cattle who followed the horses and swam back to dry land.

A pig which was in its sty in the Rhyse Lane, the water having risen so quickly, floated out of its pen and it was found near Rochford Church where it had managed to swim to safety. The tenants of The Old Toll House which used to be near Eastham Bridge, who always kept a bacon pig, had to bring it upstairs till the water subsided.

Opposite:
Riding the flood waters

Need makes the old wife trot.

The 1947 Flood

After a mild windy autumn and early winter, snow started to fall in early January, increasing in mid-January to a Siberian blizzard with drifts everywhere, and 12 to 15 feet not uncommon. Most of the schools closed, as the children from the surrounding villages could not travel or even walk to school for up to 8 weeks. Temperatures went so low, with 18 degrees of frost regularly and occasionally down to 27 degrees of frost. There was a slight thaw from time to time followed by freezing rain. This froze on the telephone wires which carried ice at least an inch thick. The weight of ice, with some posts carrying 10 or 12 wires, was so great that it snapped the telegraph poles off, particularly down the Teme Valley between Tenbury and Eardiston.

This was the winter that the older generation said was the worst in their lifetime. Lots of sheep were buried for days until they could be dug out and brought to the farm buildings. In the hills, thousands of sheep and ponies perished through lack of food. Low temperatures continued until the middle of March and then the weather turned very mild; the thaw set in, causing tremendous floods all round the district. There were still snow drifts to be seen melting up to the end of May.

In flood

In 2007 Tenbury was hit by a triple whammy; the town was hit three times in June and July when the River Teme burst its bank for the first time in many years, flooding the town to a dangerous level. When it peaked between June 24 and 26 the river was in full flood and there were no boundaries for the raging river and the nearby Kyre Brook. The flood water forced a way through public buildings, shops and homes leaving over 45 devastated. The emergency services from across the region were called in to rescue people, business was at a standstill and many people were made homeless.

On July 17 it happened again. Due to a severe thunderstorm the surface water drainage was unable to cope as 15 mm of rain fell in just one hour and, in some parts of the town water levels rose to almost a metre. This was followed 3 days later by persistent and heavy rainfall resulting in a severe flood warning from The Environment Agency. In the Teme catchment area over a month's rain fell in 15 hours and the river rose to higher levels than those recorded during the June floods, reaching 5.97m, some 15 times higher than normally expected during an average summer. The wall alongside Kyre Brook which had come down during the June flood allowed a raging stream to break through into Market Street at a level higher even than in June, leaving the Victorian toilet block hanging dangerously over the once gentle brook. It has since been demolished.

Flood in High Street

Despite major efforts, it has taken almost a year to dry out and refurbish the town and it is still not yet up to scratch. Some homes, shops, eating places and small business are still suffering the effects of the flooding but thankfully life goes on in the little town in the orchard, just as it did after earlier floods and the smile on the face of Tenbury Wells is just about back to happy again.

Hawthorn bloom and Elder flowers will fill the house with evil powers.

THE INFLUENCE OF DRINK

"Drink, men of Tenbury, drink, like the clay of our country side. Drink till you have had enough and never a drop beside." From the address given by Lord Northwick on his wedding day in 1872.

It's fair to say that born and brought up in cider and hop country there is little doubt as to why the men of Tenbury liked their tipple. In the latter part of the nineteenth century the hay and harvest allowance per man was eight or nine quarts of cider a day. The following claim by Sam Coles, an employee at Lower Nash Farm, Tenbury, around 1880, was often referred to as something of a record. During harvest time he was able to lift twenty loads of wheat in a day earning him twenty quarts of cider, at one quart (2 pints) for each load. During hay and harvest time a 'day' would often last from 4 am to 10 pm and, working such long hours under the sun it is quite possible for a hard working farmhand to sweat out a similar amount of liquid. It is also said should a man working hard sup that amount of alcohol it will travel to his brain; the results can be disastrous. In such a situation, alcohol combined with a slow down in energy can leave him weak willed and the brain more fuddled.

For generations cider has played a major part in the welfare and health of local farming families. At this time wages were around 12 shillings a week and despite the Truck Acts prohibiting any part of wages in kind, the weekly earnings included two quarts of cider and with the agreement of employees the law was quietly ignored. The growing problem of drink and farm workers came to a head in Tenbury about 1885 when some of the local clergy and one or two squire employers, tried to organize a Tenbury Conference to discuss the question of cider as wages. The aim was to encourage farmers and the farming work force to listen to reason and give up the under the counter habit of 'part payment in cider'. The meeting, held in the Corn Exchange, resulted in a riot witnessed and remembered by Tenbury folk for many generations. It appears that all went wrong for the organisers when some local wag intent on opposing the plan organized free drinks at all the public houses and the audience, by now well primed with cider, refused to listen. The lecturer offered the objectors a fair challenge to a personal contest in a nearby hay field with, or without, 'strong drink' involved. Fighting broke out, the meeting ended in uproar, and for a few days the Teme Valley echoed to chants for 'Zider, Zider'. Common sense prevailed when the more capable workmen realised that they would have more money to spend as they pleased if wages were all cash and wised-up employers could see that less drink produced more work and better work. Nevertheless, consumption of alcohol remained high in some quarters particularly at a farm at Greete where three men and an occasional visitor knocked back 1,300 gallons of cider in three months.

On the question of drink in general it is true to say that in the mid-1800s, there were far too many licensed houses in England and the Tenbury neighbourhood was no exception; the amount of strong liquor consumed was out of all proportion to the betterment of health and economy of the community. During a period when a license could be had for the asking, records show that in the country as a whole, one house in forty was a licensed premises and in cathedral cities, small boroughs, and market towns like Tenbury, one house in eight was the common denominator.

Local customs die very slowly in the Tenbury district and by the turn of the 20th century and until quite recent times, the secret and unlicensed selling of cider often persisted, especially on Sundays, at certain farm houses. Throughout

When you hear the cuckoo shout it's time to plant your taters out.

the Border counties, 'market peart' and 'over the mark' have long been a part of agricultural life and Market Day in Tenbury was up to the mark. Sometimes on a Tuesday evening pedestrians would pass the churchwarden who was nodding off in his dog-cart or trap on his way home. To be on the safe side the worldly wise gave him an extra six inches of the road, or more, just in case he had been at the 'tipple'. However, when spirits became fashionable as a 'top up' to the milder alcoholic liquors, changes in drinking customs brought with them the habit of 'treating'. The blackmail of the 'social class' almost wrecked many a happy and hardworking family.

Like most places, the offer of a 'cup o' cider' was considered an every day courtesy when men met up at a pig-killing, any other special job, or even a casual visit. It was custom for the postman usually to stop on his round for a mug of cider at every substantial house he served. Even when 'over the mark', men who went to a sale or market were rarely let down when it came to a bargain. When money is at stake, wits may be dulled but the instinct of self preservation soon clicks in. It is still generally agreed that a proper deal cannot be done without a glass or two to clinch it.

A more serious aspect of the question of drink is the damage done to the younger generation. A boy going out at the age of 13 or 14, on a farm, was practically forced to drink his cider or he was called a milksop. Teetotalers were ridiculed, 'Bands of Hope' groups were barred in most parishes and even the clergy, who in the earlier half of the nineteenth century had not been afraid to take on squires, remained quiet when it came to temperance propaganda.

An interesting and revealing story tells of Lord Northwick, owner of the Burford Estate. Considered a kind and generous landlord, he married late in life and on his wedding day in 1872 he invited everyone to his wedding party and addressed the local community from the top of Castle Tump, offering them the following piece of wholesome advice:

"Gentlemen, you will now be saying with the Latin poet, Horace, "Nunc est bibendum" (Latin for Now is the time to drink). But let me first give you one word of advice: Drink men of Tenbury, drink like the clay of our countryside, drink till you've had enough, and not one drop more."

The advice was not followed. Cider prevailed, and ruled for the rest of the day. The men of Clee Hill, scenting a days sport, invaded the Tenbury festivities, seized the best parts of the roasted ox; and then captured the rectory gardener who was making a drunken fool of himself in his jaunty pot hat and new broadcloth suit and rolled him in the large dripping pan. The usual riot between the men of Tenbury and Clee Hill ensued and the Festivities Committee, made up of the leading farmers of the parish, believed discretion to be the better part of valour and let the rioters fight it out. For centuries cider in Tenbury and the Teme Valley has been not only a popular beverage; for generations it has been part of the life and culture of the community. Nevertheless would Queen Victoria's 'Little Town in the Orchard' have been happier and more prosperous if the local cider was less plentiful in both quantity and alcoholic strength and would she have been amused? Old customs die hard and for some, better laid to rest. Thankfully, despite the ups and downs of its history, times have changed for Tenbury and the Teme Valley in so many ways since the Agricultural Society was founded a century and a half ago, and it shows in the quality of life and wellbeing of the community.

Cut a thistle in June it will bloom again soon.
Cut a thistle in July it will lie down and die

TAKING THE WATERS

Considered an architectural folly, Tenbury's Gothic style Pump Rooms designed by Birmingham and Oxford based architect James Cranston were built in 1862. Once described as 'Britain's sorriest building', after years of neglect falling into disrepair it had rusted away to become unusable and unsafe. By the turn of the twenty-first century it had been transformed, at a total of £700,000, from a heap of Victorian junk back to its former glory, a Chinese Gothic style Pump Rooms worthy of a place in local and national architectural history.

PUMP ROOMS

Cranston was 42 years old when the Tenbury Improvement Company awarded him the contract to design a new spa building in Tenbury and for a relatively unknown architect to have been considered for such a prestigious project was somewhat surprising. However, at the time he did have a good track record in the West Midlands and among the buildings attributed to his architectural skills was the Birmingham Music Hall, better known as the Prince of Wales Operetta House, destroyed by fire in 1941. He was also architect for the Round Market and the National School in Tenbury and his other local achievements were the Leominster Town Hall, built between 1852-55 at a cost of £8,000 including the land, and the Gothic style Corn Exchange for which he won first prize in an architectural competition.

Cranston's idea for the Pump Rooms stemmed from his own designs for greenhouses in Hereford. He had just published a book on his newly patented design for horticultural buildings; he used the same template but replaced the glass panels with sheet steel and added timber and Victorian brickwork for good measure. His unique design for the Pump Rooms turned out to be one of the first prefabricated buildings to be erected and was fixed together on site using Birmingham-made wrought iron plates and cast iron clips.

Designed for the middle to working classes, the building consisted of two halls, one a Pump Room measuring 32 feet x 20 feet plus a recess to display the fountain, the other housed the bathrooms and the attendant's cottage. The octagonal well tower and pump house was capable of producing mineral water at the rate of 20 gallons per hour; it was 58 feet from the surface and produced a smell described as being something akin to the odour of a discharged gun.

The painted french grey roof was offset by a dark shade of blue. On completion the building was described as 'Chinese Gothic', and it was surrounded by pleasure gardens offering spa mineral water for bathing and to drink from an ornate fountain at two pennies a glass.

Visitors travelled from far and wide to take the waters and enjoy the local attractions but like any other new project it had its ups and downs but a year after it was built the Bath based Withys Soda Water Company offered to carbonate the mineral water. In May 1872 a ten year agreement was reached at the Annual General Meeting of the Improvement Company to give up the lease and two months later the company, having completed its work, was voluntarily wound up. The following year the spa was re-opened for the summer season with a menu offering six hot baths at nine shillings and six cold baths for five shillings, the attendant was Mrs Griffin.

During the floods of 1886, Mrs Griffin and her son and daughter became trapped in the single story attendant's cottage and for almost 24 hours clung to chairs stacked on beds before eventually being rescued by rowing boat and taken to the Royal Oak where they spent three days recovering from their ordeal.

To cope with the influx of visitors arriving to take the waters, the Swan Hotel

Good fences make good neighbours.

was extended and the Crow turned into a large boarding house and hotel. With the increase in medicinal tourism came prosperity and before long the Tenbury Wells Spa with its quality mineral waters, artistic attractions and beautiful countryside was considered second best only to Leamington and Cheltenham Spa towns.

It remains something of a mystery as to why the Crow site was chosen for the project rather than the more popular Swan Hotel. It appears that in 1839 Septimus Godston was searching for a better quality of drinking water on his land near the Crow when he discovered a spring. After digging more deeply he hit a brine mineral water layer and had it tested for chemical content. It was found to contain iodine, claimed to have healing powers, so he bought up other possible wells in Tenbury to safe guard his investments. He then headed the search for a site to build a spa with land available for promenades, walks, hotels and boarding houses and although a number of other grand schemes were put forward for the project he commissioned James Cranston as architect and local builder Mr. Smith took on the work budgeted at £1,000. Once completed it became topic of conversation, drumming up visitors from across the region and beyond. Eventually time was to prove that there was not a big enough middle class population in the area to support a spa and doom and gloom soon set in.

Cranston took the brunt of the critism; in some quarters, perhaps out of jealousy, he was thought to have been "well past his prime" when he took on the project and grumblings that "Tenbury Spa was a mean affair", even when new, could not have helped his situation.

Slow decline soon set in and despite being put to many good uses between the two world wars Tenbury as a spa town never really caught on. During the second world war the Pump Rooms had been used as a bath house for evacuees, Roman Catholic Mass, a café and the weekly Women's Institute produce market. In 1945 Wolverhampton and Dudley Breweries purchased it with a view to complete renovation, but it was not to be.

From then on it was downhill all the way for the dilapidated, rusting now dangerous building until 1978 when a letter from Mrs. E. Morris from Eastham, called for a campaign to save and restore the 'crumbling piece of Victoriana' by bringing the "need for serious preservation and restoration" to the attention of the National Trust. It was well received. Declaring it a "building of the greatest importance and increasing national interest" the Trust's Historic Buildings Representative, Anthony Mitchell replied "We are delighted to hear of your campaign to save this extraordinary building which is so full of character. We certainly feel it should be preserved as part of the character of Tenbury Wells." He also pointed out that the local council should play their part, reminding them that help might be made available by the Historic Buildings Council of the Department of the Environment. Encouraged by the Trust's moral support, Mrs Morris copied the response to the appropriate councils, and authorities, and to the Worcestershire Federation of Women's Institutes, her campaign supporters. She told them, "With the National Trust morally behind the campaign to save the historic Pump Rooms, people will soon realise this isn't just a whim but a serious fight to save something worth saving."

In 1986 Leominster District Council, the local authority governing Tenbury Wells at the time, bought the Pump Rooms but later boundary changes brought it under the authority of the Malvern Hills District Council. The first phase of

A leopard never changes its spots.

the refurbishment, shoring up the remaining structure to make it as water and wind proof as possible, was started in the mid-1990s and cost over £300,000. Under the watchful eye of the town, architects, builders and craftspeople continued to restore the rare building to the very high standards laid down by the principle backers and, on Friday 22nd February 2001, civic dignitaries and honoured guests puffed out their chests and council officers smiled success as Tenbury's pride hit a new high. Malvern Hills District Council had taken the project forward and Council Leader Reg Farmer accompanied by Chairman Mrs Barbara Williams, congratulated everyone involved – from English Heritage, Advantage West Midlands, European Regional Development and both Leominster and Malvern Hills District Councls, to the imaginative architects and builders and the skilled craftspeople, on a job well done. Mayor of Tenbury Councillor Peter Mound declared it a great relief to have the Pump Rooms open again and hoped the town would get the spin-off it deserved.

Rebuilt and renovated, the Pump Rooms became the local office for the District Council and attractive meeting rooms for local groups and societies. Eventually it was licensed for weddings and civil partnerships and it was fitting that the first ceremony in May 2003 was the marriage of James Dovey, son of District Superintendent Registrar, Gail Dovey, and his Polish bride Joanna Partyka.

In July 2007, the building suffered serious damage when the town was hit by consecutive floods; following six months of drying out and refurbishment it was decided to relocate the administrative function to new, purpose built premises close to the town library. In February 2008 moves were afoot to hand over the Pump Rooms to the Town Council and consideration as to its futures lies in their hands. Hopes remain high that it could become the new base for Tenbury's bulging museum and, after all its ups and downs, a suitable role for a truly historic building.

Flooded July 2007

William Norris - c.1890

RAILWAYS IN AND AROUND TENBURY

William Norris was 29 when he came to Tenbury in 1850 to take over a solicitors' business in Market Square from Mr Williams Adams. From the first time he visited the town he liked it and thought that all it was short of was a railway. Over the next few years his solicitors' practice brought him into contact with local businessmen and landowners, among them Captain Rushout (later to succeed to the title of Lord Northwick) of Burford House. Norris soon had plenty of support for the railway but had difficulty getting the promise of enough funding. He set about improving the standing of Tenbury and persuading local businessmen that it would be to their benefit to have a railway in the town. His next move was the setting up and becoming secretary of the Tenbury Corn Exchange and Public Buildings Company who were responsible for the constructing of the Corn Exchange in Teme Street and the Round Market opposite Norris' office in Market Square. In addition he formed the T.A.S. in 1858, also becoming secretary, an office he was to hold until 1898. With support of businessmen in and around Tenbury and major landowners, funding was available and with the advice of Lord Northwick, who was Chairman of the Oxford, Worcester and Wolverhampton Railway, the railway was brought into the Teme Valley.

First thoughts were to put a line from Wooferton to Tenbury and then to Worcester, but after several meetings it was decided to follow the old canal to Newnham and go on to Bewdley and Kidderminster which eventually would link to Birmingham and the Black Country. Part of the Kington Leominster Canal (about 18 miles) was opened in 1796 as far as Southnett Tunnel and linked to the coal pits at Mamble by a miniature railway which was in use for about 50 years. The canal was never a financial success, funding ran out and, after the collapse of Southnett Tunnel, work was abandoned from Mamble to Stourport and the canal closed in 1859. The land it stood on from Wooferton to Newnham was bought by the Tenbury Railway Company in conjunction with the Shrewsbury and Hereford Railway Company. Using some of the old canal bed and purchasing extra land from the adjoining estates, the Railway Company laid a single track between Wooferton and Tenbury, completing and opening it in August 1861 and worked by Great Western Railways. This section crossed the county boundaries of Shropshire and Herefordshire through attractive and unspoilt countryside and crossed the River Teme and the A456 road at Little Hereford on its way to Tenbury. Though the station was half a mile from the town it was considered the best route as the next extension was planned to roughly follow the canal bed to Newnham Bridge. Tenbury remained a terminus for three years after which time the Tenbury to Bewdley section was completed and opened in August 1864, also worked by GWR. In June 1878 a three mile link between Bewdley and Kidderminster opened, which meant it was linked up to the Midland towns and Birmingham and London. Up to the opening of the railway, visitors to Tenbury and the area would have travelled by coach and horses; the Swan Hotel in particular would have been very important as a staging post and a change of horses. An advertisement in the Tenbury Advertiser in 1899, when Mr. Henry Preece ran a posting establishment at the Swan Hotel, was "offering for hire - a Landau, Broughams, 2, 3 and 4 horse brake wagonettes, dog carts, wedding and funeral carriages including a glass hearse".

When the railway first opened it would have brought considerable trade to Tenbury and even more visitors to the spa to take the waters. Being a large hop

What is sauce for the goose is also sauce for the gander.

growing area, at this time nearly every farm grew some hops and on the bigger farms (20 or 30 acres), several thousand pockets would have gone to market by rail which would previously have been taken by horse and wagon, mostly to Worcester or Hereford hop markets. Fruit had been important for several hundred years but with the coming of the railway large acreages were planted and sent to be marketed in the midland and northern towns of England as well as Scotland and South Wales. It was at this time that Tenbury became known as the "town in the orchard". Records show that around 1,000 people from Birmingham and the Black Country attended the Tenbury steeplechases for several years running when they were held at Oldwood and on the course behind the Swan Hotel, past the hospital and on to the present showground site. Practically the whole of this ground is now built on - the first phase erected after World War II and it was soon to take all the ground north alongside the A456. The railway was very busy in the hop picking season when as many as 6,000 pickers would arrive, mainly at Tenbury and Newnham Bridge, on special trains in late August and September, with 1,200 pickers alone going to Mr J. A. Partridge at Woodston. Hop picking could last up to six weeks and special Sunday trains were laid on for visitors to see their families for the day. When picking ended special trains would take the families back home complete with fruit of all descriptions, particularly apples which were given to them by the hop and fruit farmers. Most of the pickers came from the Dudley, Tipton, Cradley Heath and Wolverhampton areas.

Tenbury livestock markets were held fortnightly and cattle, sheep and pigs were bought up by butchers from Birmingham, Halesowen, Stourbridge, Kidderminster and Stourport. The sales were advertised as starting at the time of arrival of the 11.18am train. Cattle and sheep sales were held monthly, the biggest in April and October when it was usual for 750-1,500 cattle to be sold as well as large quantities of sheep. Buyers came regularly from the Midland Counties and occasionally from the eastern and Home Counties and special train loads of animals left Tenbury station for pastures new until motor transport gradually took over after World War II. In the early 1900s the local auctioneers had to ask the railway company to build extra loading pens at Tenbury station to accommodate the increase in animal sales. The next problem was a shortage of engines to shunt the loaded wagons onto the sidings and bring in more empty wagons. The G.W.R. could not spare an engine all the time for shunting, so a cart horse was used to move the trucks backwards and forwards at busy times.

Animals were loaded at Newnham Bridge but only in small quantities compared with Tenbury. However, in the fruit season Newnham was the busier station although extra staff had to be brought in at both stations for the fruit season, June until November. It started with cherries and soft fruits such as strawberries, currants and gooseberries and in late July the early Prolific plums and later dessert varieties such as Victoria and Queens Crown; these were followed by damsons and then apples of all varieties. Newnham station was close to the main fruit growing area of the Teme Valley serving Eardiston, Stockton, Lindridge, Eastham, Newnham, Knighton-on-Teme and other villages on higher ground either side of the valley. Tenbury station served villages such as Rochford, Stoke Bliss, Kyre, Sutton, Kyrewood, St. Michaels, Burford, Boraston and Nash. Most of the fruit grown up to the mid 1930s was delivered to the station by horses pulling all kinds of conveyances such as carts, drays, wagons, floats as well as some motor vehicles.

Fruit shed, Newnham Bridge c.1930. G. Powell with horse and dray loaded with chips and sieves of fruit from H. Muller

Newnham station was so busy in the afternoon when loading had to be completed by 3 or 4 o'clock ready for dispatch by different trains that a line of horse drawn and motor vehicles would stretch from the station yard down the road nearly as far as the Talbot Hotel at times, waiting their turn to get unloaded. Fruit wagons to be loaded for the Midlands and Northern towns were at different sidings in the goods yard so that they could be shunted onto the correct line for the connecting trains. Generally the Midland bound wagons were loaded on the east side and the northern bound on the west side. Loading was done by the railway staff as any damage in transit was the responsibility of the rail company. Ventilated covered wagons were used as fruit was mainly sent in woven willow baskets, namely pot hampers of various sizes, half pots, bushels, half bushels (sieves) and strikes (half sieve). These containers were usually covered over with newspaper or bracken held in place with two hazel sticks. This was to keep the dust off and to stop pilfering. In the mid 1920s twelve pound chip baskets, made from woven wicker wood with a metal handle, and soon after a waxed cardboard chip was used especially for cherries and soft fruit which had a cardboard cover held in place by two elastic bands. The twelve pound chips were stacked two deep in the trucks but the willow baskets of all descriptions were only loaded in a single layer to avoid crushing the fruit. Pot hampers seem to have varied in size over the years holding 56lbs to 90lbs of fruit.

The following letter appeared in the Tenbury Advertiser dated August 1874:-
Sir, as to frequent disputes, as to what is a weight of a pot of fruit. A pot of plums or damsons weighs 90 pounds, a pot of gooseberries weighs 90 pounds, a pot of pears weighs 90 pounds, and a pot of apples weighs 84 pounds.
W. H. Withington, Fruit Merchant, Tenbury.
These figures were later confirmed by an advertisement in the T/A dated October 1881 -
WANTED by T. H. Graves, Fruit Merchant, Tenbury and Newnham.

500 pots of best Blenheim Orange apples 10s 6d for 84lbs Net.
500 pots of best Forester apples 7s 6d for 84lbs Net.
500 pots of best Princess Pippin apples 7s. 0d for 84lbs Net.
To be delivered to his packing shed.

CHERRIES

Bushel baskets generally held 48lbs of plums or damsons or 40lbs of apples. Sieves held 24lbs of plums or damsons and 20lbs of apples and cherries.

The woven willow basket was superseded in the 1930s by the bushel and half bushel boxes which held the same weights as the willow containers, the reason being that the bushel is an international measure by volume. The advantage of the wooden box over the willow was that it could be stacked to any height without damaging the fruit and making best use of the space available. Before the fruit season started, thousands of basket containers strung together in bundles were sent to Newnham station; these were unloaded along the side of the railway line for a distance up to half a mile east of the station almost as far as Oxnalls Farm. Whereas the smaller growers of fruit would take one load a day to Newnham station, the bigger growers, such as Eardiston Farming Company would take two or three loads a day, firstly by horse drawn transport and later by

Hard work never killed anyone.

motor lorry. In the early 1800's records show that Sir William Smith had between one and two hundred acres of fruit at Eardiston as well as a big acreage of hops. Later taken over by the Wallace family and trading as Eardiston Farming Company, they picked as many as 130 tons of cherries in a season as well as vast tonnages of other fruit, all sent on the rail from Newnham.

For many years Mr T.H. Graves ran the Tenbury and Newnham Bridge Fruit Packing Company at Newnham. He had his own fruit shed adjoining the station where mainly smaller growers would sell their produce, such as fruit, mushrooms, rabbits, holly and mistletoe to him and no doubt he would have been able to select the best markets to send to. Besides the large tonnage of fruit the railway carried other farm produce including potatoes, hops, grain, sugar beet and timber in whole tree lengths from the local farms and estates. Incoming rail freight would include coal, feeding stuffs of all descriptions, tools and implements, shoddy from the Yorkshire woollen mills, used as manure and mulch in the hop yards.

The railway had served Tenbury and district very well, giving a reliable and efficient service, but with the increase of more up-to-date motor vehicles, both passengers and goods declined from the late 1940s and the line was closed to passengers in 1962 and goods in 1964. The Wooferton to Bewdley railway acquired the name Blue Bell line; running through Herefordshire, Shropshire and Worcestershire amid beautiful unspoilt countryside of meadow land, hop yards and vast acreages of fruit and to the east through the Wyre Forest with all its wild flowers and often wild deer. Dr. Beeching closed this line as no doubt it could not compete with motor transport and was losing money, but it is one of the tragedies of our time that this beautiful railway should have been closed forever. If it had been kept open there is no doubt it would have been one of the best tourist attractions in this country.

Tenbury Station opened in 1861

Some turn up their sleeves to work, others turn up their noses.

119

William Norris - c.1890

A GOOD AND FAITHFUL SERVANT

When William Norris, an up and coming solicitor from Leicestershire, brought his attractive wife Louise, a doctor's daughter, to Tenbury Wells in 1849, he was full of enthusiasm; from then on he made it his business to do his best for the town and he kept his word. He had come to Tenbury to take over the local law firm of William Adams and within a few years he was associating with landowners and businessmen in the district, none more so than Lord Northwick of Burford House and Sir Frederick Gore-Ouseley, founder of St. Michaels College. Little did he know then that his commitment to the town was to rob him of his wife.

William was born in Leicestershire in 1821; his father was the Vicar of St. Mary's Church in Harby, a small village in the Vale of Belvoir, nine miles from Melton Mowbray. Like father like son, he was brought up in the Christian faith and was soon an active member of the Church of England. He was 21 when he completed his articles with a law firm in nearby Grantham where he qualified as a solicitor. He later joined the law practice of Sewell, Escourt and Norris, in Newport on the Isle of Wight before coming to Tenbury to set up the partnership of Norris and Miles in the Market Square. Strangely, the little island off the Hampshire coast was to have a profound affect on William's domestic life.

William and Louisa had been married for 3 years or so when they arrived in Tenbury Wells; the couple lived at The Mount and for a while seemed to have settled in well despite not having children. The couple worshipped at St. Mary's Church, Tenbury, where William was a church warden and Sunday school teacher. He also took on various unpaid offices in the Hereford Diocese including work for church charities and after a while it appeared to be business before pleasure as he continually left his wife unattended.

With no children to care for and a husband 'married' to the job, we can only assume that Mrs Norris was often left alone for long periods and with time on her hands, perhaps she also left the door ajar for passing strangers.

The Rev. George Giles was no stranger to the Norris household; he had arrived in Tenbury 1854 to take up the post of Curate at St. Mary's Church and instantly formed a close friendship with William and Louisa calling on them whenever he could and enjoying their hospitality. Twelve months later George was struck down with rheumatic fever and the kindly couple unselfishly nursed him through his long illness. He eventually recovered, left Tenbury for pastures new and nothing was heard of him for two years.

That is, until February 1857 when William took Louise to the Isle of Wight for a much needed rest and a change of air. She stayed with Lady Holmes, a family relative and William, happy to be leaving his wife in good hands, returned to his business in Tenbury. However, within a month Louisa told Lady Holmes that William had called her back to Tenbury and she would be returning home. But it was the little white lie that almost destroyed her husband. Instead she took the coach to Cowes, presumably to meet up with George Giles, who it seems, was her secret lover.

When the news reached Tenbury of the awful scandal the good man of Tenbury was devastated and shocked by his wife's deceit. Determined to get to the truth of the sordid story he called in his solicitor to help track down his wife. She was finally traced to a house in Vauxhall Bridge Road, South London where she was living with George Giles under the name of Mr and Mrs Grant.

One years seeding, seven years weeding.

They had also been identified under the same name at Liddington's Hotel, Paternoster Row in the City of London.

The facts of the matter were witnessed by William's brother, the Rev. T. Norris; Dr. Sweet from Tenbury, Mr. Jones, William's solicitor, and a few other witnesses giving William no choice other than to sue for divorce.

The case turned out to be one of the first divorce hearings convened under the new Divorce and Matrimonial Causes Act passed in May 1858; it was heard by the full court headed by Lord Chief Justice Campbell, Lord Chief Baron Pollock and Judge Ordinary, Sir C. Creswell. Until then a divorce could only be obtained through Act of Parliament, passed after an investigation before the House of Lords; it was not usually available to a commoner.

When Louisa and George appeared before the court they were asked to reply to the divorce petition, they refused and stayed silent. When their lawyer asked the Court if he could make a statement on their behalf, he was refused but was allowed to cross examine the witnesses.

Lord Chief Justice Campbell was not best pleased by the defendants' refusal to answer to the petition stating "You were summoned to appear in the Court and you were at liberty to put in an answer; but not having done so and not having denied the allegations of the petition, you cannot now be heard on the case. It seems to us that a person has no right to be heard not having put in an answer; it would be most inconvenient if it were so. It may have the effect of changing the whole aspect of the case at the hearing without giving any notice to the petitioner. In this case the petitioner is entitled to the remedy he prays, viz. dissolution of the marriage. The marriage is proved and subsequent co-habitation; there is no ground for suspecting collusion and the adultery is clearly proved."

The Court awarded costs to George Giles; the Noble Lord Campbell having decided that the Court had no power to vary the marriage settlement.

After the hearing William Norris returned to Tenbury much chastened by his unfortunate experience and immediately threw his heart and soul into daily tasks. A year later he met and married Phoebe Nicholls from Shrewsbury and with her support his life improved and he enjoyed a good marriage lasting some 40 years or so.

In every respect an officer and a gentleman, in 1859, William helped to establish the Tenbury Company of the Worcestershire Volunteers incorporating the Tenbury Rifle Volunteer Company; Lieutenant William Norris was presented to Queen Victoria and remained company commander until 1884. Following his retirement from the Regiment, he was given the honorary rank of Major which allowed him to wear the red uniform of the Volunteers which he proudly displayed when the Volunteers, flying their new colours and accompanied pipes and drums, attended the start of the building works for the Pump Room in 1861. To commemorate his long military service he received the Victoria Decoration and silver inkstand sporting the figure of a volunteer.

By now, education was William's top priority and his links with the Church of England and the Tenbury National School contributed to the success of the Education Act passed in 1870. When Sir Frederick Gore-Ouseley announced his plans for a new Parish complete with a church and choir school in Oldwood, the Rev. Bennett, Vicar of Tenbury objected, testing William's loyalty. William sided with his friend Ouseley, at the time curate at St. Mary's and after giving the plan careful thought he failed to understand why such a good man

(Ouseley) with principles backed by the Bishop, should not go ahead with his St. Michaels' project. In the event, both church and college were built and Norris and Miles became legal advisors to St. Michaels College.

Throughout his life, promotion and improvement of Tenbury Wells was always top of the list for William Norris; his main motivation, to increase prospects for farmers and land owners and bring prosperity to traders and businesses in the town. His first major aim, to bring the railway into the Teme Valley by extending the line from Wooferton to Tenbury, almost hit the buffers. Although he had plenty of support for his idea, funding it was a major problem; to establish his credibility and prove his worth, he became Secretary of the Tenbury Corn Exchange and Public Buildings Company responsible for building the Corn Exchange in Teme Street and The Round Market. He was also the prime mover and shaker in the founding of the Tenbury Agricultural Society in 1858 and becoming the first Secretary, a post he held for 40 years. But it was the railway that fired his imagination; his commitment and persistence paid off when his good friend, the influential Lord Northwick, came up with funding and the railway came into town in 1861. To celebrate the occasion he was given a gold pocket watch and silver candelabra.

During his life time William Norris held various appointments in the community, including; Clerk to the Tenbury County Court and to the Magistrates of the Tenbury and Burford courts, Chairman of Tenbury Parish Council, Trustee of the Bailey's Charity, a member of the Board of Health, the Foresters Court and the local Odd Fellows Lodge.

Despite being devastated by his wife's adultery, William, supported by his second wife Phoebe, continued with his good works for as long as he could. Age and poor health forced him to reduce his public activities but he continued with his legal work. During the afternoon on December 27, 1904, he left his office at Norris and Miles at approximately 3.30pmn and went home to The Mount where he died an hour later at the ripe old age of 83, from heart failure; a heart he gave unconditionally to the people of Tenbury and the Teme Valley.

In a mark of respect for a very great man, window shutters and blinds were closed as the funeral cortege, fittingly lead by the Tenbury Volunteers, progressed through Tenbury's silent streets to the sound of muffled bells. Members of the local Lodge of Oddfellows and the Ancient Order of Foresters followed behind and the people of Tenbury Wells lined the route to Oldwood. When the long procession reached the end of William Norris's final journey, it was met at the gates by the Warden of St. Michael's College and a large gathering of town's people anxious to pay their respects. When all were seated, the service, attended by the Bishop of Hereford, ended suitably with the hymn "Now the labourer's task is o'er."

The good man of Tenbury was laid to rest at the eastern end of St. Michael's Church, close to the grave of his old friend Sir Frederick Gore Ouseley. "Well done thou good and faithful servant."

He carves his meat so thin it tastes of the knife.

Some County Poems

WRITTEN UP AS ORIGINAL

2003

From an original painting by Robin Wheeldon from a country calendar - 2003

Go to bed with the lamb and rise with the lark.

A BRITISH FARMER'S
THOUGHTS AND AFTER THOUGHTS

(TAKEN FROM THE
TENBURY ADVERTISER OF 1903)

I'm an old British Farmer, and "Hereford bred",
Though I've ne'er a white face, nor horns on my head.
I live quiet and snug, on a sizable farm;
And to never a neighbour I wish any harm.

Time was when from sunrise till close of the day,
My spirits were good, as I paced the old way.
But nowadays things are unlike what they were.
If they rose in their graves, how our fathers would stare;

I once loved the life of a Farmer, but now
I'd as lief be a bullock, or horse at the plough;
Yes, as well as a turnip, kohl-rabi or swede,
As go on a leading the life that I lead.

I remember the time when tight breeches and boots
Was a good enough dress for a grower of roots;
My father afore me, and his afore him,
Would have scorned to have pantaloons on a limb.

But my Missus, says she, on one Sunday last year,
"You can't go to church in those garments, my dear.
No John, I insist, to your room you'll go back,
And put on a suit of respectable black".

So now every Sunday I walk by her side,
As black as a Bishop, to humour her pride.
My feelings, of course, I endeavour to smother;
For when Madam says one thing, who dare say t'other.

My daughters, Miss Emily, Susie, and Fanny,
Have all been to school, and learnt the Pianny;
And what with their music, fine dresses, and learning,
Won't tuck up their sleeves to do washing or churning.

My boys, Tom and Dick, ride in patent top-boots,
And no baccy will touch, but cigars and cheroots;
At a glass of good beer they turn up their nose,
For French stuff as sour as 'twere made out of sloes.

In long Ulster coats, like men in the ark,
They run up to town on the 'spree' and the 'lark';
The money they spend on their pleasure, I'm sure,
Had better be spent on the farm in manure.

Then the taxes and rates, win or lose, all the same,
There's the Income-tax paper – I call it a shame;
Nay, it's worse than a shame, darned if 'tisn't a sin,
To take Income-tax out, when there's nought
coming in.

Twelve shillings per bag is the price of good wheat;
The market is full of American meat;
Says my landlord, "If barley and wheat doesn't pay,
Turn ploughland to grassland, and cultivate hay".

But I think of the days which won't come back again,
When a farmer could get a good price for good grain;
When taxes and rates were what folks could afford,
And we didn't build schools just to please the
School-Board.

I know what I'll do, I'll just pack up my kit,
Sell my stock to my landlord, give notice to quit,
And take the wife and children (though perhaps
they won't come)
Across the Atlantic to seek a new home.

Yes I'm off, bag and baggage; I'm tired o'taxation,
Free trade, strikes, and unions, and co-operation,
So I'll start for New York by the very next mail,
And goodbye to Old England, roast beef and good ale.

~0~0~0~0~0~0~

Wait a bit, like a farmer, my growl I have had,
About all I see going, or gone, to the bad,
But now my growl's over, to own I am free,
Though things may be bad, that still worse they might
be.

We've had some hard years; but how do I know
But next year may be good, and pay all that we owe;
I don't like high rates and School-Board education;
But I daresay it's all for the good o' the nation.

My Landlord's a trump, and my Missus she suits,
Though she hasn't good taste in the matter of boots.
My children, no doubt, are too fine for their Dad,
But young'uns are young'uns, and ours aint so bad.

Old England has faults; but, from all that I hear,
There are things in America wonderfully queer;
So I'll sing "Rule Britannia" and drink "Speed
the plough",
And stick to the Farm, as we've stuck to till now.

Beer on cider is not a good rider. Cider on beer makes you very queer.

A Countryman's Prayer

Lord, who makest corn to grow, The hens to lay, the cocks to crow, And cows to milk and sheep to lamb, Fat pigs providing us with ham,

Pray spare us simple country folk The burden of the Whitehall folk.

From rust and mildew in the corn, From maladies of hoof and horn, Mastitis,murrain,colic, cramp,

From leaking roofs and rising damp, Protect us; and [our voice is small] From faceless men in far Whitehall.

Preserve us from those sundry ills Like bailiffs men and unpaid bills, The tax demands and kindred cares That aggravate our small affairs, Especially such gents as call

"Upon instructions from Whitehall".

From motorways and speed and noise, Transistors, pop, and long-haired boys, From broken bottles, plastic bags, And hay-fires from discarded fags, Deliver us - but most of all -

From town-bred planners in Whitehall.

Grandmother's Bible

This is grandmother's Bible,
Just as she left it when.
She went upstairs in the darkness,
Not to come down again.

Night after night we saw her,
Deep in her thoughts and prayer.
Then came the night we missed her,
Looked as she was not there.

Not there – yet the candle was burning,
Her glasses lay on the book.
The chair in the chimney corner,
 Looked just as it used to look.

When we went to her room to find her,
She was kneeling down by her bed.
Just as if she were praying,
But life and spirit had fled.

Eighty years in God's service,
Daughter, mother and wife.
Now she has gone to praise him,
Still in that higher life.

Somebody closed the bible,
Somebody moved the chair.
Out of the chimney corner,
That we might not miss her there.

Yet we feel she is somehow still near us,
Not quite has she gone away.
From her children and children's children,
Who learned at her knees to pray.

Something helpful and holy,
 Lies like a fragrant smell.
Betwixt the cover of Grandmother's Bible,
Whose pages she loved so well.

This poem was recently recalled by Rosemary Pritchard's 91-year-old mother, Minnie Price, from the days when she learned this and a number of other recitations, whilst going about her duties as a dairy maid when she was 16 years old. She would prop the words up and whilst churning the butter, learn the recitations which she later performed at concert parties held at Lingen village hall. Minnie Price passed away on April 2nd 2008.

GRAVE WORDS

Here lies my husband, he was
Dishonest, erratic, erotic,
Irresistible, irrepressible, wanton,
Untrustworthy, and a liar.
Sadly missed by his ever loving wife.
R.I.P.

JOHNNY LUMP'S VISIT TO TENBURY WELLS

My names Johnny Lump Iz'e a bit of a clown,
And Iz'e come on a visit to Tenbury Town;
That sweet place in the orchard as travellers tell,
Where they've lately discovered a wonderful well.

Now this dear little spot, as history tells,
Can boast of a hero as great as its wells;
Caractacus here first drew breath, as fame goes,
On the spot they tan hides, as apt he tann'd his foes.

When to Rome, by his foes this great hero was sold,
The grief of his friends was so great I am told
That their tears made fountain of this healing spring
That ages unborn of its virtues might sing.

Now this highly favour'd, this neat little town,
Which I prophecy shortly will rise to renown,
With its river for fish and its country for game,
And its springs, so transcendent, shall raise it to fame.

The cure the consumption, the asthma, the gout,
Nay, every disorder they fairly drive out,
They give vigor to youth and the old they make young,
And the virtues for ever shall live in my song.

I've tried Cheltenham Waters, the Buxton also,
But the "Tenbury Wells" will be soon all the go,
I can speak for myself, when I come to this place
I scarcely could walk; - I can now run a race.

Now among other things dame Nature supplies,
A clear crystal spring that is good for the eyes,
I know from experience it strengthens the sight,
Only try it yourself, and you'll find I'm quite right.

For the kindness I've met with in this charming place,
No time nor no distance can ever deface,
My gratitude ever shall sing in your praise,
And I'll think of your goodness the rest of my days.

May your town and trade flourish, you wells and your shops,
Your orchards and fields yield you plentiful crops,
May prosperity ever among you be seen,
Life long to Prince Albert and God Save the Queen.

Written about the time of the opening of the railway
1864.

It's always been the same since Adam was a boy.

THE FINAL INSPECTION

The soldier stood and faced his God
Which must always come to pass
He hoped his shoes were shining
bright
As brightly as his brass.
"Step forward now soldier, how shall
I deal with you
Have you turned the other cheek.
To my church have you been true".
The soldier squared his shoulders
and said:
"No Lord, I guess I ain't
Because those of us who carry guns
can't
Always be a saint.
But, I never took a thing that
wasn't mine to keep:
Though I worked a lot of overtime
When the bills got just too steep
And I never passed a cry for help
Though at times I shook with fear,
And sometimes, God forgive me
I've wept unmanly tear.
I know I don't deserve a place
Among the people here,
They never wanted me around
Except to calm their fears.
If you've a place for me here, Lord,
It needn't be so grand,
I never expected or had too much
But if you don't, I'll understand".
There was silence all around the
throne
Where the saints often trod
As the soldier waited quietly
For the judgement of his God.
"Step forward now soldier,
You've borne your burdens well,
Walk peacefully on heaven's streets
You've done your time in hell".

LOGS

Beachwood fires are bright and
clear,
If the logs are kept a year;
Chestnut only good, they say,
If for long it's laid away.
Make a fire of Elder tree,
Death within your house shall be;
But Ash new or Ash old
Is fit for Queen with crown of gold
Birch and Fir logs burn too fast
Blaze up bright and do not last;
It is by the Irish said
Hawthorn bakes the sweetest bread;
Elmwood burns like churchyard
mould
E'en the very flames are cold;
But Ash of green or Ash of brown
Is fit for Queen with golden crown.
Poplar gives a bitter smoke,
Fills your eyes and makes you
choke;
Apple wood will scent your room
With an incense like perfume.
Oaken logs, if dry and old,
Keep away the winter's cold;
But Ash wet of Ash dry
A king shall warm his slippers by.

Anon.

THE GREEN WOODPECKER

When I were a-coming
Back home for my tea,
I hears an old Yaffle
Up top of a tree.
His cap it were scarlet,
His jacket were green –
The finest old Yaffle
That ever were seen.
He laughed and he laughed
As he sat on his bough,
But I couldn't make sense
Of that Yaffle nohow.

You silly old Yaffle,
I started to bawl,
A sitting there, laughing
At nothing at all.
And Yaffle he answered –
I swear this be true;
You silly old juggins,
I'm laughing at you.

Traditional Farm Buildings

TRADITIONAL FARM BUILDINGS

In the Teme Valley farm buildings are an important feature of the country landscape. The assortment of farm buildings of different ages found within the Tenbury Wells area, where traditional mixed farming has been practiced for many years, record centuries of historical change not only on the farm and in the countryside but also in society and the economy.

A farmstead is defined as the farm buildings and house and are usually found in grouped settlements either in villages or hamlets and a small number are isolated. Their location is the result of centuries of development and change and those which remain in villages today are the survivors of a much larger number. Isolated farmsteads are normally the result of either the occupation of previously unfarmed land by a single farm up until the late nineteenth century or the movement of a farmstead out of a village following enclosure of the open fields. Sometimes a field barn consisting of a threshing barn, usually with a shelter shed and foldyard for loose cattle, was built to serve land lying some distance away from the central farmstead. The farmer could then avoid lugging the corn back to the farmyard for threshing, could fatten cattle on site and spread the farmyard manure on the surrounding land. This practice was linked to mixed farming and the first outlying barns were built in the seventeenth century. When portable threshing machines started to be used in the nineteenth century, these outlying barns ceased to be necessary as ricks were threshed and built in the fields.

The U, E, or T-shaped layouts were favoured by our forefathers and there was much to commend them regarding the efficient use of labour. Whether the farmyard could be seen from the house was also an important part of the farm building design. The photograph below shows the original U-shaped range of Victorian buildings at Lower Quinton Farm, Leysters, which are overlooked by the house.

Lower Quinton Farm, Leysters

It looks black over Bill's mother's.

Lower Quinton Farm Buildings, Bockleton, Tenbury Wells

The farmhouse and buildings were built around 1870 by Arabella Prescott, the widow of a merchant banker. She owned the Bockleton estate which covered approximately 5,000 acres. In 1927 William and Mary Prescott (great grandchildren of Arabella) inherited the estate and continued to run it until the 1960s when one by one the farms were offered for sale to the tenants. The farm buildings are of red brick, all of which were made on the Bockleton estate. These buildings were all built to exactly the same high standard as the house and the craftsmanship is evident in the detail over the doors and windows.

The farm was offered for sale in 1905 and the sale particulars listed the original buildings as being comprised of a range with fowl house, bull house, timber built calves house and a four-stalled stable; another range of buildings included a cider house with granary above, barn, calves cot, cow house for six head, cow house and a further range of, cattle shed for nine head, two pig cots and a boiler house. At that time Lower Quinton Farm was only 100 acres.

Farm buildings were generally constructed in the local vernacular style. During the nineteenth century more uniform designs spread through the nation, however some estates decided to create or maintain their own distinctive style of building.

Generally re-modelling of farm buildings is expensive and farmers over the years have normally contented themselves with gradual adaptations and improvements which have preserved much of the old farmstead pattern. Whilst the design of farm buildings has changed only gradually in the past, the rate and type of change has been very much greater since the Second World War with the increased mechanisation and automation. Most farmers have inherited more buildings than they have erected and, though medieval and Tudor buildings may be individual rarities, a substantial proportion of farmers' buildings in the locality are Hanovarian and Victorian. We are most fortunate in the Tenbury Wells area to have a good variety of traditional farm buildings, many of which are in very good repair. A number of these old farm buildings have sadly become redundant, including a fine Grade 1 Victorian range of buildings at Sutton Court Farm, which have recently been sold to a property developer for conversion into four residential homes.

Grade One redundant building at Sutton Court

The Industrial Phase of the Agricultural Revolution

Between 1820 and 1880 the demand for food increased steadily as the population of England and Wales rose from 12 million in 1821 to 16 million in 1841. There was a further increase from 20 million in 1862 to 26 million in 1881.

Throughout most of this period it was the responsibility and profitable privilege of the British farmer to feed this growing market with little help or competition from overseas. This resulted in a major economic achievement in British history: the development of a farming system which raised the standards and efficiency of British agriculture to an all time high. However, towards the end of this period, even this 'High Farming' failed to keep pace with the demands made on it and by 1880 Britain was importing half of all bread and a quarter of all meat consumed.

From the beginning of this period it was clear that the resources and methods of the eighteenth century Agrarian Revolution could no longer keep the growing population fed. Reclamation of land continued, but the use of such land could only make a limited and ever shrinking contribution to the national food supply. It was obvious by the time of Queen Victoria's accession that any large increases in food production could only come from more intensive farming of existing farmland. The building of new farmsteads on new farm land, which had been so conspicuous during the reign of George III, then largely dwindled. The new age of farming necessitated the development of existing farmsteads to cope with the demands of a more sophisticated and productive agricultural system. Sir James Caird refers to this in a letter to Sir Robert Peel of 1850: 'It would be in vain to drain the land and fit it for the culture of green crops if no suitable housing is provided for economically converting these into a marketable form and for preserving and accumulating manure'. The growing productivity of the farmstead reflected an improvement in the quality as well as an increase in the quantity of the equipment, crops and livestock stored and housed there. The complicated and expensive farm machinery which the farmer was now buying merited better protection than the cruder implements of the past. The improved cattle of the period also required upgraded housing if they were to repay the time and skill which had been invested in them. The traditional type of steading with its obsolescent barn and dark, dirty and ill–ventilated stables and cowhouses could not meet these increased needs.

The Industrial Farmstead

The Victorian farmer sought new technical allies in order to produce more food from a limited acreage. In particular he delegated many of his traditional responsibilities for the design and erection of the more complicated buildings to professional architects and engineers. As farmers in the early Victorian period used the resources of industry to solve the problems in the farmstead, the modern concept of the farmstead as an agricultural factory began to emerge.

Land improvement companies were empowered by an act in 1849 and various subsequent acts to make capital investment in agriculture, including investment in farm buildings. These loans were largely designed to placate landowners and farmers for the repeal of the corn laws in 1845, which had deprived them of their traditional tariff protection, in the interests of a triumphant industrialism. Nevertheless the new industrial approach didn't lead to changes in the general design of farm buildings. Sir James Caird's criteria for a good farmstead were concerned with the degree to which it provided stock with warmth and shelter, allowed ease of working and made possible the conservation of rich manure. These were the concerns of his grandfather although the following generation gave higher priority to economising labour. The siting of farmsteads continued to be based on inherited principles including the need for a reliable supply of water which was as vital as in Saxon times. The basic needs and relationships of workmen, materials and livestock were not changed as it was still necessary to convert stacked corn into grain and straw, to store the grain safely, and cart straw to the yards and stock buildings. It also remained necessary to face cartsheds north to protect timber from sun and rain and to site stables near cartsheds. Victorian farmsteads were built of factory–produced materials and fitted with factory produced equipment, yet they continued the basic Hanoverian design with the old pattern of the north range with wings of livestock buildings forming south-facing yards.

Dairy Buildings

Until the middle of the nineteenth century the inherited dairy system continued unchallenged. Dairy farms mainly produced butter and cheese and the urban cow keeper provided the townspeople with milk. The familiar cowhouse with its row of individual stalls where cows were tied in winter and milked all the year, remained the accepted form of housing. Following the cattle plague in 1865, when almost a quarter of a million cattle were slaughtered to prevent its spread, an increased volume of milk was transported to London by rail. Agricultural inspectors appointed to supervise the control of the disease were the first officials to inspect the London cowhouses and their revelations led to the introduction of sanitary legislation. These new regulations initially controlled the London cowhouses but soon afterwards were applied to all cowhouses in the country. The railways enabled the Victorian farmer to take the first step towards the modern dairy system. In the 1860s American factory cheese imports into Britain began to compete with the produce of the English farmhouse so strongly in both price and quality that the Royal Agricultural Society of England sponsored the establishment of a cheese factory. This opened in 1870 and within six years ten factories were in operation. Between them they processed the milk of 7,000-8,000 cows. Future farmers would generally no longer process milk into butter or cheese themselves but instead sell it as a liquid. One result of this change was the end of the farmhouse dairy. Another consequence was the abandonment of pig-keeping in dairy areas, for the end of butter-making and cheese-making on the farm meant an end of the rich byproducts which provided cheap and convenient feed for pigs.

The Steam Engine and the Barn

The traditional barn was adapted to accommodate the new mechanical threshing equipment which became widespread in the 1820s. A variety of sources of motive power were used to drive both threshing machines and other barn machinery. Horses, water and wind were used but by the mid-Victorian age, steam power finally triumphed and the steam engine became common on large arable farms. Steam engines were used to grind and crush corn and beans, break oil cake, cut chaff and roots, whilst its heat could steam potatoes and chaff, boil linseed, and cook pig feed. The new barn equipment required new buildings as well as the adaptation of old structures. The changes generally

When the elm leaf is as big as a penny
you will have to plant if you are going to have any.

involved the addition of a loft to accommodate a chaff cutter. This allowed the chaff to fall to the floor where it was mixed with pulped roots. The steam engine for some years remained harnessed to certain limited static operations in the farmstead. Farmers realised that it was much more convenient to take the threshing machine to the corn stacks instead of carting the corn to the barn. This encouraged the development of portable threshing machines. These were driven at first by portable steam engines which were also hauled by horses but later by self-propelled traction engines which could pull as well as drive. By the early 1830s portable steam engines became popular on farms as they could be used to drive machinery anywhere. They were used much more than the fixed steam engine and were widespread in the Midlands in 1854. The portable steam engines could stand outside the barn, with belts to drive a wheel on the end of the barn machinery shafting. Most new barns built around the 1850s no longer included a stationary steam engine with a chimney. Instead a small building for a portable steam engine was constructed alongside the main barn which was now designed for the accommodation of hay, straw and feed preparation. In a generation the barn lost its ancient function as the site of the processing and storage of the corn crop and instead became the centre for the storage and processing of livestock feed.

The Barn

The barn was used to house and thresh the corn and to store pulse crops, hay and threshed straw. Most threshing barns had at least one threshing floor with bays for housing the crops either side of it. The doors to the threshing barn floor are the most prominent external feature and the most common type are the large, wide double doors which can be sub-divided horizontally to give four sections. The high doorways were necessary in order to enable loaded wagons to unload from the threshing floor into the bays. They also allowed good lighting for threshing and air for winnowing the husks from the threshed grain. Barn doors often stopped between 1 and 2 feet above the ground with a separate series of boards below. These were held in place by a groove in the bottom of the door jamb, which projected slightly for the purpose.

The 'lift', as it was called, enabled the doors to clear the manure in the yard and kept any roaming pigs off the barn floor whilst the doors were open. Air vents were incorporated to prevent any crops that had been harvested when damp from going mouldy. These were normally in the form of single holes or slits in stone barns. Brick threshing barns were more easily ventilated than stone barns as it was possible to omit a half-brick or less, without affecting the structural stability of the walls and half-brick holes could readily be arranged in rows. Geometric shapes appeared in the early eighteenth century and are the most widespread type with some vents being grouped to form the appearance of a window. Owl holes between 6 – 9 inches across were often set high in the gable end of barns to allow owls in to catch mice.

Dutch Barns

Even humble buildings illustrated the increasing complication and intensification of Victorian agriculture. Greater production and rising values encouraged expenditure on the protection of farm produce such as the building of Dutch barns which became popular in the early 1800s. Dutch barns were usually open on both sides and had brick or stone pillars to support the roof.

Sutton Court Farm showing shafting used to drive machinery

Sow four grains in a row. One for the pigeon,
One for the crow, One to rot and another to grow.

They varied in size from one to ten bays and were built to store hay, straw or sometimes unthreshed corn. Most were built after the late nineteenth century as they were previously considered an extravagance. After 1885 their use increased considerably when landowners built modern iron-framed barns with corrugated-iron roofs to combat the effects of the agricultural depression by ensuring crops were properly protected. During the 1880s a local firm situated in Tenbury market yard sold Dutch barns.

Cartshed

Until the nineteenth century, farmers' horse-drawn equipment was limited and consisted mainly of carts, wagons, ploughs and harrows. Thereafter more specialised equipment appeared which included drills, threshing and reaping machines and cultivation equipment. There was a consequent need to protect these machines from the elements and so implement shedding became more common. Cartsheds were probably only found on larger farms before the eighteenth century. The most common type surviving are open-fronted buildings with brick or stone piers, timber posts, or cast-iron columns which separate the 8-10 foot openings with a shallow arch or timber lintel above. They rarely open onto the foldyard but more often back onto the yard and face north to avoid the sun. Access to these somewhat deeper cartsheds was from the end under the gable and this type is quite common in Worcestershire. Granaries were sometimes situated over cartsheds as this allowed plenty of fresh air to circulate below making them suitably dry places.

The Granary

The granary was a very important farm building used to store the grain after it had been winnowed or threshed. The floor was usually raised above ground level by approximately two feet in order to keep it dry and to provide some protection from vermin. Entrance to the first floor was often accessed by an external staircase and the recess under the stairs was typically used as a dog kennel and sometimes a hole was left in the granary door for a cat.

The best manure is the farmer's foot.

133

Hop Kilns

Hop Kilns were used to dry the harvested hops before they were marketed. Most of the hop kilns in the area are the square or circular nineteenth century type with a characteristic tall conical roof terminating in a cowl. Square kilns were built in Herefordshire by the 1870s but not used in the southern areas until shortly before the First World War. These had brick walls and inside there was an open brick box to contain the fire. The drying floor was between 10-11 feet above and was made of laths or battens set slightly apart which allowed the hot air to pass between to the hops above which were spread out on a horsehair

Burford Mill pressing the hops into pockets

Hop Kilns at Burford Mill Farm, some dating back to 1600

134

God loves the crow as well as he loves the nightingale.

cloth. After 1885 a few rectangular kilns with a steep gable roof and a ventilator which ran the full length of the ridge appeared in Herefordshire. The upper floor of the two storey building adjoining the kiln was used for receiving the hops and for spreading the dried hops out to cool prior to compressing them into long sacks called pockets. The lower floor was only required for stoking the fires and to allow space for the pockets to hang. At other times the space was used for cider making, housing livestock or as a cartshed.

There were numerous hop growing farms around Tenbury Wells in the nineteenth century. Since the gradual demise of the hop industry in this region, however, many hop kilns have been sympathetically converted into residential properties.

Burford Mill Farm showing pockets with owners name

Dovecotes

By the eighteenth century the importance of keeping pigeons to provide fresh meat declined with the increase in farm livestock. Nevertheless, during the nineteenth century pigeons were often kept for their picturesque appearance. Initially the right to build a dovecote was strictly limited to landowners as the birds fed on any standing crops but small freeholders and tenants were later also permitted to do so.

The Stable

On larger farms separate stables were built often adjoining one another, one for wagon horses which were used for agriculture work and one for horses used for riding or pulling the carriage or trap. The amount of stable accommodation was dependant on whether or not oxen were used as draught animals, (a practice which had mostly died out by the early eighteenth century) and also on the amount of arable land farmed and whether this was light or heavy. The enclosures of open fields during the eighteenth and early nineteenth centuries reduced the number of horses needed. However with the increase in farm work during the mid nineteenth century, including the use of horse engines, more

Dovecote built in the roof area above the loft in meal house, Bickley House Farm

horses were again used on farms. Single storey stables were built towards the end of the eighteenth century, as stable lofts which were set at approximately eight feet high were thought to prevent good ventilation. In contrast, loftless cowhouses only appeared in the early nineteenth century. Many original lofts survived, however, as they helped to insulate the stable and enable it to warm up more quickly once the horses had returned from work. Lofts were also used for storing hay which was readily fed into the wooden hay racks below. Cast-iron hayracks and troughs were normally only found in hackney stables. Feed troughs which were situated below the hayrack were made from wood, brick or stone with the latter to often having a timber lip to protect the horse's mouth. Most stables had single stalls with wooden partitions high at the head and normally the full length of the stall to prevent the horses kicking and biting each other. Stalls were set five to six feet apart to enable feeding and room for the horse to be groomed whilst tied up. The stable, like the yard and cowhouse, changed little in conception and plan but greatly in detail with its improved standards of flooring, drainage and ventilation due to a growing appreciation of livestock needs. Windows in stables were large compared to cowhouses at the time, as the importance of light and ventilation in stables had been recognised sooner. Some stables had a separate harness room but most only had a number of wooden hooks which projected from the wall behind each horse. Feed rooms were mostly shared with the cowhouse or combined with the harness room. Many stables on local farms have long been redundant and either left empty or used for alternative enterprises such as calf rearing or lambing. The stable stalls at Bickley House Farm face across the building, a design which allowed more horses to be housed with better supervision.

Stable Stall at Bickley House Farm

The better the day the better the deed.

The Pigsty

In the 1850s pigs were kept on most farms as they were able to fatten quickly from food which would otherwise have been wasted. Pigsties were often built near the house for ease of feeding. By the eighteenth century most pigsties were of one type consisting of a small sty with an opening into a slightly longer yard which allowed the pigs to access both areas. There was however little interest in new buildings for housing pigs and the period of the woodland pig herd had mostly passed into history. Although in Shropshire during 1868 a combination of a good acorn year and a poor grain harvest revived the old tradition and children were sent to collect acorns for pigs at a time when they were mostly fattened in the traditional pigsty with a pen and run. A hen loft was occasionally built over the pigsty which helped to keep both pigs and hens warm. Single sties were usually only large enough for one or two pigs or a sow and her litter. Pigs are now only kept on a few small farms in the district including one free range unit at Brimfield. This may be due to the fact that farmers' wives have discontinued farmhouse traditional cheese and butter production. There are nevertheless a good number of redundant pigsties from the Victorian era remaining in the area.

Cattle Buildings

The cowhouse was the most important type of housing for cattle and was equally suitable for milking cows, fat stock and draught oxen. Cowhouses were normally approached from the main yard in the farmstead, as this allowed for ease of collecting the manure which was cleaned out daily from behind the cows and tumped in the yard. A large proportion of the cowhouses built after 1800 were open to the roof as lofts didn't allow the heat generated by the cows to escape and as a result cattle often suffered ill health. Water troughs were fitted in some cow houses by 1845. Racks for hay or straw commonly used before 1840 were replaced with mangers which were used for feeding roots, chaff and other chopped fodder. Since 1945, government regulations led to the replacement of fittings for tying and feeding cattle in dairy cowhouses. In the most common cowhouse design the cows faced across the building in a single row. The wooden

Original cow house
at Bank Farm, Rochford

An apple a day keeps the doctor away.

137

partitions were usually fixed between every two cows and lower and shorter than in the stable. A feed passage between 3-4 feet wide in front of the cows was found in many cowhouses as this speeded up the feeding process and reduced the waste of feed.

Shelter sheds were built to shelter loose cattle and related either to a yard or a field.

Cattle yards were the most popular type of cattle housing in the early twentieth century as farmers continued to fatten bullocks in the yards built in the nineteenth century. The front wall was normally open, the roof being supported by piers or posts built from timber, stone or brick and troughs and racks were usually fixed along the back wall. Open yards were more common in rearing districts as young stock required sunshine and also in areas where rainfall was high and straw plentiful. By the 1860s the roofing of yards was well established in most parts of the country, as this provided both cattle and manure with better protection. However, they remained a mass-production unit where the larger cattle prevented the smaller ones from feeding efficiently. The improvement of yards therefore was accompanied by an increase in more intensive systems of boxes or stalls. This allowed the individual treatment of stock, where each animal could eat and rest undisturbed and feed could be more carefully rationed and manure properly conserved.

Bickley House Farm, Knighton-on-Teme, Tenbury Wells

Bickley House Farm has one of the finest examples of 19th century farm buildings still in use in the Teme Valley. Their history goes back to the 1820s. A wealthy family member involved in the wool trade in Yorkshire had a son with TB. They needed to find him an environment with clean fresh air. Bickley House Farm was available for sale and they bought it. At that time the farm had a small house and very few buildings. They first enlarged the house to accommodate the son's carers and then between 1825 and 1835 built the best of modern farm buildings using local bricks and incorporating the era's latest technological features. The main part of the buildings comprises four yards in one block, each carefully designed to provide shelter and protection from snow, driving rain and prevailing winds. Alongside the yards were stables, milking parlours, bull pens, stores for produce, a mill and a large barn. An attractive feature of the complex is the farm's dovecote. Great attention was paid to every detail including intricate brickwork and substantial hinges and catches to doors which are still in use today. Two other interesting features, added in 1863, are a fine vaulted cellar for storing cider below three kilns for drying and pocketing hops. At a later date, probably around 1900, another storage building was erected to house carts and implements. Fortunately, in good times and bad the buildings were maintained and used and the roofs were repaired from time to time at great expense.

So the original structures are still largely as they were in 1825, although usage has changed to reflect the needs of modern farming. Other than the addition of two Dutch barns in the 1950s there were no changes until 1982 when a large grain store and livestock shed were built. This building won the Country Landowners' Association award for its design and the sympathetic way that it sits alongside the much older buildings. Today all the buildings are in good working order and are at the heart of the operations at Bickley House Farm.

Hop Kilns at Bickley House Farm

Cattleyards at Bickley House Farm

Half the pedigree goes in at the mouth.

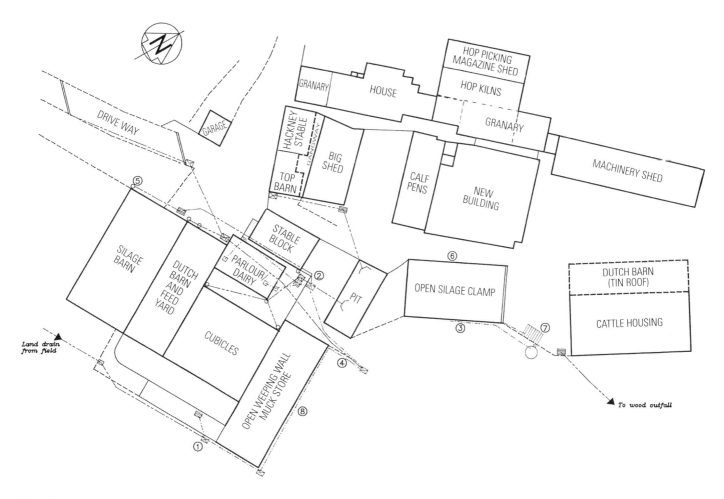

Farmhouse:

Georgian built in three stages. Attached to each end of the house is a granary so you can imagine the passage of vermin from one end to the other! Thanks to pest control that has been curtailed.

Hop Kilns:

Incorporated with the lower granary are the hop kilns and a hop-picking machine shed. Hops were reintroduced to Bank Farm in 1947 and the hop-picking machine in 1959. This enterprise came to a halt in 1998 due to cheaper hop products coming from abroad.

Machinery Shed:

This was erected in 1990 principally for machinery but since cattle numbers have increased a section is used for their wellbeing.

The Hackney Stable:

As the name suggests it was where the hackney horses were kept. These horses were kept to pull the trap or gig. It still has the partitions and the loft above.

The Top Barn:

This barn has a driveway through the centre with two large double doors each side. Sheaves of corn were stored in bays on either side and the passage in

A gallon of milk from the cow is worth two from the bucket.

the middle was used to thresh the corn. When the corn was threshed by flail, the wind blowing through would have helped to discard the chaff.

The Gangway:

This is more or less redundant, but years ago the cows would have been tied up here and calves multiple-reared on them.

The 'Big Shed':

This is not very big really. It is a corrugated half-moon building, now used as a 'maternity ward' as it is close to the bedroom window.

Original Cowhouse:

This building has been used for various enterprises over the years.

It originally had spaces to tie up 20 cows for milking and a loft above where hay was stored to feed them and mangers in front for corn or cake.
Cows were milked by hand until a bucket milking machine was introduced.

In 1975 a more modern set-up was built, so the cowhouse was gutted and the 24 single calf pens were fitted where calves were reared on the bucket.

In 2004 dairying ceased at Bank Farm and a Single Suckling Beef Herd was introduced so the calf pens became redundant.

In 2005 Mr. David Powell converted it into a 'Museum of Farming Interests'.

New Building:

This building was erected in the late 1980s and it took the place of a three sided range of open-sided brick buildings with tin roofs. There was an open yard in the middle. On the fourth side was a wooden barn which housed the chaff cutter and root pulper which were driven by an engine. The wooden structure was taken down and numbered and is supposed to be erected at Avoncroft Museum.

Stable Block:

As the name suggests this was where the cart horses were kept. There was a hay loft above and in the winter the hay was fed to the animals below through an opening from the loft into the mangers, in front of the animals. The stalls are still in it but are generally redundant, though they prove useful to get calves in for dehorning.

There was a lean-to on the back where the chaff and treacle used to be mixed for the horses' rations. It also housed the saddlery.

Dairy Unit and Cubicles:

Before the dairy unit was put up in 1975 this area had a big wainhouse with a fireplace in. Hop pickers in the 1920s slept in it. In the 1950s the men, all 16 of them, would sit around the fire in winter to have their breakfast. It was later used to store potatoes over winter and the lean-to sheds that adjoined it housed tractors and implements. An interesting brick shed was the 'Goose Cubs'. There were about 8 cubicles 2'6" square with doors on. Sitting hens were put in there to hatch out eggs. Adjacent was the 'hovel' where anything was stored! All this was flattened to make way for more efficient milk production.

Dutch Barn:

This escaped the bulldozer and was incorporated into the dairy complex. It is now used as a feeding area for cattle.

Open Silage Clamp:

This was used for containing silage to feed the dry stock. It has now been adapted into a general purpose building.

If you'd live to be old, strip before you sweat and dress before you are cold.

The Dutch Barn:
  This is original with its tin roof and is now used to house cattle in the winter as was the lean-to which was built in 1974.

Garage (falling down):
  It was originally used for hop pickers to sleep during the 1920s and the fireplace remains in situ.

Stable range for wagon horses at Bank Farm, Rochford

141

Games and Pastimes

PUMP ROOMS ARCHITECT'S CRICKET CONNECTION

Architect James Cranston's claim to fame can still be seen in and around Tenbury Wells where his unique, prefabricated design for the Chinese Gothic style Victorian Pump Rooms remains an architectural gem for some, an unrequited folly for others. In the same year, 1862, he also designed the more oval than round Butter Market and in 1855 Tenbury's National School.

As well as churches and chapels in and around the Teme Valley and in neighbouring Herefordshire, Cranston also designed the 'Italianate' Town Hall on the High Street in Leominster and the Corn Exchange in Corn Square plus a number of interesting secular and non secular buildings in Birmingham and the West Midlands. However, what may not be known is that he was the proud father of an England 'ashes' winning cricketer.

James Cranston Junior was born in Bordesly, Warwickshire, in 1859. Educated at Taunton College, he took up cricket and at the age of 17 he was selected to play for Gloucestershire County Cricket Club. Between 1876 and 1899 he played 103 first class matches for the County as an amateur in a team captained by W.G. Grace. He also played a couple of seasons for Warwickshire before the club gained first class status. He also turned out for the 'Gentlemen of England'. Considered to be one of the best left handed batsmen in England, and a fine fielder, there was little between him and Grace when it came to averages and aggregate. The height of his success came in 1890 when he was brought into the England side at short notice for the final test match at the Oval. He played a vital role in a low scoring game, his two innings, played with a straight bat, brought his team 31 important runs in the two-wicket victory against the Australians, resulting in the home side taking the Ashes.

His innings, recorded at the time in Wisden, was described as masterly under trying conditions against the Australian bowlers Turner and Ferris; nevertheless it was to be his first and last game for his country. A year later his career almost came to an end when he suffered a fit during a county game but surprisingly eight years later he was able to play in representative matches. His last appearance was for the M.C.C. in 1901. During his first class career James Cranston scored 3,450 runs in 188 matches, his top score being 152. Three years after his final match, at the age of 45, he died in Bristol on December 10th 1904.

All goes to the Devil when the shepherd is evil.

WHEN THE BEATLES CAME TO TOWN

When the Beatles came to Tenbury in 1963 it was a sell-out occasion and a wonderful musical moment that lingers in the memory of local people today. But for young Andrew Lowe it was the greatest event in the Teme Valley since Caractacus defeated a Roman Legion at Tenbury in AD49. But he missed it. The visit of the fabulous Beatles to the Riverside Dancing Club at The Bridge Hotel in April 1963 came the year after his family had moved out of Tenbury to live in nearby Rochford and he had little chance of getting into the event without help or the consent of his father. Still considered today by some people to have been the most exciting moment in history of the town, the show had an enormous impact on many of the young residents at the time, including Andrew. He was just a lad when the Beatles came to town, but he remembers the Easter weekend of 1963 very clearly. He recalled: "It was largely remembered in our house for the chaotic preparations for the first annual Worcester/Tenbury Walking race; my father, Eric Lowe, was involved with the organisation and he had littered the place with maps and plans, but as a 12-year-old pop fanatic I was completely taken over by the impending visit of a pop group about to become the biggest phenomenon since Cliff Richard."

The Tenbury gig came just three days after the release of their third single, 'From Me To You' and their first album, 'Please, Please Me'; the Liverpool Four changed the face and the sound of popular music were now the cream rising to the top of the pops and the big hit number 'Love Me Do' went 'top of the pops' in autumn 1962. The following February the 'Fab Four' spent two weeks at number one with 'Please, Please Me' and on April 6th they received a Silver Disc. They appeared at the Bridge Hotel just over a week later, on Monday, April 15, 1963. It was a Bank Holiday and the support band, El Riot and the Rebels, a popular Midlands group, eventually changed their name to the famous Moody Blues.

The Tenbury event was down to two local lads, Tony Ward and Kevin Davies. They had convinced the Riverside Dance Club committee that it would be worth 'splashing out' their largest fee to date, £100, to get the Liverpool band to perform at the club. How right they were. Tickets were set at 3/6 for members, 5/- for visitors and three days before the gig, the Tenbury Advertiser announced "Sorry - all visitors tickets sold". Tony Ward was the DJ on the night and was lucky enough to go back stage to meet the Beatles and have a chat with them. "Paul was the spokesman for the band, Ringo was his usual self and George was the quiet man but it was John who stood out. He was wearing glasses for the first time and seemed a bit moody."

It is nothing short of astonishing that Beatles manager, Brian Epstein, insisted that the group honoured the engagement, made a year before Beatle mania exploded onto the popular music scene, to play in a small market town in Worcestershire on an Easter Bank Holiday weekend. The Beatles had already overtaken American pop idols, Tommy Roe and Chris Montez as 'top of the bill' and were well on course to fame and fortune; yet they still kept a commitment to appear at Tenbury Wells during a break between their second and third national tour co-starring with the great Roy Orbison.

Only the day before the Tenbury event they recorded a third appearance on the massively popular show, 'Thank Your Lucky Stars' featuring the very best pop artists both sides of the Atlantic which was screened weekly by the then Independent Television Channel (ITV). The programme was recorded at the

Advert in Tenbury Wells Advertiser - 1963

Teddington Studio in West London and afterwards the Beatles went on to the Station Hotel in nearby Richmond-upon-Thames to rub shoulders with and watch the mighty Rolling Stones perform live on stage.

Declaring himself 'not obsessive', nevertheless since the 'not to be forgotten' night at the Bridge in 1963, Andrew Lowe has followed the twists and turns of life with the Beatles, even as far as going to Liverpool University in 1969, seeing George Harrison on stage with Eric Clapton at the Liverpool Empire and gatecrashing the World Premiere of 'Let it Be', on a 'borrowed' press pass. Forty-five years on and now living away, Andrew Lowe remains a Tenburian at heart and hopes one day to base a book on his memories of the Tenbury concert and how a small market town was hit by a sensational musical event still vividly brought to mind by so many people today.

● RIGHT: Yes it's true...the Beatles outside Dale Cafe in Tenbury on Easter Monday, 1963. The photograph was taken by John Hillier and featured in Howard Miller's book 'In and Around Tenbury'.

Don't spoil the ship for a ha'porth of tar.

CROQUET AND TENNIS

Croquet was a very popular summer sport played by two or more competitors round a course of 12 numbered hoops laid out on well prepared, level lawns. The aim, played under strict rules, was to drive a ball through the hoops in rotation to advance their own ball or obstruct an opposing player's ball. The first player to strike the final peg wins the game. Most of the rectories and vicarages in the district had their own croquet lawn and competitions; the ladies of the house were expected to organise the matches.

The Tenbury club played matches throughout the district including at Ashford House, Bockleton Court, Bockleton Rectory, Coreley Rectory, Court of Hill, Easton Court, Kyrewood House, Leysters Rectory, Lydiates, The Parks, St Michael's Vicarage and Mr Sweets, Tenbury. Ten or so matches were played from May until September, the winners receiving prizes of books, vases, fancy boxes, field glasses and inkstands, all donated by the owners of the houses hosting the event.

At the last meeting of 1872 held at Leyster's parsonage, the top prize a painting was won by Mrs Prescott Decie. It featured a lady sitting on the poet's stone in the foreground, Leysters Rectory in the middle distance and the Clee Hill as a background and bears the initials E.M.P. It is a view that could still be painted today.

The poet's stone referred to is where William Wordsworth brought his fiancée in a pony and trap from a nearby house where they were staying; a local vicar had the initials W.W. carved on the stone which can still be seen today. The stone lies on the by-road between Oldwood Common and Leysters Church.

By 1875 lawn tennis was coming into its own and very soon croquet lawns were being converted to tennis courts. It became so popular that The All England Croquet Club at Wimbledon added Lawn Tennis to the title. The Tenbury club soon followed as tennis began to over take croquet as the popular summer game. In the 1930s the Burgage Tennis Club took up residence on the Burgage recreation ground. The name was later changed to the Tenbury Tennis Club and tennis is still played there today on three council-owned hard courts.

ICE SKATING AT KYRE PARK

The idea of developing a pastime based on gliding across the surface of a frozen lake came from Scandinavia and although 17th and 18th century paintings feature ice skating, it wasn't until the 19th century that it really caught on in rural areas as an outdoor winter recreation for all the family. In Victorian times Christmas cards often pictured skaters wrapped up against the cold, scarves flying in the wind as they whizzed along on purpose made iron skates. But it wasn't an unusual pastime.

Frozen lakes and ponds were the ideal and natural places to try out figure skating, ice dancing and speed races and it wasn't long before competitive ice hockey came into its own.

Some years ago the Banfield family were great ice skaters and with other Tenbury enthusiasts went skating whenever the local pools froze over in the winter. They were also regulars at Kyre Park which had a pool with a 20 acre surface and it soon became a favourite venue for winter sports. With the permission of the owner, Mrs Baldwyn-Childe, skaters came from near and far but could not go on the ice until the more experienced Banfields had checked

Mrs Ronnie Hipkiss with the iron hoop she played with as a young girl in the 1930s. This hoop was made by John Newall at Eastham Blacksmiths shop. He made lots of hoops for children, often as a reward for the child working the bellows on the forge when he was making horse shoes.

out the thickness of the ice. It had to be at least four to five inches thick before it was pronounced safe for people to skate on.

BOWS AND ARROWS

For hundreds of years archery has always been something of an historic and long standing outdoor sport and Tenbury once had a double World Champion and an Olympic Team Manager living in Archer Way. Roy Matthews twice took the World Gold Medal and to mark his achievement, Archer Way, where he lived with his wife Mary was named in his honour. Both stalwart members of the 'Archers of the Teme', Mary Matthews was also a member of the British Olympic Committee from 1971 until 1981 and Manager of the British Olympic Team for 15 years. For his Gold Medal winning performances at archery, Roy Matthews was awarded an MBE in 1977; Mary Matthews was awarded the same accolade in 2003 for services to archery.

OTHER POPULAR SPORTS

Other popular sports in and around Tenbury Wells include hockey, football, rugby, cricket and bowls and many of the clubs, founded in the late 1850s, are still active today. Both Tenbury United Football Club and Tenbury Rugby Club play on Palmers Meadow, Penlu is home to the Cricket Club and the Bowls Club 'rolls up' on the Bowling Green in the Burgage.

ALL THE FUN OF THE MAY FAIR

When the annual May Fair came to Tenbury, it was an event not to be missed. Packed with attractions and amusements, it toured the towns and villages of Worcestershire and the surrounding counties of Herefordshire and Shropshire and it was, and still is, an eagerly awaited pleasure ground for all. Through the ages, towns and villages regularly celebrated religious festivals and feast days; Shrovetide, Easter, May Day, Saints Days, Christmas and Epiphany among the most popular. These were usually held annually on the village green or in the churchyard where buying and selling took place; people would also barter - a system often used to exchange goods and services. Small groups of travelling musicians and Morris Dances provided entertainment and hand bell ringers competed village against village. Cider and food was served a the end of the day.

The hey-day for fun fairs was in the 19th and early 20th century when the May Day Fair came into its own. It would set up on a pre-arranged site in Tenbury for a day or two and when it opened there were long queues to be the first on the latest rides like the Big Wheel, Roundabouts and Swing Boats and the Helter Skelter. The atmosphere was heady and exciting; hurdy-gurdy music pumped out of colorful steam organs, noisy side shows attracted keen customers, and the shooting galleries and boxing booths challenged the brave to compete for cash prizes. It was the highlight of the working year for all the family, an occasion for the hard working farming community to let down their hair and enjoy themselves. And they did.

Flashy showmen and mouthy barkers pushed pay-night punters into spending all their wages on freak shows, ghostly goings on, fire eaters and the tiniest crowd pullers of all, the performing fleas. These were usually fed on blood from the arms of the owner. To a gambler's delight fleas harnessed by a thread of hair

Dressed up like a dog's dinner.

to various purpose made contraptions like tiny water wheels and mini handsome cabs raced about while bets were placed and the winner took all.

Showman and impresario Mr Studt was considered to be the best in the business; he was always on the lookout for more challenging rides and his great circular switchback, more popularly known as the 'mountain climber', was said to have cost him around £3,000. It made its first appearance in Hereford and it soon became the big attraction for daring lads and lasses across the region. It whirled round and round at a fast speed accompanied by frenzied music causing terrified girls to cling onto brave boys in nervous excitement. However, the more timid preferred his elaborately decorated roundabouts which moved up and down imitating horses at the gallop. These were so popular that the moment the fair opened people headed for the horses and it became known as 'the Zulu Rush'. Photo booths, 'quack' doctors, conjurors, jugglers and haunted houses were some of the most popular side-shows and, to bring the feel of a breezy seaside day trip, a unique contraption dispensed ozone into the crowd.

Afterwards the cider would flow, a pig and ox was roasted over an open fire and the singing and dancing began. Under cover of darkness, usually in the early hours of the morning, the May Fair would pack up, move on and disappear like the magic it is until the next time; a tradition still prevalent today.

TENBURY RACES

One of the most popular sporting events in town came under starters orders during the mid-1800s when the race course on Oldwood Common was set aside for steeplechases. It proved to be a very popular sporting day attracting people from all walks of life and in time race days became great social events with stalls, side shows and refreshment tents. The lavish Stewards Dinner and Ball was held at the Town Hall and the Worcester Theatre Company performed every evening during race week. In the beginning all the races were run over a flat course designed for riders and runners with little experience; race meetings were financed by subscriptions and an official Steward was appointed to oversee events and cash prizes were donated by local worthies.

The first available Tenbury paper announced on June 25th 1874 that Tenbury Races would be run over the Oldwood course, one of the oldest racecourses in England. On Friday May 6th 1887 Tenbury Hunt Steeplechases were held on the racecourse adjoining the Swan Hotel, owned by Mr. Hardeman who had taken over the Swan, and after a lapse of seven years steeplechasing was revived on the original ground adjacent to the railway station. A special train brought eight to nine hundred race-goers from Birmingham, some of whom were of the questionable type but the police arrangements seemed to have kept control. It was at this meeting a horse called Iron Master, ridden by Mr Brocklehurst, fell and broke its neck at the open ditch, about half a mile from home. The rider was taken, in an unconscious state, to St Mary's Hospital but was able to leave next day. There were no races at the Swan in the following spring; the Hereford Agricultural Show was held at Tenbury that year and the races had to be postponed until the autumn.

The next recorded Tenbury Hunt Steeplechase was on May 8th 1890 again at the Swan Hotel course; there were five races attracting twenty-nine entries and a letter was received from a punter complaining that the stands obstructed the view of the finishing post. There were also reports of steeplechases on May 19th

For the want of a nail a shoe was lost. For the want of a shoe a horse was lost. For the want of a horse a rider was lost.

147

the following year and after the event, local auctioneer Mr G. H. Winton sold the grandstand timber and fixtures, the fencing, the doors and the gates. It seems that a temporary grandstand had been built for the races and the timber had to be auctioned after the races.

The weather was very good for the 1894 steeplechases held on May 4th; attendance was above average and included a good number of petty criminals of the "light fingered fraternity" but thanks to the vigilance of the police they were prevented from carrying out any shady dealings. The Tenbury Steeplechases continued to be held at Oldwood Common until the turn of the 20th century and in 1901 two jockeys were taken to Tenbury Hospital, one with broken ribs and the other with a crushed foot. One of the Tenbury Races at Oldwood took place on June 11th 1906; six runners were listed for the Maiden Plate, which offered prize money of £50, and five runners for the Plate, open to all ages.

Once described as one of the oldest and best race courses in England it was finally closed, and Grandstand Cottage became a private dwelling. The nearby Booth Cottage, used for selling refreshments on race days, was sold to Sir Fredrick Gore-Ousley, founder of St. Michaels College, and used as a school for children; it later went into private ownership as a house. Largely covered in bracken and left to grow wild, the course was, for a time, used as a makeshift golfcourse. During the Second World War it was cleared and used to produce food. Grassed over Oldwood Common is an attractive, natural open space with wild flowers and trees enjoyed by children at play and dog walkers.

1885

Mutton dressed as lamb.

THE WILD BEAST SHOW

In the 19th century people rarely left home except perhaps to seek work. Social life depended upon market days, hiring fairs and travelling entertainers, that was until Wombwell's Menagerie, a sort of travelling Zoo, came to town. Considered one of the best shows of its type in the country and for many years it was a regular and popular event for Tenbury and the Teme Valley when, for one night only, it pitched the horse drawn heavy, caged wagons, complete with many 'wild beasts' on a pre-arranged site. Around thirty different animals, including lions, tigers, giraffes and elephants, all trained by the fearless Captain Fred Wombwell, said by many to be the best animal trainer of all time, came to town. Excitement built up as his regular visits got nearer; his 'daring do' travelled ahead of him and huge crowds gathered to cheer his arrival, see his spectacular 'wild beast show' in action and watch in fear and trepidation as he encouraged the animals to perform even more fearsome tasks.

Also remembered is the remarkable story of Lizzie, the elephant who never forgot. It happened during the Wombwell's visit to Tenbury of 1874. She had been drinking large amounts of cold water which had become heated as she walked; this brought on an attack of spasms and so she was taken to the local pharmacist, Mr. Turley, for treatment. He applied a large blister to her side to help relieve the pain and this simple method of treatment did the trick. Five years later the menagerie came again and as the animals paraded through town Lizzie spotted her medical advisor in the doorway of his shop and remembered what he had done. She stepped out of the ranks and greeted him by placing her trunk around his hand, drawing his attention to the side where he had applied the blister. This was repeated two years later when Lizzie saw him again but this time she gently lifted Hurley from the ground in a sort of elephant hug which only goes to prove, perhaps, that elephants never really forget. This event was reported in the New York Times.

Wombwells elephant and show girl

If March comes in like a lion, it goes out like a lamb.

People, Places and Social Institutions

THE WOMEN'S INSTITUTE

Tenbury Women's Institute was founded in September 1922 at the old Parish Hall, Church Street. The subscription was set at two shillings and over seventy members enrolled on the first night.

The first President was Mrs Elton, there were two Vice Presidents Mrs Winnyates and Mrs Higginson; Miss Augusta Davis became Secretary and Mrs Mattock, the Treasurer. Eighty-six years on members meet in the Methodist Hall in Cross Street and annual subscriptions have risen to £25.

Like most Women's Institutes, Tenbury has always been a very active organisation and it isn't all Jam and Jerusalem; a busy weekly W.I. market is held on Tuesday mornings in the Scout Hut at Palmers Meadow from 9.30am. A regular flow of customers snap up the wide range of seasonal produce including plants, cut flowers, cakes and other farming produce on sale and local shoppers drop in for morning coffee and a chat with friends.

Monthly meetings are friendly and informative; the business agenda is discussed, reports from the Regional and National Federations are read out and the monthly competition judged. Interesting guest speakers are invited to entertain members on subjects ranging from local history, world wide travels and fashion hints. There are also cookery demonstrations, quizzes and musical moments.

The W.I. is a great supporter of the local community providing help where needed at village and country shows, as well as the Tenbury Show. At the bigger Three Counties Show at Malvern they have their own marquee for demonstrations and sales. They also do their bit in times of emergency.

W.I. members don't stay in one place; they enjoy a programme of outings to the theatre, country houses and gardens and shopping expeditions, planned well ahead to fit in with domestic and family life. Many publications have been written by members on various subjects like cooking recipes, gardening hints, local walks and historical events - books for future generations to read.

Educational courses of all kinds are organised nationally at the W.I's own, nationally acclaimed residential college near Abingdon in Oxfordshire.

Denman College, an independent Adult Education Centre set in 17 acres of stunning countryside is named after the first National Chairman of the Women's Institute, Lady Denman. A programme of 2, 3 and 4 day courses on just about every subject from arts, crafts and drama, to wine tasting and complimentary therapy with so much more in between, is open to all members of the Federation, some with bursaries attached.

Tenbury Women's Institute is affiliated to the Worcestershire Federation.

As wise as an owl.

THE YOUNG FARMERS

It is generally accepted throughout farming communities that the Young Farmers' Movement is one of the finest organisations in existence. It not only teaches its members so many different crafts and skills but it brings confidence in learning, conversing and socialising, and is no doubt the biggest matrimonial contact in the countryside.

It all started in the 1930s when competitions took place with animals resulting in the formation of Calf Clubs. These clubs steadily grew in number until eventually the National Federation of Young Farmers' Clubs was established around 1948 which enabled clubs to compete with each other in organised countrywide competitions. As the clubs developed, over the years competition became more complex and wide-ranging and nowadays YFCs enter a variety of competitions ranging through public speaking, debating, stock judging, ploughing, hedging, cooking, flower arranging, handicrafts, cake icing through to musical and dramatic entertainment.

Each county holds an annual rally or show, where the clubs within the county Federation compete against each other; the winners in some sections going on to represent their county at National level. Exchange visits are arranged between clubs in other parts of the country as well as from abroad and some from this country are chosen to visit countries abroad.

Tenbury Wells Young Farmers Club was founded in 1943 by Mr S.H. Mattock, Mr H.J.Spilsbury and Mr H.F. Robinson; others who helped the club in the early years were Mr W. Baldwin, Mr H. Bentham, Mr J. Nott and Mr W.H. Sinnett. Originally it had been in existence since about 1938 under the banner of the Tenbury Young Farmers' Association when it carried out a tremendous amount of work for charity during the Second World War. The first Chairperson of the Tenbury Wells Young Farmers Club was Nancy Spilsbury (Wozencroft), and the Secretary was Richard Robinson. Membership was 3s.6d and 5s.0d for seniors. Over the years Tenbury Wells gained the reputation of being a very successful club noted for winning the annual county rally on many occasions.

Although called a Young Farmers' Club, it is not restricted to the farming community. Members can come from all walks of life to participate in and enjoy the wide variety of club activities. It has also been said that these days clubs are not as strong and well supported as they were years ago for example, in the past Tenbury YFC would have had up to 60 members. But in comparison, it's fair to say that there is a lot more going on for young people nowadays; they are able to travel around more and it is also difficult for family farms to release their young workers as more young people are going on to higher education at college and university, taking them away from the farming communities which years ago depended upon them.

Membership of Young Farmers' Clubs is open to girls and boys aged from 12 to 26. Meetings are usually held weekly in the winter months with the business discussed first followed by a visiting speaker talking on a variety of topics. Regular visits to outside venues like ten pin bowling are programmed, dances, discos and parties are organised to raise funds for the club and its chosen charities. In the summer months there are farm walks, visits to factories, seaside trips and, of course, practising for the annual rally.

Membership of the Tenbury Wells Y.F.C. often runs through the family; parents as well as children and siblings have shared key responsible positions,

Love and a cough cannot be hid.

passing them down through the generations to eventually become presidents and vice presidents at local and county level.

In 1997 Tenbury was given the honour of hosting the 50th Annual Rally of the Worcestershire Federation of YFC and in 2008, the 150th anniversary of the Tenbury Agricultural Society; they will be fittingly hosting the 60th Annual Rally.

Many changes may have taken place since it all began way back in 1938; old crafts and skills have given way to mechanisation and the enthusiasm of youth for socialising in some quarters of the Young Farmers movement has been known to get a bit out of hand. Young Farmers are known to work and play hard and still come out on top when it comes to dedication in the fields, leadership, commitment to the movement, and top of the pops when it comes to charity fundraising.

Hedging competition,
Worcester Federation of
Young Farmers - 2008

Little strokes fell great oaks.

BANFIELD'S

To walk into a long established hardware shop is like walking into a veritable house of agricultural and social history. Bits and pieces from past and present times line the shelves and experienced employees have more than a few handy tips and a tale or two to tell about the old family business.

James Gay Banfield came to Tenbury in the mid 19th century to run an ironmongery shop in Teme Street. He had a wife and 13 children and traded in the town for many years, supplying farm machinery, household goods, builders' materials and water supplies for a century or so. The business also carried a wide range of spare parts for just about every farm machine or household appliance imaginable. As early as the 1870s, the Tenbury Advertiser carried adverts for Banfield's turnip and chaff cutters, pulpers, oil cake mill and all kinds of agricultural machinery, and in the 1900s for mowing machines, swath turners, side delivery rakes, horse rakes as well as hop washes and sulphur for use in hop drying. They had their own metal turning lathes and as early as the 1920s claimed that they were able to produce any spare part for a motor vehicle or farm machinery. The building had its own forge where the windmills to drive the well pumps were made. They always employed a team of first class workmen who had been with the firm for years, which included carpenters, joiners, fitters and plumbers.

Like most business in those days the firm would have been passed down from father to son but today James Banfield's great grand daughter Sadie Chalkley runs the business.

In the early days of radio, a fashionable crystal set, complete with headphones and aerial sold for 30 shillings but these were soon superseded by the valve radio set powered by an accumulator. To be on the safe side wise owners bought two accumulators, one in use and the other on charge at where else but Banfield's.

The shop is virtually the same apart from a few minor changes and is more like a museum than a trading place, stacks of original wooden cupboards and drawers decorate the old walls and there are the same wooden counters to lean on to place an order.

Interestingly, the Banfield family were also keen ice skaters and because of their experience when the local pools froze over in winter they were usually called in to make a decision on the safety of the ice.

Sadie Chalkley with Iain Duncan Smith and Tenbury M.P. Bill Wiggin

Keep a thing for seven years and you'll find a use for it.

Allan Mason making a pot hamper
in the 1930s

MR MASON, THE BASKET MAKER

Fruit picking baskets, hop bushels, hampers and baskets – A.J. Mason, Rochford.

Tim Mason says his grandfather Joe and father Arthur were basket makers in Rochford from 1860 to the 1950s. He remembers his father employing three or four basket makers on a regular basis and in busy times up to ten. These extras included German prisoners of war in the First World War (Rochford House) and also vagrants or tramps who slept on the wooden floor of the workshop. He said one of the POWs could make up to ten pot hampers a day and this was well above the average worker. During the First World War, A.J. Mason made pannier baskets to fit mules taking shells to the front line. Fruit picking baskets, fruit containers, including several sizes of pot hampers, half pots, bushels, sieves (half bushel), strikes (quarter bushel), peck baskets with handles, and rim peck which held 14 pounds (usually soft fruit and cherries) were always in demand, as were hop bushels, laundry baskets of all sizes, post office baskets, poultry and pigeon baskets, cycle baskets, shopping baskets and railway baskets. Invalid carriages (three wheels and steering which would be of metalwork), pony carriages, panniers for horses; all these would have been very important in days gone by for salt trail and pack horse. Other items made and sold were balloon baskets, tradesman baskets for bicycles, fish and lobster traps, chairs and furniture.

Willow called osiers, is the annual growth of a willow stub grown in wet land around pools or streams and generally called osier beds. These are often shown on old maps and usually cut during the late winter months, dried and stored under cover until required. Some were used with the bark on, but most were stripped of the bark by pulling through a metal frame the width of the gap getting narrower at the bottom to accommodate the taper of the osier. This stripping was done while the wood was still green and before storing. Some had to be boiled for several hours before stripping and allowed to dry out before storing in an airy shed. Before the basket maker could use the stored rods it was necessary to soak them in water to make them supple again.

Tim, (who is well in his 90s) said his father cut his osiers at Rochford, the old brickworks near Eastham Bridge (presumably where the clay was taken from to make the bricks) and a big osier bed near Ludlow which is now part of the Ludlow bypass (A49) and also at Church Stretton.

THE POT HAMPER

THAT EXTRAORDINARY MEASURE 'THE POT' VARIED NOT ONLY WITH THE KIND OF PRODUCE BUT ALSO FROM DISTRICT TO DISTRICT, IN 1891 HARVEY HUNT PUBLISHED FOR HIS MARKET IN EVESHAM THE WEIGHTS OF FRUIT & VEGETABLES ACCEPTED FOR THIS CONTAINER:-

APPLES 64lb.	ONIONS 64lb
CHERRIES	PARSLEY 20lb.
CURRANTS } 63lb.	POTATOES 80lb.
GOOSEBERRIES }	TURNIPS 60lb.
PEARS } 72lb.	
PLUMS }	
BEANS	
PEAS } 40lb.	
SPROUTS }	

Whats in a 'pot'

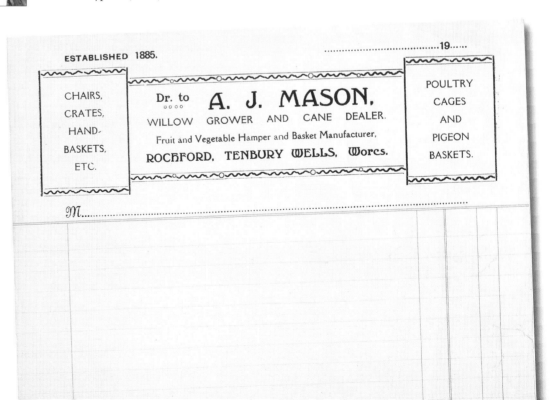

ESTABLISHED 1885. ....19......

CHAIRS, CRATES, HAND-BASKETS, ETC.	Dr. to **A. J. MASON,** WILLOW GROWER AND CANE DEALER. Fruit and Vegetable Hamper and Basket Manufacturer, ROCHFORD, TENBURY WELLS, Worcs.	POULTRY CAGES AND PIGEON BASKETS.

M.................

154

BILL DIPPER – JACK OF ALL TRADES

When a job needed to be done, Bill Dipper was your man. Bill lived at a smallholding in Sutton Mill Lane, Rochford, and like most smallholders he carried out seasonal work on the local farms. When they were first available, he was one of the first men to have a shearing machine, a Lister hand turned model with the big wheel and a flexible cable. Earlier machines, such as the Burman and Cooper-Stewart, had a solid shaft drive with a joint halfway to the hand piece which made them very hard to turn. Bill was a very tidy shearer and could shear 60 or 70 sheep a day, whereas the ordinary farm worker would work hard to get 20 or 30 done, mainly because they were much less experienced.

He rode his motorcycle and sidecar to transport his shearing machine and whatever tools he needed for each farming season. In hop picking time he would be employed as a hop busheler; this was a very skilled job and difficult to please both the picker and the grower when it came to payment per bushel. The art was to fill the bushel level full when gently compressed. However, it was possible to over compress the hops by the using the elbow, probably on the boss's instruction, to pack in plenty more.

Bill Dipper showing corn dollies - 1878-1964

It was common for the pickers, mostly women, to tell the busheler to keep his bloody elbow out and in extreme disputes it was not uncommon for threats to put him in the river or some sort of physical violence if he failed to play fair.

Among Bill's special skills was thatching; at the drop of a straw bale, he could thatch ricks of hay and corn, often adding a decoration, such as an animal or bird, fox or cockerel to finish off the rick. For a hobby he would fashion corn dollies and create shapes from odd bunches of straw and today several local people are proud possessors of Bill Dipper models.

In winter time he would travel far and wide on his motorcycle to trade as a pig killer and as soon as the weather was cool enough, usually November through to early March, Bill would be booked up to kill three or four farm pigs if several workmen lived in or the farmer had a big family with five or six children.

Up until the 1950s most cottagers, farm workers or local tradesmen kept a pig and, on a pre-arranged day, Bill would arrive to find three or four strong men waiting for him. After passing the time of day he would fix the pig bench on level ground near the pig sty and arrange his tools on a nearby box. Then he made a noose from a strong piece of cord, and talking quietly to the pig, would slip the noose over the upper jaw and pull the cord tight. This gave him control of the head, and the pig would be guided outside to the bench, where it was physically pulled onto the bench sideways and the cord tied to a leg to secure the pig's head. Quickly Bill would sever the jugular vein with a sharp knife.

It's anyone's guess as to how long it took for the pig to lose consciousness, probably not long; suffice to say, it was quite upsetting for the younger members of the family faced with the high pitched squealing of the pig. Thankfully, by about 1950, it became law that all slaughtermen had to be licensed and all animals stunned by humane killer before being bled. Everyone within a couple of miles would know when the pig was killed.

After bleeding, Bill would place straw on the ground, the pig was laid out and covered with straw which was then fired to burn the bristles off; it usually took three burnings to get it thoroughly clean. It was then hoisted up by the back legs, often into a fruit tree if there was nowhere convenient in a building. The pig would be washed off, and the liver, lights and veil, the membrane around the

Remove not the ancient landmark which your fathers have set up.

entrails, saved. Some times the entrails would be thoroughly washed and used for sausage skins. The carcass would be hung for at least 24 hours and Bill would come back to cut it up into joints to suit the owners requirements.

To do this it was lowered onto the pig bench, the carcass cut and sawn to take out the chine –backbone and each of the two sides would be cut into, ham (hind leg) and flitch (front leg and belly) and then carried to the salting slab in the house ready to be cured with salt. Several weeks later it was hung on a beam and dried in a warm room, and used throughout the year. Nothing was wasted; the off cuts, including the head, became brawn, faggots, pork pies and sausages.

At a time of plenty it was usual for gifts of pig meat to be given to neighbours and friends and to receive some back in return when their own pig was killed. Bill was also a pig castrator; both hog and sow pigs not required for breeding were castrated, but these days most are left entire.

Bill might have been a Jack of all trades, and as far as the community was concerned was a Master of all of them, and a hard working, talented man.

THE HISTORY OF BOWKETT'S IN TENBURY
by Roger Bowkett

Grandfather, Bill Bowkett, did his butchery apprenticeship at Upton-on-Severn, riding his bycle there on a Sunday evening and returning to Tenbury on a Saturday afternoon. The butcher who owned the shop at Upton-on-Severn had a butcher's shop in Tenbury and, when the position of manager arose, grandad was given the job and he moved to Tenbury in 1908. The shop was where Gallimores, the estate agents, and Beauty Lane are now situated.

Father, George, was born in 1908 at Rochford Post Office, where his mother was the post mistress.

During the First World War father would help at the shop, delivering orders in a pony and trap as far away as Clee Hill, Stoke Bliss and Eastham, in those days a considerable distance. At the end of each week, any meat left over was either put into pickle or cooked in a large boiler during Saturday night and, on Sunday morning, people would come and collect the broth for free, so at least some people had the chance to have one hot meal a week. Also, father would take pieces of meat to the houses in Cross Street opposite the Methodist church which was home to mainly elderly widows, who, like a lot of people, had fallen on hard times.

In 1919 grandad bought his own shop at 1, 2 and 3 The Square, the existing site of Bowkett's supermarket today. From the age of twelve George did the books for the business and at the age of fifteen left school to work there full time.

In May 1924, George had an accident; he was shot and lost the sight of one eye and restarted work again in October the same year. Father met my mother in 1927 and married in 1934. They bought a house in Bromyard Road, opposite the Co-operative shop. He started making pies and by trial and error made excellent pork pies and later sausages. Sales expanded and it was not long before the production was moved to the Square. In 1938 my father took over the business and with his mother made the business successful and profitable. The same year he bought a deep freeze which was later to prove a valuable asset to the business.

With the start of the Second World War in 1939 the situation changed dramatically for the business. In 1940 meat rationing was brought in and this

Roger and Ben Bowkett - 2008

It will all be the same a hundred years hence.

continued until 1954. The weekly allowance was 6 pence (pre-decimal money) per person, per week, which was made up of 4 pence fresh meat and 2 pence of tinned corned beef, mainly from Argentina. Not all meat was rationed but all prices were controlled. Offal, chickens and rabbits were not rationed and were always in demand, which lead to some black market operations, with the police and food inspectors always on the look out. Whale meat, venison and reindeer were also not rationed and large supplies could be bought and stored in the deep freeze so as to allow a continuous supply of goods. During rationing, father made contact with a London company who could supply meat that was not rationed and because father was making pork pies before the war, he was allocated a quantity of pork (usually from New Zealand) to allow him to continue production.

1954 saw a change in the direction of the Bowkett firm. It divided into wholesale and retail. During this year, father built the first private abattoir in the country with encouragement from farmers and local butchers; this was built on land at Bromyard Road. Bowkett's had always bought their animals in Tenbury market or from farms in the district, now with their own abattoir they purchased stock in several markets as well as from farms for 20 miles around. Demand for their meat, which came from this noted stock raising district, was so great that they took on the new Hereford City Abattoir and at one time had a throughput of 500 cattle, 1,000 pigs and several thousand lambs weekly. With the waste from the two abattoirs they started a bone and fertiliser factory and this was very successful for many years. At one time Bowkett's employed 250 people. Trade expanded and soon a cold store, capable of storing 1,000 tons of meat, and a boning plant were built in Tenbury, which supplied a supermarket chain but it was subject to regular price reductions which eventually made the wholesale business uneconomical to run. The decision, by the family, to close the abattoirs was much regretted by local farmers, who supplied the stock, and by butchers who bought the meat. Successive governments have done their best to close all small abattoirs and now very few exist. The problem with this is that live animals have to be transported many miles to large city abattoirs causing them unnecessary stress. This was probably at its worst during the last Foot and Mouth disease outbreak in 2000, when lambs from our Tenbury market were being sent regularly to Truro in Cornwall, a journey of around 300 miles.

The retail side of the business has continued and, over the years, has been improved and upgraded.

2008 sees two special occassions for Bowkett's, the first is my father will be a hundred years of age and the second, a member of the Bowkett's family has been butchering in Tenbury also for a hundred years. Bowkett's still supply local restaurants; a large part of the business is supplying products for home deep freezers. Bowkett's have won awards for their home products and have gained a reputation for supplying good quality meat.

So, Bowkett's is still trading 100 years after grandad Bill Bowkett first came to Tenbury to manage the butcher's shop.

It is important for the public, when buying meat, to know the origin and how the animals have lived. This area of the West Midlands, renowned for its quality livestock, offers some of the best meat available. Buying local meat from a local butcher not only ensures a first class product, it also supports the local rural economy, ensuring the health of the countryside as a whole.

There are more people rust out than wear out.

HARRY HIGGINS
COLLECTOR OF CLOCKS

Harry Higgins' father was the Manager of the Tenbury Union Workhouse. As a young man Harry was apprenticed to the ironmongery trade with J.G. Ban field and Sons in Teme Street, Tenbury Wells before setting up his own business opposite the Ship Hotel in Teme Street where the little arcade is now.

Harry was also a successful and popular sportsman and for several seasons he played football for Stafford Rangers and well into middle age he played hockey for the local team. When the River Teme flooded the whole town during the great flood of 1947, Harry swam the full length of Teme Street.

Alongside his main business he also bought and sold second hand furniture and good quality antique items which he stored in various buildings in the town. On entering his premises the smell of creosote was almost overpowering but Harry quickly explained it away by blaming it on the wood worm. Whenever his workmen brought old furniture into the building, the legs and back panels were often infected by woodworm and left to stand in a container of creosote for several days and then liberal coatings were painted onto badly infested parts. At the time creosote was the most effective deterrent he had found against woodworm, cheap to use and more important usually did the trick.

From time to time Harry struck lucky and managed to acquire many beautiful items of furniture, much of it sold locally, but in later years, when antiques became more valuable, he sold them on to London dealers for exporting to the Americas.

However, clocks were his passion; in the 1940s and 50s he claimed to have had enough grandfather clocks to fill the many local farm buildings he rented for storage.

It was generally accepted that clocks were very popular in most households during this period and just about every farm or country cottage had at least one clock and Harry relied on messages to say that a grandfather clock was waiting collection from a local cottage sale and perhaps two or three from larger farm sales. Like all good dealers, he had an arrangement with local auctioneers (Russell Baldwin and Bright, Cattell and Young) and others in the area that if he could not attend a clearance sale they would bid for him. Mostly all farm and cottage furniture was sold by public auction on the premises and Harry willingly gave £5.00 for eight day and £2.10s for a thirty hour grandfather clocks providing they were in reasonable condition.

Eventually there was very little demand for grandfather clocks and, as his stores filled up, he had to tell the auctioneers that he did not want any more clocks unless he left instructions to bid.

Harry Higgins was a real country man, a popular local character remembered by people today. When he was 80 years old he went to a pheasant shoot at Eastham Park and impressed other members of the party by killing two birds, one with the left barrel and one with the right, all with one body movement. Afterwards he announced, "That will do me for today, I just wanted to know if I could still shoot straight".

There is more than one way to skin a rabbit.

JOHN MORRIS' FARM
FROM HIS NOTEBOOK
1859-1874

Touching John Morris' notebook with its neat brass clasp is like touching history. It is clear from its content that the tenant of Burford Farm was a fastidious record keeper and astute businessman keeping detailed accounts of his dealings, his workers and his stewardship of the land, on a day to day basis. His farm was on the Burford estate owned by The Right Honourable Lord Northwick, situated about a half mile north of Burford church. It was a mixed farm with cattle, sheep and working horses and wheat, barley, oats, beans, peas and hops grown on the arable land. There were also at least five orchards of fruit, mainly apples.

John Morris

Like most farmers he kept a bull - most likely a Hereford - charging his neighbours five shillings each time the bull was put to service; he also noted down the service dates of his own cows — Spot, Cherry, Fillpail, Dina, Alderney, Pigeon, Mottle, Huberton and Daisy. He bought and sold sheep, sometimes using them to pay a bill or two. After all it was common practice for farmers to let their meat bills increase for a couple of years and then sell the butcher a fat beast, sheep or pigs to clear the debt. Amongst his working horses were several mares used for breeding; Darling, Jewel, Buxom and a hack mare were put to a stallion and Mr Morris was charged one pound for each mare serviced. In 1864 he sold a mare and colt for twenty pounds and in 1870, six years later, he sold a working horse for £17.10s to the local builder, Mr. Haddon Hewitt. He also took horses, colts and sheep at tack, grazing them for a weekly fee.

Some of his other income came from letting out his land for potato growing and during one year in the 1860s he recorded letting out 194 rows of potato ground to 46 people. They were able to grow up to eight rows at three shillings and sixpence per row, possibly for people to plant their own seed in prepared ground. In 1863, Farmer Morris was still having his corn crops cut by hand using a traditional sickle and scythe; he paid the reapers, often Welsh and Irish men plus several local reapers, a total of nineteen pounds and six shillings for the task. They also received 174 gallons of cider, valued at eight pence per gallon but it is not clear if this was included in their wages or charged for. A thatcher was generally employed; growing a large acreage of corn required some of the crop having to be put in ricks and stored outside until threshing, hence the need for thatching.

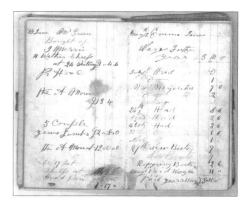

Income also came from sales of wheat, barley and beans to local farmers and cottagers and often in exchange perhaps for a pig or poultry; he also had similar arrangements with several owners of local water mills at Burford, Newnham and Boraston. Corn for his own use was usually ground at Burford Mill for which he was charged one shilling to one shilling and sixpence per bag which could have weighed in at one and a half to two hundredweight at a time. Straw was usually sold by the bolten - a bundle - or by the thrave, believed to be the equivalent of 24 boltens or about a cart load for thatching.

Wheat and beans were sold mainly at 16 to 22 shillings per bag and hops more often than not, sold by the pocket to local innkeepers to brew his own beer. The cost of coal needed to fire the kilns used for hop drying are recorded in detail; from the early 1800s this was mined at Mamble and transported from the colliery to the Burford Farm by canal. The waterway had served the district

To err is human, to forgive divine.

159

well for 50 years, by the time the railway came the canal had already closed and a railway track laid in its place; this resulted in John Morris having to send a team of horses and a wagon to Mamble colliery to collect the coal.

At the time coal could be bought for about eleven shillings a ton but from time to time prices fluctuated; he purchased two loads at different times which varied between ten shillings and sixpence and eighteen shillings and eleven pence. On top of the basic cost, the wagon and team at ten shillings per load and turnpike fees at two shillings and sixpence per single load were added plus a possible fee payable to a toll house at Burford, Newnham Bridge and Mamble for using the road.

Apples were sold by the pot -56 to 84 pounds and by the barrel - 6 pots to the barrel to Tenbury fruit dealers Mr. Graves and Mr. Higginson which added to the farms income; fruit was sold directly from the trees in John Morris's five orchards on two occasions and he sold quantities of cider in 100 to 500 gallons at 4 to 6 pence a gallon. In June 1871, the sale of 450 faggots, (bundles of brushwood off the tops of trees), fetched eight shillings per one hundred bundles and when dried out they could be used to fire up the bread oven or as kindling wood to light the open fires which kept the household warm.

Male and female workers were hired on an annual basis usually at the May Fair. In 1868 John Morris hired Ezra and Edward Homes who may have been living in a cottage near the farm at a wage of ten pounds each. Most of the other workers seemed to have been 'live in' young male and female workers hired at between three and six pounds per year, which would have included their board and lodging. His notebook carefully records every payment made to them during the year and paying any balance owing to them at the end of the year. On May 29th 1872, Henry Humpris was taken on at one shilling and sixpence per week and as most of the workers were unable to write they used a cross as a signature. However one girl could write well enough to sign her own name.

Domestic spending included boots, leggings, waistcoat, hat, dress shirt, an umbrella and sometimes tobacco. Other expenditure included sixpence to go to the circus, a shilling on race day at the Tenbury steeplechases and a further shilling for his brothers at Christmas. Considering John Morris' little notebook covers just 15 years of the 19th century, it is amazing how much information it contains. The writing is neat, very tidy and easily readable and the reader will see the spelling is most amusing.

John Morris' farm also had an excellent range of farm buildings, probably built in the late 1700s; hop kilns were added some 100 years later and the Dutch barn was built about 1900.

Today the farm is no longer owned by the Morris family but the memories still linger in the old farm buildings at Burford. Current owners Mark and Anne Yarnold have converted the old corn and threshing barn into living accommodation without spoiling the character of the old buildings; the Dutch barn has been converted into an office and workshop. The end result proves an excellent example of how 300-year-old redundant farm buildings can be sympathetically renovated to meet 21st century living requirements. May future dwellers continue to enjoy touching the history of a remarkable Tenbury farmer and perhaps one day produce their own notes on John Morris's farm.

For more details see page 178.

MARKET DAY

Market day in Tenbury has always been Tuesday with special cattle and sheep sales on various other days. Up until 1900 everybody would have driven to market in a horse drawn trap, cart, wagon, gone on horse back or on foot. After having trotted or walked up to five or ten miles by the time they had reached town, the horses would have been all of a lather and it was important to unhook the vehicle, take the harness off and stable the horse so it did not get a chill, and then feed and water it. The hotels and inns in Tenbury all had stabling, probably catering for some 200 horses.

The Rose & Crown, the Swan, the Bridge, the Ship, the Crow, the Royal Oak, the Bell, the Market Tavern, the Kings Head, the Barn & Barrel and Pembroke House, as well as a few which have since ceased to exist, had stabling. Most of them employed an ostler who would be there to receive the horses, rub them down if necessary and feed and water them, then harness or saddle them ready for the homeward journey.

Most of these establishments had a market room where tradespeople could send grocery and other shopping which had been ordered earlier in the day for loading into assorted horse drawn transport.

Market day was always a very social occasion, but business came first. The farmer would go to the livestock market and meet various tradesmen and merchants at the corn exchange and his wife took her butter, cheese, eggs, live and dressed poultry and seasonal fruit and produce to one of the two markets or sold direct to the various dealers who had travelled by train from the industrial Midland towns.

Later in the day, when business was completed, the ladies would go to their favourite cafe for refreshments and meet relations and friends and most of the farmers would go to a local inn for bread and cheese and enjoy a pint of ale with their neighbours and associates. It was not uncommon to see a horse and trap returning home to some distant farm with the driver asleep helped by the rhythmic jogging action of the trotting horse and on arrival at the farm, the horse waited at the fold yard gate or stable door until someone arrived to loose him in. The local term given to men and women who stayed too long drinking with their friends was that they were "market peart".

When one considers that there was room for about 200 horses in Tenbury on market day it must be remembered that at this time there were about 30 farms or smallholdings in each village, but by the end of the 20th century there were only about 6 farms in most villages and very few small holdings with even fewer working horses.

By 1910 a few motor vehicles were to be seen around the district, owned mainly by the upper classes. In 1909 Mr Wall opened a garage in Teme Street where he sold petrol, carried out vehicle repairs and hired out cars. All the early cars and lorries had solid rubber wheels but in 1925 a 'for sale' advertisement in the Tenbury Advertiser offered a "new 1925 Ford car with balloon tyres."

By 1920, the Baths Garage in Cross Street started their Bluebird Bus Services and, as well as running local buses around Tenbury, they timetabled market day buses to Ludlow on a Monday, Hereford on Wednesday, Kidderminster and Bromyard on Thursday and Leominster on Friday; the return fare to Hereford or Worcester was 5s6d.

Several other bus companies, Yarranton Bros, Eardiston, Owens Bros, Abberley, Burnhams, Clifton-on-Teme and others in surrounding towns, started

Donkey Davies market carrier who lived at Rochford

You can't teach an old dog new tricks.

up around the same time. The first market buses had a roof rack and a step ladder up the side of the bus where the driver would put crates of garden produce, baskets of fruit, crates of poultry, bicycles and tools. In the fruit season the weight on the roof was very heavy but for cottagers it was the only way to get their produce to and from market.

A true story of a Yarranton's bus going to Kidderminster market happened just before the Second World War. It was climbing Stockton Bank in low gear when the roof began to sag under the weight of produce on top; the quick-thinking driver was forced to stop, borrowing an axe from a cottage to cut a couple of wooden props from a nearby wood which he used to support the roof of the bus.

It was during this period that the wireless was gaining in popularity with country people but, as many homes were without electricity, households had to rely on a battery accumulator to power up their wireless. It had to be charged about once a week and most families had two; one in use and the other was transported on the weekly market bus to Tenbury to be re-charged. For the return journey the market bus would be piled high with shopping, especially grocery, poultry and pig food, chickens, both day old and growing pullets and cockerels. There were also the empty baskets for the next week's fruit and of course a stack of the charged up, heavy accumulators. The driver could always expect a good tip for his efforts up and down the roof ladder after which he very often popped into a house or two for a quick glass of cider. By the end of the 20th century, very few country buses ran because most people had their own transport.

The local Tenbury produce and fruit market in Teme Street closed around 1980 and the livestock market finally closed in 2004. Some produce is still sold in the Round Market on a Tuesday.

Market Day - 1900s

162

TENBURY MARKET PLACES

The establishment of Tenbury as a market town came about in 1249 when Henry III granted Roger de Clifford and his heirs the rights to a market and fair at Tenbury. Market Street and Market Square would no doubt have been the centre for trading in Tenbury. The present Round Market, built in 1856, replaced a very ancient butter market on the same site. Until a proper sale yard or smithfield was established, animal trading took place in the streets leading into the Market Square; records show that the first proper marketplace in Tenbury was established in the paddock or little field opposite the Swan Hotel.

ROUND Market

The earliest Tenbury Advertiser available, 1874, advertises G.R. Winton's autumn sheep sale. Besides local entries it includes 200 grand Shropshire ewes from the Felton and Wigley flocks (Ludlow). At this time these sheep were considered to be among the best known flocks of the Shropshire breed and would probably have been walked to the sale from Ludlow, confirming that Tenbury was now well placed as an important livestock market.

The auctioneer, George Henry Winton, had an office at the Post Office in Teme Street but lived at Vine Farm, Sutton. For several generations his family had farmed at Perry Farm, Kyre, and as well as the Vine Estate they also owned Mileshope Farm and Sutton Court Farm. Regular sales of livestock, fat and store went under the hammer and with the coming of the railway in the 1860s special monthly sales of store cattle and sheep were added. He also held occasional sales of cart horses at the Swan sale yard. This little market, between the River Teme and the Swan Hotel, must have been a very busy place. Selling always started soon after the arrival of the 11am train which brought buyers from the Midlands to compete with local butchers and farmers.

Unlike today, fat appeared to be more acceptable in those days; a report in the local newspaper recorded "At Tenbury Christmas fatstock - now referred to as primestock - show and sale held on December 8th 1874, two extraordinary grand fat oxen, five very prime fat oxen, five very prime oxen, forty fat oxen, heifers and cows, three fat bulls and two hundred fat sheep were sold. Oxen at this time were still being used to plough and cultivate the arable land and were usually worked, starting at three years old until they were six or seven years old, and then fattened to be sold to the butcher. This may account for the former description. As well as holding sales of store cattle and sheep at Tenbury, G.H. Winton also held spring and autumn sales at the Hundred House sale yard, Great Witley, for many years.

Tenbury was proving to be a very popular market, but change was in the air. In 1877 the name of Messrs. Backhouse and Baker, auctioneers, of Cleobury Mortimer began to appear in the local paper, offering for sale the property known as Titrail at the Knowle, and then twelve orchards of fruit on the trees at Field Farm and Lowbourne, Knighton-on-Teme. Further newspaper reports confirmed that the company were to hold regular sales of livestock at the Rose and Crown sale yard - later known as the Station sale yard.

On an old map of Tenbury and Burford, this site appears to be in a field on the west side of the Rose and Crown extending to the entrance to the old station yard, currently the site of Kerry's food factory. Although Backhouse and Baker did not seem to have had an office in town, entries for future sales could be left with Mr Robinson at the Rose and Crown.

Plans for a new Winton auction yard were announced in the press in September 1877, when local iron founders and similar traders were invited to

More haste, less speed.

Edwards butcher in Market Square on site of Bowketts supermarket - 1902

Family Goodall & Sons grocers

Royal Oak in Market Street, Tenbury Wells - 1892

tender for providing and fixing a quantity of wrought iron, sheep and pig pens, strong tubular fencing, asphalt and brick paving. This referred to a site with the entrance opposite the Ship Hotel in Teme Street and not to be confused with the one by the old fire station; this was the entrance to the workhouse yard and infirmary.

A year later, G.H. Winton held a Christmas fatstock show and sale at his new Teme Street market, and to commemorate the occasion local farmers presented him with an engraved silver plate. The cattle, sheep and pig pens removed from the old livestock market in 2005 would have been the ones installed in 1878. They must have been big cheese eaters in those time; six years later, Mr Winton sold two tons of cheese in lots after the livestock sale.

By June 1885 competition among the auctioneers was hotting up. Backhouse and Baker had split up, resulting in a new company, Backhouse and Horton; they worked out of the Station sale yard leaving T.R. Baker and Son to run the Swan sale yard. Two years later the two firms of auctioneers had exchanged sale yards and competition was fierce, with three sale yards selling on the same day, and all sales advertised in the local press to start soon after the arrival of the 11 o'clock train. It's possible they agreed a rota on who started first, but whatever happened, Tenbury was a very important place as a livestock centre.

The local paper regularly reported up to twenty-five truck loads of sheep and cattle leaving Tenbury station. All these animals would have been walked to market in the morning and those that did not go by rail would have been walked to their new homes, anything up to ten or fifteen miles away. There were plenty of drovers who would undertake the work, finding overnight grazing and resting ground before the animals continued their journey next day.

In 1891 Mr Winton tried to sell the Teme Street sale yard. The following advertisement appeared in the Advertiser, "Freehold Sale-yard, one of the best in the Midlands, entered by double, handsome iron gates from Teme Street, opposite the Ship Inn, and comprising cattle enclosures and sale ring, large calf's house and ranges of sheep and pig pens on asphalt with iron fittings". It was offered for sale but did not reach the reserve price; the best offer was £4,000. Undeterred, Winton continued his usual livestock sales and was still selling in 1894. Unfortunately, there are no local papers until 1899 when it was announced that Messers. Warne and King had taken up selling in Mr Winton's market off Teme Street.

In 1901, Warne and King dissolved the partnership and then became Warne, Griffiths and Boyce; Arthur E. Griffiths of Worcester, had, for two years previous, been selling at the Swan sale yard and taken Mr Boyce into partnership. Two years later G. Herbert Banks took over the Rose and Crown sale yard and in the same year, Jackson and McCartney held livestock sales in a meadow, better known as the cricket meadow, adjoining the Swan Hotel. The Tenbury Great April Fair of 1903 was held over the three market sites on the same day when nearly 1,200 cattle and 1,000 sheep were sold.

In 1905 Griffiths and Boyce took Mr Cooper into partnership; he had worked for the firm for some time and in 1908 a local press announcement stated that: "John Cooper begs to inform his clients and friends that he has now taken over, by mutual agreement, the business carried on by Griffiths, Boyce and Cooper, and taken into partnership Archer Ernest Baldwin of Underley; he later became Sir Archer Baldwin M.P. and that the name of the firm will be known as Cooper and Baldwin selling at Tenbury, Teme Street market and in Leominster."

Many hands make light work.

In 1909, Morris, Marshall and Poole, auctioneers at Ludlow and Craven Arms, purchased the Tenbury business of G. Herbert Banks and the Swan sale yard changed hands again. At the Great Annual April Fair in 1909, Cooper and Baldwin sold 747 cattle and 600 sheep, Morris, Marshall and Poole at the Swan yard sold 550 cattle and 350 sheep and for the next five years or so business was brisk. Later, Morris, Marshall and Poole pulled out of Tenbury but continued selling at Ludlow and Craven Arms for many years. By 1913, Edwards, Russell and Baldwin had become the foremost market name in Tenbury. It seems that Edwards and Russell, an old established firm of auctioneers based at Hereford, had joined with Mr. Baldwin to form a new firm with sales at Tenbury, Leominster and Hereford.

The Swan Hotel - 1900

Store sales during the First World War continued but fatstock prices were controlled; animals were allocated to local butchers by the Ministry of Food who used the local markets as a collecting centre. In 1919, Edwards, Russell and Baldwin covered in part of the Teme Street market and started a weekly sale of fruit and farm produce. This may have taken the place of the fruit and produce market which had been held at the Swan Hotel for some years before. The old established Round Market, where a variety of produce including poultry, eggs, butter, vegetables, rabbits, mushrooms and fruit in season were sold, had been run for many years by Mr. Drew; he later took Stanley Cattell into partnership and the weekly produce auction attracted a wide variety of vendors and plenty of wholesale and retail buyers, many coming by train from Birmingham and the Black Country towns.

A market report in the local paper for March 1929 recorded: "Edwards, Russell and Baldwin sold 30,000 eggs this week, Drew and Cattell sold 20,100."

By 1938, up to 5,000 dozen eggs were being sold in the Round Market, and at Christmas, 500 turkeys, 250 geese and 1,500 cockerels and ducks. In the same year, the Teme Street market of Edwards, Russell and Baldwin saw weekly sales figures of 800-1,000 couples of rabbits, rising to a record 1,372 couples sold in one week in 1939. The rabbits were legged together in pairs and hung over two metal rails running the full length of the produce shed and as well as being sold in large quantities at both markets, rabbits were also bought by several fruit and produce merchants in Tenbury Wells, directly from farmers. It would not be an exaggeration to say that during the winter months, 4,000 to 5,000 rabbits were sold each week and it was said that in the 1930s some farmers could catch and sell enough to pay the rent for the year; however, once the weather warmed up in April, the value of the rabbit dropped suddenly. This steady trade in rabbits continued until the outbreak of the deadly myxomatosis in 1953; it raged through the countryside like wildfire wiping out 95 percent of the rabbit population in the United Kingdom and numbers have never recovered.

Further changes in the management of Tenbury market came in January 1939 when Edwards, Russell and Baldwin invited Geoffrey Bright, a specialist in antique furniture, to join the partnership to become Russell, Baldwin and Bright.

During the Second World War, Tenbury market, along with all other UK markets, became a collecting centre for all cattle, sheep and pigs going for slaughter. On behalf of the Ministry of Food, auctioneers organised where the animals were to be weighed, assessed for quality by a grader and allocated to butchers around the West Midlands; meanwhile store cattle and sheep sales continued.

It's an ill wind that blows no good.

It was in April 1940 when a record entry of over 1,600 cattle went under the hammer in one day at Tenbury. This was at a time when farmers had to plough up extra grassland to produce more wheat, potatoes and sugar beet and were forced to sell the cattle because of the shortage of grazing. After years of food shortages, in the early 1950s food rationing finally came to an end leaving farmers free to farm as they wished. Much of the arable land in the area was put back to pasture and animal production increased again.

Tenbury market, run by Russell, Baldwin and Bright, was big enough to cope with the normal sales of animals, except the two big autumn store lamb and breeding ewe sales which attracted a total entry of up to 18,000 head; the sales were held on the Palmers Meadow, mostly on land where the swimming pool and car park is now and continued on the site until about 1980. Six years later Russell, Baldwin and Bright sold the property side of their business to Hogg Robinson who also took the name but the agricultural and market side of the business carried on trading as Russell, Baldwin and Bright Markets. However, to avoid the difficulties caused by the two separate firms using similar names, the name was changed to Brightwells and they continued with their auction business at a number of livestock markets stretching from Tenbury Wells in the east and across the Marches into Wales. Tenbury market, run by Managing Auctioneer Nick Champion with the loyal support of the local farming community, continued to trade successfully.

The big crunch for Tenbury and the Teme Valley came in 2004. Amid uproar and outrage in the town, Brightwells finally decided to sell off the livestock market, also famed since Victorian times, as a site for the traditional holly and mistletoe sales. Rumours of supermarkets, housing and assorted development invaded the town, but eventually the market site was bought by Leominster based Tyrell's, producers of up-market potato chips.

The final livestock sale in Tenbury market on 16th December 2004 attracted great crowds into Tenbury Wells. A mock funeral, complete with coffin, pall bearers, mourners and muffled drum, brought a sad and final end to the famous Tenbury Livestock Market but the show goes on for auctioneer Nick Champion, also current secretary of the Tenbury Agricultural Society. He has set up his own business in the town and in these difficult days for the farming community, strives to keep the farming tradition going by holding two or three sheep sales a year in a field on the Worcester Road. He couples this with his nationally respected holly and mistletoe sales, held in November and December since Victorian times in Tenbury Wells.

Looking back over the years, seasonal sales of livestock were held at village sites in the Tenbury area, some going back as far as the early information in the local press in 1874. For well over 100 years a sale at the Hundred House, Great Witley, staged first by G.H.Winton and until the end of the 20th century by Nock and Joseland of Kidderminster, was held on a green field site using temporary penning. The latter firm also held sales in a yard at the Lion Hotel, Clifton-on-Teme during the 1930s.

In April 1879, George Green held a stock sale at the Falcon Hotel, Bromyard; this may have been before the town's own livestock market was built. From 1925 and for some years after, auctioneers John Norton and Bright, from Ludlow, held seasonal sales of livestock at Woofferton, in the Smithfield, adjacent to the Salwey Arms Hotel as well as holding sales of ewes, lambs and cattle at the Angel Inn, Clee Hill.

Butter wouldn't melt in his/her mouth.

Messrs. Millard and Urwick of Ludlow held horse sales at Leintwardine and Brampton Brian in 1878, and in 1881 a consignment of horses from Ireland went under the hammer at Ludlow. As well as Tenbury, Leominster, Ludlow, Craven Arms, Knighton, Kington and other Welsh Border markets became important centres for breeding ewe sales, mainly Kerry Hill, Clun Forest and Shropshire's, with the numbers sold peaking in the 1950s and 1960s.

Craven Arms boasted an annual turnover of 60 to 70 thousand ewes but by the end of the Millennium, the market sites and saleyards went the way of many others countrywide, developed into housing estates and today the main ewe sales are now held across the Welsh Border at Builth Wells and Welshpool.

But it's the sad demise of Tenbury's market scene that finally closes the pages of market history. The now sorry state of the old livestock market leaves an empty feel to the town and so far there appears to be little future for the remains of G.H. Winton's famous sale yard, quietly crumbling away on the bank of the River Teme. Apart from a few parked vehicles, what is left of the now empty, run down market-place stands as a silent memorial to the ghosts of a once bustling economic farming community.

THE SHOWMAN
BOB WEBB of ASHFORD CARBONELL

Few can boast such long held links with the Tenbury Show as Bob Webb, born in the spring of 1927. In all probability, he has attended most, if not all, the shows held during his lifetime and, in the majority of cases, as an exhibitor of livestock.

Bob's earliest memories of the Tenbury Show are of visitors using the pony and trap as transport, with hardly any cars on the Show site. He well remembers the show of 1935 when the eight-year-old was asked by Bill Homes, of Bosbury, to parade his Ryeland ram lamb before the judge. Bob jumped at the chance and won fourth prize. Bob retained the prize card with great pride for many years, as a memento of the occasion. This introduction certainly sowed the seeds of 'the showman' in Bob's mind. He returned to Tenbury and, through the years, has attended many other events around the Country, competing with his livestock.

The Ryeland breed has played an important part in the Tenbury Show over time. It was one of the first sheep breeds to have Pedigree Classes, scheduled at the Annual Show of 1922 and has been included ever since. The Ryeland is certainly one of the oldest breeds established in the UK, probably originating from Roman times. It is likely that they were developed from the importation of breeds like the Spanish Merino which no doubt had a great influence in establishing the Ryeland breed as a noted fine wool producer. Indeed, during the early 1600s, the Leominster area was noted for its wool production, so valuable was wool to the area that it was known as 'Lemster Ore'. The Ryeland Sheep Society was founded at a meeting held at the Green Dragon Hotel, Hereford on 2nd December 1903. Eight breeders and the first secretary, John Pinches, were present. The Society's first President, William T. Barneby, of Saltmarsh Castle, near Bromyard, was elected in 1905. The first Ryeland Sheep exported to New Zealand were from the Saltmarsh Flock. The whole flock was dispersed in 1909 when it consisted of 460 sheep. The breed's first Flock Book was published in 1910, detailing the breeding lines of members' animals. The Ryeland was most widespread from the early 1920s until the early 40s but, soon after, its popularity tailed off, no longer considered commercially viable by a growing number of

When pleasure do become a business it usually turn sour.

sheep flock owners, even though the breed had retained its well-shaped conformation and early maturity. However, during the 80s and 90s up to 230 members were recorded, the increase being very much due to the attraction of the easy-care nature of the breed to new sheep-keepers. Also during this period, the Coloured Ryeland was developed, although not to the satisfaction of all the Ryeland Society's members. These sheep carry wool of a darker colour, which has gained favour with wool spinners.

In 1937, the Webb family set off to the Tenbury Show from their Ashford Carbonell farm with a promising Ryeland ram lamb, loaded in their horse cart. On arriving at the Palmers Meadow showground, it was clear that the more experienced exhibitors were concerned about the competition that the newcomers were presenting. However, closer examination revealed that the Webbs were not registered breeders of the Ryeland sheep and were therefore barred from competing. Not many days passed before their membership application form was sent away in the post!

The Second World War years intervened when no shows were held. The show of 1948, the first after the hostilities, was held on Castle Meadow at the Linnage Farm, Burford. The following year, it returned to the Palmers Meadow.

The Webb family became regular exhibitors with mainly Ryeland Sheep but over the years they have also prepared Clun Forest sheep, Black Welsh Mountain, Shropshire, Suffolks and more recently Coloured Ryelands. They have also exhibited cattle from their pedigree Hereford herd including a dairy heifer in 1960. Bob recalls the purchase of this very promising British Fresian and taking her to the Show. She took first prize and Reserved Champion in the dairy section of some 40 entries, when the judges were R.F. Goodwin of Earls Croome and J. Turner of Kings Pyon.

Stock lorries had become more common just before the Second World War, but for some time after it was difficult arranging transport for animals. However, Bob recalls Harry Wragg, of Little Hereford, providing a lorry, shared by numerous exhibitors for Show day. The homeward journey always included a stop at the Rose and Crown for refreshment! More recently, Bob has become a familiar figure, turning up at the Show and other events, with his tractor and stock trailer.

Harry Wragg's business was founded in 1957 with a seven-ton Bedford livestock truck. His father had established a haulage business in the late 1800s based in Sheffield, using heavy horses and specialising in felled timber. Harry's workload developed over the years to include general haulage and the transportation of holly and mistletoe to Sheffield Market. The family gave up the hauling of livestock in the late 1970s. This coincided with more farmers using their own transport, often stock trailers towed behind Land Rovers. The company is now run by Harry's son, Malcolm, and involves the use of fifteen articulated 44 tonne units. The fleet was the first in the UK to adapt its trucks to run on low polluting rapeseed oil. More than 100 years on, the Wragg family's haulage activities have turned full circle with regard to low environmental impact.

To develop the best lines in livestock breeding requires great patience. Devoted stockmanship and sound judgement is required to deliver the successes achieved by producers like Bob Webb. Nothing in stockbreeding is instant and there can be many disappointments along with the glory times. Nonetheless, talented breeders with the right sort of breeding stock, who are prepared to put in a great deal of hard work, can get the results. Bob stresses the importance of

Make hay while the sun shines.

good preparation for successful livestock showing. With regard to sheep, possible entries have to be identified early in their lives and adult prospects should be shorn soon after the year start. A careful feed regime follows to ensure adequate condition without getting your charges 'over the top'. Then follows a sequence of trimming and working on the fleece to ensure optimum presentation. Bob likes to 'freshen-up' his show sheep in a weak solution of sheep dip the week before an event and then tidies them up with a final trim. Trimming sheep is a great skill and, in Bob's case, he prefers to use a set of hand shears that he has had since 1940! It has become commonplace today that some breeds of sheep are exhibited in a more natural form. Bob suggests that one of the toughest taskes in the whole procedure is breaking the animals to halter and getting them parading well. Usually, a three or four day crash course does the trick. Sheep can test the patience but often cattle are more difficult! However, the rewards are great. The pleasure of accepting a prize card, the honour of taking part in the Grand Parade, and the extra kudos it all brings to your stock, are the rewards of the successful breeder and showman. For Bob another rewarding feature of his work is the interest shown by his children and now grandchildren, thus representing the fourth generation of the family experienced in the art of the show ring.

Bob has fond memories of the time he has spent supporting the Tenbury Agricultural Society. He commends the organisation for its friendly nature. Bob has not only been an exhibitor, but also a Committee member, a Steward, particularly of the Hereford cattle section in the 1960s and 70s. He has also judged the Tenbury Ryeland Sheep classes on two occassions and has been invited to officiate at the Royal Show three times. Bob feels that the success of the Tenbury Society is due to the support of so many good people over the years and he recalls with great affection Sir Archer Baldwin M.P., an absolute stalwart of the Society, who was always interested in what supporters were doing and who himself exhibited Ryeland sheep, the flock founded in 1915 and Hereford cattle, the herd founded in 1872, from his farm at Underley. There is no doubt that the prime stock raising area around Tenbury Wells owes a great deal to those who have raised the standards and profiles of their charges. One of them is Bob Webb of Ashford Carbonell, the Showman.

A.H. CALDICOTT & SONS

A.H. Caldicott and Sons was established in 1919 by Albert Henry Caldecott, son of a farming family, who decided his destiny was not in farming, but was to become a carpenter and wheelwright. After leaving school he completed an apprenticeship with the Allen family, at the blacksmith and carpenter's shop in Brimfield, to become a master carpenter and wheelwright.

When the First World War started, he was called up to register for service but, unknown to him, they were requesting carpenters and especially coach builders, a profession making carriages for horse drawn vehicles. Following an interview of registration, he was directed to take lodgings in Birmingham and work at the Wolsley works making cabs, bodies and propellers for aircraft and vehicles. After cycling from Birmingham to Brimfield every weekend to see his future wife Esther, he decided to marry her and they set up home in Ward End, Birmingham.

After the war ended, Albert Henry worked for Birmingham based Mulliners, a prestigious company making bodies for Rolls Royce, Bentley and other motor vehicles. He was awarded a diploma for making the body of a Rolls Royce for an Indian Maharaja who actually signed the diploma. However, it was always Albert Henry's intention to return to Brimfield or Tenbury Wells and he eventually relocated to Market Square, Tenbury, recently vacated by the Bowkett family. Working hard for long hours, he made a reasonable living.

Reading through the Tenbury Advertiser, Albert Henry and Esther found a large empty house with land to rent at Sutton near Tenbury, for their increasing family of five, from where he could also set up and expand his blacksmith and carpentry work. In time Ninevah House, at Sutton was developed into a large business with carpentry, wheelwrights, blacksmiths and undertakers. They cut up large elm and oak trees and dried them for customers and then made their coffins for them.

The family increased again, making a total of five sons, Harry, Cyril, John, Arthur and Alan and two daughters, Esther and Gladys. Albert Henry decided that the two eldest sons, Harry and Cyril, should join larger building companies to gain valuable experience and knowledge in the building and carpentry trades, which would help develop and support the family business. They built the first council houses in the local area, including at Upper Sapey, along with many other private and commercial properties and they eventually employed a workforce of around thirty people.

Granville House, in Cross Street, was purchased by Albert Henry in 1956 along with the Bell Yard workshop, which was specially adapted to the making of coach bodies; the floor above could be lowered by pulleys to allow coach bodies to be taken up to a dust-free room for painting etc. Albert Henry purchased many other properties apart from Bell Yard which was bought from auctioneers, Messrs. Cattell & Young who held their holly and mistletoe sales on the site.

Sadly, Albert Henry died in 1956 and did not get the chance to move into his retirement home at Holland House, in Market Square. Harry and his brothers continued trading at Cross Street as equal partners and successfully developed the building and funeral business. The company prospered, employing around 50 employees at one time, working on many building projects, including parapets to hold the steel Bailey bridge over the River Teme, at Little Hereford, considered to be a spectacular achievement.

170

In 1980, Harry and Cyril retired and so the family business was run by brothers John, Arthur and Alan. The brothers relocated to 15, Market Street to join up with Caldicott Bros. Builder's Merchants. Sadly, only John, Alan and their two sisters, Esther and Gladys remain and ownership of A.H. Caldicott & Sons is currently being transferred to the third generation of the family, the sons of Arthur, John and Alan who will, no doubt, continue to trade in Market Street for many more years to come.

Heard Under The Bridge

A TENBURY WAG

A popular Tenbury character made a bet that he would ride his horse from Bewdley to Tenbury, and, starting at the same time, would reach Tenbury station as soon as the train. Accordingly, he took his horse to Bewdley in a railway van. On arrival there preparations were made for disembarking the horse. 'No' said his owner, 'leave the horse where he is'. When the train was due to start, the equestrian mounted his horse in the van and majestically sat on the saddle until they all reached Tenbury station not later than the train itself. Thus at a small extra cost he duly won his bet.

Victorian Convenience collapses into the river

AN UNFORTUNATE INCONVENIENCE

In 1924 Tenbury Town Council discussed two proposals to erect public conveniences on council ground in Market Street. One was to use glazed bricks inside the urinals at a cost of £425, the cheaper plan, £370, was to plaster the walls and use washable paint. The Bayley's Charity had offered to pay two thirds of the cost of building works and the finance committee would make up the difference by increasing the rate by one and a half pence. Several councillors wanted the cheaper version, thus saving the rate payer extra costs (there must have been an election due) but the Town Surveyor stuck to his guns and insisted he could not do anything to make it cheaper as glazed bricks were far better for wiping clean the objectionable writing often found on urinal walls. Councillor Maund did not agree with spending such a large sum of money as the toilets were for the convenience of the town and not the country people. The Chairman could not see why it was only for the convenience of the town but Mr Maund insisted it was for the use of visitors chiefly and these benefited the town. People coming in from the countryside only stayed for two or three hours in the town and for years before had done so without such a place. Nevertheless, the Edwardian public toilets had stood the test of time and, with a public campaign to bring them up to 21st century standards, the toilet block was refurbished in May and June 2007 at a cost of £4,500. Sadly, in the following July the adjacent wall collapsed and a little bit of Tenbury's architectural history was flushed away in the floods. Plans are underway for a replacement.

'COW IN THE BEDROOM'

'On Tuesday morning last the movements of a cow being driven to market were followed. It was quietly coming down Berrington Road towards Cross Street until it reached the house occupied by Mr E. Bolas. Here it stepped in at the entrance to the garden and walked round to the rear of the house. Finding the door open, it walked into the kitchen, and with becoming politeness closed the door after itself. While preparations were being taken to prevent the animal from doing much damage, the cow, to the amazement of those present, went upstairs and took up its abode in the front bedroom. Here the animal behaved in a very quiet way, but it took some time for the helpers to persuade the quadruped to leave its cosy surroundings. However, without doing very much damage the distinguished visitor departed, much to the relief of those who had been honoured by the visit.

If wishes were horses beggars would ride.

173

Facts and Figures

NEWS IN BRIEF FROM THE TENBURY ADVERTISER

1878 - A sea lamprey was caught in the Teme near the church at Tenbury, in July a second sea lamprey was caught soon after. It had never been known before.

1880 - At a farm sale at Moor Park, Ludlow, four Alderney cows were sold; this Channel Island breed is now extinct. At the same sale 18 Shetland heifers went under the hammer, the breed still exists in small numbers.

1883 - Alderney cows and a pedigree bull were sold at sale at Easton Court, Little Hereford.

1883 - Large white pigs, first mentioned in this district, went up for sale at a farm at Whitton.

1899 - Mrs W.S. Davis from Stanbrook House, Burford, erected a water fountain and drinking trough where man and beast may slake their thirst near the Rose and Crown.

1899 - A mushroom weighing over three pounds was grown by Mr J.W. Rose of Harpfields, Burford.

1901 - An advertisement in the Tenbury Advertiser offered for sale 40 to 50 wagon loads of gorse at 7 shillings per load, ready cut from Simmonds, St. Michaels.

1901 - Also saw a young Anglesey cow to calve shortly for sale at Linnage Farm, Burford.

1911 - A notice in the local paper stated that - 'W. Nott begs to announce that he has taken Sutton Mill (water mill) and will continue to carry on the milling business formerly carried on by Mr Geo Brown.'

1911 - At the licensing sessions it was stated that there was a licence to sell beer and cider at the rate of one per 176 persons, including children, in the Tenbury district. It was stated that in some parts of Worcestershire it was one to 800 persons.

1911 - An advertisement in the Tenbury Advertiser – 'At service, Pedigree Curly Coated Lincolnshire boar – terms two shillings and sixpence – S. Davis, Kings Head, Tenbury.' According to the BBC Country file broadcast in January 2007, this breed of pig became extinct in 1976.

1913 - The name Tenbury Wells to be used to avoid confusion with towns of a similar sounding name like Tenby.

1915 - Local vets Mr J. McKay - White M.R.C.V.S. arranged for a locum, Mr P. Kearney, to look after his practice during his absence serving with the British forces in France. In 1919 Captain James McKay-White M.R.C.V.S. was demobilised and resumed practice in Tenbury.

1919 - Whit Monday. At a sports meeting held at Rhyse Meadow, Tenbury – visitors were taken on passenger flights in a three-seater Avro aeroplane.

1921 - A Pitmaston Duchess pear, six and a half inches long, thirteen and a half inches round and weighing 33 ounces was grown in Tenbury.

1925 - A freak calf was born at Clifton-on-Teme with one head, two bodies, eight legs and two tails.

1931 - A third sea lamprey was caught in the Teme near the church.

1937 - Witley Court was destroyed by fire.

1938 - Under a Tenbury Slum Clearance Order 3 houses in Scotland Yard, Church Street, 6 houses in Corn Exchange Yard, Teme Street, 7 houses in Trumpet Yard, Cross Street were demolished.

A farmer should live as though he was going to die tomorrow and farm as if he was going to live for ever.

TENBURY HOSPITAL

19.10.1929 - Proposed to sell Tenbury Hospital, invest the proceeds and build a Nursing Home.

16.11.1929 - Tenbury Hospital to be sold.

25.1.1930 - Hospital meeting – a proposal.
"That this meeting of the parishioners of Tenbury strongly condemns the proposal to sell Tenbury Cottage Hospital and recommends a reconstruction of the committee and officers and the re-opening of the institution".

15.2.1930 - A letter about Tenbury Hospital in the Advertiser says –
"If a guarantee of finances does not come forward, the sale of the Hospital will go ahead. There is a need to spend 300 pounds on the Hospital and about 500 pounds per annum to run it."
Several letters hoping to save it.

8.11.1930 - Big meeting to re-open the Hospital.
Two meetings in November 1930 – Good attendance and a scheme to finance the Hospital was approved by all the parishes.

7.3.1931 - Tenbury Hospital – 90% of householders supports the scheme to open it again.

29.8.1931 - Hospital re-opens.

THE OLD AGE PENSION

The old age pension, five shillings per week, was first paid from 1st January 1909 through the Post Office. At Little Hereford, old age pensioners held a tea party to celebrate the granting of old age pensions to "veterans of labour".
It was noted that the pension was to be five shillings per week yet it cost eight shillings and four pence per week to keep a person in the workhouse.
If a couple had to go into the workhouse they had to live separately as men and women were segregated.

THE TELEPHONE

It was first suggested in 1903 that Tenbury Post Office be connected to the telephone system. A letter from the Postmaster General dated February 1909, asking the Tenbury Council to guarantee any deficiency that might arise in the establishing of a Telephone Exchange at Tenbury and connecting it to the National Trunk System as the number of subscribers in a recent canvass was less than expected. A proposal that a guarantee be given was not seconded and after discussion the resolution fell through. However, by June 1909, the telephone was connected to Tenbury Exchange and two years later was extended round the town and within a few years into the surrounding countryside.

THE HUMANE KILLER

The R.S.P.C.A. demonstrated the Humane Killer gun at two slaughterhouses in Tenbury in 1909. It was recommended to replace the poleaxe for stunning animals. The butchers, Mr Eaton and Mr Barnes, believed the meat would not keep properly because some of the blood was retained after using the humane killer and they still believed the poleaxe was the best method. In March 1924 the R.S.P.C.A. asked the Tenbury R.D.C. to make it compulsory for butchers to use a humane killer.

Sometimes young horses die. Old horses are bound to.

ELECTRICITY

At a meeting of the Tenbury Union Gas Company in January 1924 the question of electricity being supplied to the town and immediate neighbourhood was discussed. It was resolved that if sufficient support was forthcoming, the company would consider the provision of such a supply in connection with its own undertaking.

EARLY CLOSING

From 7th May 1891 all businesses in Tenbury will close at 2 p.m. on Thursdays, all the year round. This was agreed at a special meeting of tradesmen at the Corn Exchange to discuss early closing and a half day holiday for the shop assistants. Up until this time the shops were open 6 days a week, often until 8 p.m.

TENBURY WATER SUPPLY

In March 1894 the Tenbury Advertiser reported that a meeting of Tenbury Town Council had been called to discuss a new water supply for the town. A recent report from the health inspector stating that the present water supply was not fit for human consumption was discussed and consequently a new water supply taken from springs on the Clee Hill, probably the Knowle spring, was eventually installed.

In 1901 it was again reported that because of a partial failure of the water supply from the Knowle spring, in the interests of economy there was to be no watering of gardens. At the same time the new Élan Valley water pipeline to supply fresh water to Birmingham was being installed; this included two tunnels and an aqueduct 200 yards long on 15 arches on Clee Hill.

Later that year it was confirmed that during the laying of the Birmingham water main the supply from Clee Hill had been accidentally severed, this considerably reduced Tenbury's water supply from around 53,000 gallons per day to barely 1,000 gallons. This led to a possible crisis situation and to cope with the lack of water the town council bought an engine and pump to extract water from the Teme directly into the Clee Hill pipeline. It came with a public health warning that "the water would not be equal in quality to that obtained from Clee Hill and must be boiled before drinking; it would however be most welcome to those who indulge in the luxury of an occasional bath".

This seemed to get over the problem and to avoid the possibility of being sued, the Corporation of Birmingham allowed Tenbury to connect up to the main Elan water supply and provide a reservoir on the Clee Hill road north of Tenbury. This vital supply of fresh water continued for many years until the steadily increasing population of Birmingham needed extra water and an alternative supply was installed.

While the new pipeline was being installed in 1901, a report in the Tenbury Advertiser, headed "Living in a Birmingham Water Supply Pipe," said "*the local inspector told the court that he had found a family of 5 persons occupying one of the large steel pipes to be laid on the water track, the pipe was 42 inches in diameter and 24 feet long. The three children were swarming with vermin, their hair was matted together and their clothing in a very dirty condition They appeared to be under fed and conditions were filthy to the extreme.*"

Apparantly it was not uncommon for navvies to use the pipes as sleeping quarters.

As artful as a wagon load of monkeys.

THE TENBURY FIRE BRIGADE - *Extracts taken from the Tenbury Advertiser*

In January 1874 the Tenbury Advertiser printed an article about the need for a fire engine and invited subscriptions from the public. Whether this was for the first ever fire appliance is not known.

Three years later, the Advertiser reported a disastrous fire at Clifford's farm, the home of Mr Edwin Corfield who had been threshing with a machine belonging to Mr Brown of Coreley. At about midnight, Mr Corefield awoke to find the rickyard ablaze; it is supposed that a smouldering of dust inside the threshing box had ignited and caught fire. A messenger was despatched to Tenbury for the fire engine but by the time it got there everything, ricks of beans, wheat, barley, seed clover and two wagons, was ablaze. When the fire engine did arrive the pumping apparatus was frozen and could not be used. However, the firemen did save one rick of wheat by throwing water on it with buckets and bowls. The threshing box was completely destroyed, nothing but the iron work was left and the damage was estimated at £300.

"September 1894. On Friday last a fire broke out in the kitchen of Mr H.Pullman of Burford. After the inmates had retired to bed it is surmised that a spark from the grate fell among some clothes. A loaded gun which was hung up in the room was exploded by the heat and the discharge shattered two or three panes of glass in the window. This aroused the occupants and the fire was put out but not before the contents of the kitchen had been greatly damaged."

June 1901. A fire at Fern Farm Nash. The fire engine was called drawn by three horses belonging to Mr H. Preece, the Swan Hotel, who runs a posting establishment there.

Fire, especially at hop drying time was very common, in fact, there will not be many hop kilns that have not been burned down at some time, and replaced, before the arrival of the motorised fire engine. For many years the procedure, in the event of fire, was to send someone on horseback or bicycle to Tenbury to raise the alarm. One of the firemen would go for the horses, sometimes housed in the stables at the Swan Hotel or in a paddock close by and occasionally from the Clock House. They were taken to collect the fire engine, kept in a shed near the church, pick up the other firemen and make their way to the fire as quickly as possible. If the fire was any distance from Tenbury, the firemen did not stand much chance of saving the buildings, it was more a case of stopping it spreading to other properties. It was such a problem to get horses to pull the fire engine in the 1920s that it was suggested that if a farmer had a fire he should send his own horses to fetch the engine. All the early fire pumps were hand operated, needing three or four men on each side as well as men directing the hosepipe onto the fire. Eventually, the telephone came to Tenbury and was extended to most villages by the 1930s and, with the new motorised fire engines of this period, the alarm was raised and the fire dealt with so much quicker.

Tenbury has much to thank the early firefighters for, those men who struggled to get to the fire with horses over bad roads, using very basic equipment. Today firemen and women are not only expected to fight fires but also attend all kinds of accidents, rescue people and animals from floods, using the latest up-to-date engines and equipment. Their dedicated and committed team work serves the community well.

REPORTED CRIME FROM THE TENBURY ADVERTISER

09.09.1884   This year saw a rowdy meeting at the Corn Exchange, the purpose of the meeting was to curb the supply of cider to farm workers. It was suggested that farmers should pay the equivalent value of cider in extra wages. Several anti-drink campaigners thought the farm workers should only drink tea or coffee. Angry farmers and farm workers shouted them down and told them they did not understand that hard physical work such as haymaking and harvest, as well as work in general needed cider to quench their thrist and these people did not know whay they were talking about.

27.01.1885   Drunkenness, game trespass and petty stealing appeared every week from the start of the Tenbury Advertiser. Animals straying, not sending children to school, suicides, overcrowding a small house – Fines for obstructing the highway with a horse and cart – Cruelty to horses – Trespassing in search of game.

11.02.1890   Sad accident to a child – A horse and trap belonging to Mr. Reece Davis, Butcher, was standing outside his shop in Teme Street when it suddenly ran away at great speed. After knocking down a little boy it continued on at a fearful rate and when passing over Teme Bridge the left wheel of the trap came in contact with the iron railings of the bridge, several of which were completely smashed. Also at this place a sad accident befell a little girl named Alice Bennett who had been living with her grandmother in Church Street. Before she could get out of the way she was knocked down by the horse and trap and the wheel inflicted dreadful injuries to her head. She was picked up unconscious and taken to Tenbury Hospital. The other children coming over the bridge escaped by taking refuge in a recess by the railings.

22.07.1890   Riding without reins – Thomas Teague of Netherwood was charged with riding on the shafts of a wagon without reins at Kyre. The defendant pleaded guilty, but said that he had been ploughing the whole of the day and that he had got to go at night to Bayton for a load of coal and that his feet were so sore he was compelled to ride, and his master had not sent a boy with him – fined 5 shillings.

23.06.1891   Nine boys were fined for playing football in Cross Street. It had been reported that the boys were playing on a Sunday when the police were not about – fined 1 shilling each.

06.10.1891   Breach of the peace – John Mobberley, drover from Kidderminster and Edwin Ashford, farmer, were charged with fighting at Burford – bound over for the sum of £5 each to keep the peace.

01.05.1891   At the May Fair – Early in the evening, a young man named Pound of Rochford met with a serious accident through a fall from the swing boats.

24.03.1903   People fined for horses and cattle straying off Old Wood Common also for having no dog licences. Charles Maund, an insurance agent of Stoke Bliss was charged with not ringing his bell on a bicycle or giving proper warning of approach at Rochford. P.C. Moody said that the defendant ran into him, knocked him down and dislocated his shoulder and broke his arm. The road was thirteen feet wide. Defendant was fined 11s 6d or in default seven days imprisonment.

24.10.1910   A boy of fourteen was found guilty of stealing a carbide lamp and regularly misbehaving. He was too young to be sent away for corrective training but was sentenced to six strokes of the birch rod.

Tramps and Vagrants - Several cases of fires on farms, thought to have been caused by tramps smoking. Building destroyed and only the ash of the person in the rubble.

It was very common for families with six or eight children in two up, two down cottages to be fined for overcrowding.

29.09.1914   Jane Burden (Jinny) appeared before the magistrates for the 18th time for being drunk and disorderly – sent to prison for 1 month.

Teme Street - C.1920s

179

THE WORK HOUSE AND POOR - *Extracts taken from the Tenbury Advertiser*

07.09.1880   Cost of relief of paupers for Tenbury Union.
There are 372 paupers receiving indoor or outdoor relief upon January 1st 1880.
First mention in 1872, £1,010 was expended on relief of paupers.
In the half year ending Lady Day 1880 the sum was £515.

25.01.1881   Death of a 79-year-old man in a barn – died of exposure to severe cold. Several cases similar over previous years including young children who died of lack of nourishment.

08.03.1881   Suicide at Lindridge – Edward Davis of Mamble cut his throat with a razor. He had been charged with stealing some swedes and it had preyed on his mind.

14.02.1882   Martley Workhouse has 111 inmates, against 110 last year.

05.05.1886   Mr and Mrs Higgins (Somerset) – Master and Matron of the workhouse.

15.11.1887   A very sad case of a man dying in Tenbury workhouse – he had been hop picking at Hilltop, Rochford and was taken ill - John Parker, aged 35, described as a travelling tinker. He came from Newport, Shropshire. His wife had died recently; he had three children and had taken to the road, all sleeping by the roadside at night. He was earning a small amount of money by grinding knives and razors. The seven-year-old son, John (an intelligent lad), answered the Coroner's questions. The family had recently been at Malvern where police found the three children asleep by the road and the father had fallen and injured his head. After working six days at Hilltop, on the hops, he became ill and was taken, with his three children, to Tenbury workhouse, where he died the next day. Verdict – Death by abscess to the brain.

21.02.1888   John Fay, a tramp, was charged with stealing three sacks from a farm at Bockleton – asked by a policeman, why he took them, he said "I took them to wrap myself up in as it was so cold". He had been sleeping in a cart in the wain-house at the farm.

07.01.1890   Christmas Day in the work house - Every year there was a special Christmas dinner – Christmas cards, a liberal allowance of tobacco for the men, tea and sugar for the women, the boys a scarf each with cake, fruit, sweets and nuts and to the girls, toys, cake, fruit, sweets and nuts, which occupied their thoughts until breakfast time. Dinner was customary old English fare of roast beef and plum pudding with an allowance of beer. With dinner over and Grace sung, hearty cheers were given for the Board of Guardians. No doubt the guardians and local shopkeepers contributed to make this a special occasion.

15.09.1894   Police Court – Before Mr G.R. Godson. - The tramp and his eye protectors.
George Evans, a tramp, was charged with refusing to break the quantity of stone allotted to him whilst an inmate in the Tenbury workhouse. On that morning, Mr. Enos Higgins, the Master of the Union, stated that he informed the defendant, when admitted, that he would be required to break stone with the other casuals on the following morning. He made no reply or complaint then, but refused to break stone the next morning unless a pair of eye

180

protectors were given him on account of his eyesight being bad. On his repeated protestations, witness sent for a constable and had the defendant locked up. Mr. Sweet, the surgeon was sent for, and on examining the defendant's eyes pronounced them bad and the sight defective. He certainly thought that protectors for the eyes should be furnished by the guardians. Upon the surgeon's finding, the magistrates had no alternative but to dismiss the defendant.

03.01.1899   Tenbury Board of Guardians. (Workhouse)
Inmates – 26 men, 12 women, 12 children and 33 vagrants relieved.

26.03.1901   Tenbury Workhouse.
A proposal that the frosted glass should be replaced by clear glass so that the inmates could see what was going on in the street. Mr. Ballard, who proposed, thought the life of the inmates was a very miserable one, and that they were there through no fault of their own. Their existence seemed to him to be that of waiting in the workhouse only to die, and he thought that by having the windows replaced it would add a little interest to their lives as the men seemed to have nothing to do. The chairman was against it, it was not wise to make the lives of the inmates too happy. The master was called in and stated that the inmates would be at the windows all the time and pulling faces at the public outside. It was decided not to change.

24.02.1903   A letter in the Tenbury Advertiser from a resident complaining that she had been struck on the cheek, just below the eye, by a chip from a stone being broken by a vagrant outside the workhouse in Teme Street.

18.08.1903   Absconding from work.
The Tenbury workhouse is at present being inundated with vagrants, many of whom have a particular aversion to work, especially that of stone breaking. One of the fraternity, who gave his name as John Hughes, was charged with absconding from the workhouse and refusing to do his allotted task. He was sent to prison for seven days.

14.05.1907   In the Workhouse - 19 men, 21 women, 7 children.
This is about the average over the years. There have been 162 vagrants in the last fortnight (staying 1 night only). Average 11 per night besides the inmates.

11.04.1908   104 applicants for the position of Master and Matron of Tenbury Union workhouse. A list of 5 were interviewed.
Vagrants were allowed to stay overnight at the workhouse on condition that they broke a certain amount of stone (used for road mending) or some other allotted task before they left next morning.
Vagrants were allowed 8ozs bread and water (sometimes warm) or 6ozs bread and a pint of gruel.

02.03.1909   Dr. Mary Williams (Sanitary Sub-Committee) says that a lot of milk is not fit for human consumption and blames it for a lot of tuberculosis in children.
Mr. Waite claimed that one eleventh of the cost of pauperism was due to consumption (TB).

Nothing is certain but death and taxes.

It seems that a poor rate was levied on Tenbury and surrounding villages to support the union workhouse. The staff included Master and Matron, nursing staff, cook and domestic and tenders for food, coal etc. were called for regularly.

04.01.1910   Christmas Show in the Workhouse.
A magic lantern show was given to the inmates, showing excellent local views followed by many of a humorous and amusing character. This was after a substantial dinner of roast beef, plum pudding, mince pies, beer, cider and minerals. A supply of tobacco was provided for the old men, with three dozen churchwarden pipes for their use. Sweets and oranges were given to the children and extra tea and sugar for the women. At night each of the old men were given a pint of beer.

22.02.1910   A boy of 10 years old, whose home was at Leysters, was charged with begging at Oldwood. He was remanded and sent to the detention hall at the union workhouse. At the next court, the mother stated that she had no control of him. The bench sent the boy to the Working Boys Industrial School at Hereford until he attains the age of sixteen years.

03.01.1911   A joint of beef weighing 70 pounds was carved at the workhouse on Christmas Day.

11.03.1913   Tenbury Union Workhouse – Inmates 80 compared to 51 last year. Vagrants in the last two weeks 94 against 106 last year.
Vagrant numbers are low in winter and increase in the summer with the warmer weather and a chance of finding work. It was estimated to cost 13 shillings a head to keep a pauper per week in the workhouse at this time.

03.07.1920   Board of Guardians – Inmates 28, vagrants 28.
These numbers are a lot less than pre-war.

09.09.1922   Workhouse – 40 inmates, vagrants 267.
Workhouse - 29 inmates. The number of vagrants in the last month is 303 which equals 10 to 11 per night.

16.05.1925   Tenbury Board of Guardians
£3,496 collected from the parishes to fund the workhouse.

21.09.1929   Tenbury Guardians – inmates 23 (the lowest so far) and 276 vagrants.

18.01.1930   Tenbury Guardians – an inmate at Powick Mental Hospital, from the Tenbury district, admitted in January 1868, died aged 89. The clerk remarked that the deceased had been in hospital for 62 years and had cost the rate payers some thousands of pounds.

09.08.1930   Proposal to close Tenbury workhouse and transfer inmates to Kidderminster. Several people expressed concern about how vagrants would be looked after, especially in hop picking time when large numbers were reliant on a night's lodging and food.

27.09.1930   Tenbury workhouse closes – The Matron moves to Martley – inmates go to Martley or Kidderminster. Several members of Tenbury Guardians to still serve on Martley committee. Tenbury would be open for tramps for a time.

11.06.1932   Tenbury Workhouse and Hospital and Isolation Hospital for Sale. This must have been the time when E.R.& B bought their offices and isolation hospital to use as a café.

They couldn't hit a barn if they were standing inside it.

14.01.1939   Martley workhouse closes – Patients go to Worcester or
             Bromsgrove. Martley workhouse buildings not up to standard.
             Between the 1st and 2nd World Wars, during the summer time
             especially, large numbers of tramps (vagrants) wandered through
             this district looking for work. They often begged for food when
             work was short; most people would feed them in return for doing
             some work, like chopping sticks for the fire, digging the garden
             etc. Most of them had fought in the First World War, some had
             been gassed, shell shocked, injured, or lost an arm or leg. They
             drifted from workhouse to workhouse, getting seasonal
             employment, particularly on the farms, hop picking, fruit picking,
             and other work at hay and harvest time.
             Over the years, they knew where to call and they came for years
             to the same farms. Being ragged and often unshaven, they were
             quite frightening to children. They would often arrive with a
             bundle on their back, on a stick slung over the shoulder.

JOHN MORRIS' NOTEBOOK
(Spelling used from original text)

3/4 day thrashing – Edward Powell – Paid 19s 6d

194 rows of potato ground to various people (1 row to 4, 5, 8 rows) at 3s 6d per row. This looks to be for people to plant their own seed in prepared ground. (46 tenants).

He takes horses, colts and sheep at tack (so much per week) colt is spelt coult (1s 6d per week).

His household expenses are noted including meat from the butcher and a sale of animals (sheep) to the butcher to pay the outstanding bill.

He regularly sold wheat, barley and beans to local farmers and cottagers (for their pig and poultry) and to several owners of water mills, Burford Mill, Barretts Mill, Newnham Mill and Boraston Mill.

Boltens and thraves of straw ? could be for thatching.

He kept a bull and charged his neighbours 5s 0d for each service. He notes down the service dates of all his own cows – Spot, Cherry, Fillpail, Dina, Alderney Hfr, Pigeon, Mottle, Huberton, Daisy.

Mares to the stallion (usually two each year) - Darling and Jewel.

Women's wages for working in the hops.

Bought 1 ½ cwt white Dutch clover seed.

Sells cider in quantities up to 500 gallons.

Sold 5 couple yews and lambs at £2-8-0d – the amount £12-0-0d.

Emma Jones – Wages for the year £3-10-0d. She received payments taken out of her wages throughout the year as needed – 2 pairs of boots @ 9s 0d per pair. Repairing boots 2s 6d. At the end of the year there was 11s 0d to come to make up to £3-10-0d.

Paid Tinker £1.

He had a load of coals	10s 6d.
Cost for drawing (transport)	10s 0d.
Turnpikes	2s 6d

29th November 1862 – G. Pardoe –
500 gallons of cider @ 6d per gallon - £12-0-0d.

Bill from Burford milling his own corn – looks to cost 1s to 1s 6d per bagg and booked as baggs of flowers.
1st May 1863 – John Turner – wages for the year £5-10-0d.

2nd May – John Turner – wages for the year £5-0-0d (could possibly be relative of the above or hired for second year).

5th May – Mary Blakeway agres to serve Mrs Morris for 12 months at £6-0-0d. Sub – new dress 5s 8d and several 2s 6d.

7th May – John Owens agres to work for 3s 6d per week for 6 months in the summer and 6 months in winter for 3s 0d. Pair of boots 12s 0d.

Birds of a feather flock together.

Horse – Mr Wall. Tack 2s 6d per week.

1863 – Lewis Taylor wages £4-0-0d.

30th September – Load of coals 18s 11d
Turnpikes 1s 9d
Teme (? team) 10s 0d Total = £1-10-8d.

1863 - Paid to Reapers:-

Welshmen	£8-15-0d
Irishman	£3- 5-3d
Homes	£2- 7- 6d
Greggs Lot	£4- 4- 0d
Hill	13s 6d
Gates	10s10d
174 gallons of cider	£5-16- 0d
5 days William Clark	10s 0d
Thatching – Gregg & Heath	9s 0d
R. Hill, worck	5s 0d
Measuren Cooper	2s 6d
Tranter Discount	5s 0d
	£27-13-7d

Paid to Reapers	19s 9d	
Paid to Stemer Men	12s 0d	
Samuel Rider 2 days	3s 0d	
40 baggs of wheat @ 17/6 Mr Wheeler	£35- 0-0d	
40 baggs of wheat Mr Wheeler	£34- 0-0d	
Mr Wood, Burston Mill (? Boraston)	£49-10-0d	
Mr Davies, Park (? Dean Park)		
20 baggs of wheat @ 16s 0d	Paid	£16- 0- 0d
Mr Pound, Barretts Mill –		
11 baggs of wheat @ 16s 0d per bagg	£8-16-0d	

1864 – Sara Dovey, wages for the year £4-0-0d.

July 1864 – He appears to have bought a wheat crop at Sutton off 2 farmers, Normans £130-0-0d and Davis £81-10-0d. His expenses seem to have been £255-9-9 ½d inc purchase price and he received £256-11-0d.
21st July 1864 – Mr George Morris bought a mare coult for £20-0-0d

2nd January 1865 – Mr E. Owen bought 100 gallons of cider @ 4d per gallon – £1-13-0d.

30th November – Mr Pound, Barretts Mill – one load of beans @ 16s per bagg
20 baggs - £16-0-0d.

30th November – Mr Wheeler, Burford Mill – 20 baggs of beans @ 16s per bagg - £16-0-0d.

2nd December – Mr Wood, Burston Mill – 20 baggs of beans @ 16s 6d per bagg - £16-10-0d.

Mr Wheeler, Burford Mill – 5 thrave of straw and 2 thrave of straw £3-10-0d
At 10s per thrave.

Cut your coat according to your cloth.

Mr Smallman – one horse a day to all (haul) manure for Mr. Tudor 5s 0d. 2 days, 3 horses £1-10-0d.

Sold lots of 1 or 2 baggs of beans and wheat, probably to smallholders or cottagers.

1st May 1867 – Edward Homes agrese to serve me 12 months for £9-10-0d. He had subs throughout the year – shirt, tobacco, wascot, hat and at the end of the year was paid £4-10-2½ d to make the money up to £9-10-0d.

8th May – Mary Norgrove agrees to serve me for 12 months for £6-10-0d. Subs – Umbrella 6d, circus 6d.
She may not have served the full year as she was paid 16s 0d on 27th June and is not mentioned again.

16th July 1867 – Betsy Jones agrees to serve till May next for £4-0-0d and her signature is written clearly.

11th October 1867 – Sold to Mr Higginson 20 pots of apples @ 2s 9d per pot £2-15-0d.

14th November – 17 barrels, 6 poots in each barrel, the amount 102 pots £14-0-6d.

November 1867 – Mr Phillip Morris, Butcher bought 30 sheep £60-10-0d. This looks to be to cover a meat bill for £57-2-9d. This was quite usual for the butcher to come and buy some animals to settle the outstanding bill.

1st May 1868 – Ezra Gittins agrees to serve me for 12 months £6-6-0d Ezra Gittins signed with a X. Subs included tobacco, leggins 7s 6d, pr boots 14s 0d. At the end of the year he was paid £3-2-0d which was owing on 1st May 1869.

1st May 1868 – Edward Homes wages for the year £10-0-0d. Subs – tobacco, 1 row of potato ground 4s 9d. Over Crismuss 10s 0d, leggins 7s 6d and received £2-4-6d to make up the total at the end of the year.
1869 – Mr Page, Bridge Hotel bought 3 pockets of hops at £6-10-0d per pkt – 2cwt 3qrs 0lbs £17-17-6d.

12th November 1870 – Mr Haddon Hewitt, the builder, Tenbury bought a black mare of Mr John Morris for £17-10-0d.

1st May 1871 – William Homes engaged to me for 12 months £7-0-0d. For is X mark. Subs – For his father 6s 0d, to go to Tenbury, small amounts. Had to go at Crismus £1-0-0d. Went to see his brothers 1s 0d. Whip 6d, pare boots 13s 6d, Tenbury steeplechase 1s 0d. Row of potato ground 3s 9d.

16th May – Hack mare to Mr Davis horse £1-0-0d.

13th June - Buxsom to the horse £1-0-0d.

7th June – Emma Shutt engaged for £4-0-0d.

21st June – Mr Wheeler, Burford Mill 100 of faggots 8s 0d.
   Mr Lloyd, Greete 200 of faggots 16s 0d.
   John Ryder ½ hundred of faggots 4s 0d.
   Mrs Goodman, Bedenall ½ hundred of faggots 4s 0d.
   Mr Mullard ½ hundred of faggots 4s 0d.

Good ale will make a cat speak.

Faggots were usually brashwood of the tops of trees, often used, when dried, to fire the bread oven or kindling wood.

29th September 1871 – Sarah Walwin engaged for 12 month for £6-0-0d. Her mark X.

1871 and 1872 – Mrs Turner – hop tying, turnip pulling.

1871 – Mr Graves, the fruit dealer, Tenbury bought the fruit on the trees of 5 orchards for £43-5-0d.

1872 – Also sold fruit to Mr Graves and some wool.

29th May 1872 – Henery Humpris engaged for 1s 6d per week.

12th October 1872 – Mr Meakins bought six bullocks @ £12-15-0d - £76-10-0d.

17th October – Mary Butts engaged to serve Mrs Morris, now till May £3-0-0d a month's notice to be given for either – her signature.

10th December – William Homes agrees to serve me for the year - £8-15-0d. His mark X.

1873 – Sold to Mr Wheeler Burford Mill –
15 bags of wheat @ 22s 0d	£16-10-0d
20 bags of pease @ 17s 0d	£17- 0- 0d

6th May 1873 – Thomas Griffiths agrees to serve me till
6th May 1874 £4-0-0d.
Subs – Tenbury races 1s 0d. On the 6th May paid £1-18-0d.

21st August – Mr Graves bought fruit on the trees - £40-0-0d and received final payment in January 1875.

3rd November – Sold to Mrs Bowen, Crown Inn – 1 pocket of hops - £7-10-0d.

6th December – Mr Peney, Malster, Ludlow bought 3 pockets hops - £33-13-9d.
37 bags of barley @ 18s 0d -	£33 - 6-0d
	£66-9-0d

and paid in instalments with final payment 4th January 1875.

9th December – Mr Jones, Rose & Crown bought 2 pockets hops £15-5-0d.

PAST PRESIDENTS AND SECRETARIES FOR THE TENBURY AGRICULTURAL SOCIETY

1858 - SIR W. SMITH, BART. (EARDISTON)
1859 - THE RIGHT HON. LORD NORTHWICK
1860 - E.V. WHEELER, ESQ.
1861 - GEORGE PARDOE, ESQ.
1862 - SIR JOSEPH RUSSELL BAILEY, BART.
1863-1866 - NAMES MISSING
1867 - SIR T.E. WINNINGTON, BART. M.P.
1868 - R. PRESCOTT DECIE, ESQ
1869 - NAME MISSING
1870 - JOHN BARBER. ESQ.
1871 - NAME MISSING
1872 - H.J. BAILEY, ESQ.
1873 - E.O. PARTRIDGE, ESQ.
1874 - E.V. WHEELER, ESQ.
1875 - G. PARDOE, ESQ.
1876 - THE RIGHT HON. LORD NORTHWICK
1877 - SIR E.A.H. LECHMERE, BART. M.P.
1878 - J. BARBER, ESQ (THE JEWKES).
1879 - CAPTAIN SEVERNE, M.P.
1880 - MAJOR CHARLESWORTH
1881 - G.R. GODSON, ESQ.
1882 - CAPTAIN GREATOREX
1883 - SIR BALDWYN LEIGHTON, BART. M.P.
1884 - E. VINCENT V. WHEELER, ESQ
1885 - JAMES RANKIN, ESQ
1886 - COLONEL R. PRESCOTT DECIE
1887 - COMMANDER HILL-LOWE, R.N.
1888 - H.J. BAILEY, ESQ.
1889 - R. JASPER MORE, ESQ. M.P.
1890 - SIR W.M. CURTIS, BART.
1891 - JAMES V. WHEELER, ESQ.
1892 - EDWARD F. WILLIAMS, ESQ.
1893 - ALFRED BALDWIN, ESQ. M.P.
1894 - CHARLES W. WICKSTED, ESQ.
1895 - THE REV. E.G. BALDWYN-CHILDE
1896 - MARTIN CURTLER, ESQ.
1897 - CAPTAIN CRICHTON-BROWNE
1898 - THE RIGHT HON. THE EARL BEACHAMP
1899 - W. NORRIS, ESQ.
1900 - H.J. BAILEY, ESQ. (ROWDEN ABBEY)
1901 - H. WAKEMAN NEWPORT, ESQ.
1902 - S.H. COWPER COLES, ESQ.
1903 - S.H. COWPER COLES, ESQ.
1904 - SIR W.M. CURTIS, BART. M.F.H.
1905 - W.T. BARNEBY, ESQ. (SALTMARSH CASTLE)
1906 - LEWIS WALLACE, ESQ. (EARDISTON HOUSE)
1907 - F.E. PRESCOTT, ESQ. (PULBOROUGH)
1908 - MICHAEL TOMKINSON,
        (FRANCHE HALL, KIDDERMINSTER)
1909 - STANLEY BALDWIN, ESQ. M.P. (WILDEN)
1910 - GERALD E. GODSON, (TENBURY)

1911 - R.H. WINGFIELD CARDIFF, ESQ.
1912 - G. BALLARD, ESQ.
1913 - NO SCHEDULE.
1914 - SIR CHARLES RUSHOUT
1919 - SIR CHARLES RUSHOUT
1920 - W. BALDWIN, ESQ.
1921 - A. ROWLAND CLEGG, ESQ.
1922 - H.T. NOTT, ESQ.
1923 - CAPTAIN HILL-LOWE
1924 - C.G. PARTRIDGE, ESQ.
1925 - A.E. BALDWIN, ESQ.
1926 - MAJOR F.E. PRESCOTT
1927 - COL. E.V.V. WHEELER
1928 - H. INGLEBY, ESQ.
1929 - E.B. FIELDEN, ESQ. M.P.
1930 - M.G. ROLLO, ESQ.
1931 - J. BATLEY, ESQ.
1932 - K.D. BRIGGS, ESQ.
1933 - LT.COL. W.R. PRESCOTT, M.C.
1934 - CAPT. J.W.D. EVANS
1935 - BRIG-GEN. W.C. ANDERSON, C.M.G.
1936 - MAJOR A.G. PARDOE, M.C.
1937 - BRIG-GEN. H.C. REES, C.M.G. D.S.O.
1938 - CAPT. R.J.E. CONANT, M.P.
1939 - T.E. SMART, ESQ.
1947 - T.E. SMART, ESQ.
1948 - T.E. SMART, ESQ.
1949 - T.E. SMART, ESQ.
1950 - COL. T. FILLERY
1951 - COL. E.G. WALLACE
1952 - SIR HUGH ARBUTHNOT, BART. M.F.H.
1953 - LT.COL. E.A. FIELDEN, M.C. D.L.
1954 - DR. J.E. BLUNDELL-WILLIAMS
1955 - J.B. SUMNER, ESQ.
1956 - J. NOTT, ESQ. M.B.E.
1957 - T.E. SMART, ESQ.
1958 - G. NABARRO, ESQ. M.P.
1959 - T.D. SHAW, ESQ.
1960 - T.D. SHAW, ESQ.
1961 - F.H. DALE, ESQ
1962 - J.R. HUGH SUMNER, C.B.E. D.L. J.P.
1963 - LT.COL H.M.V. NICOLL, D.S.O. O.B.E.
1964 - R.H.B. INGLEBY, ESQ.
1965 - SIR TATTON BRINTON, M.P.
1966 - LADY ROUSE-BOUGHTON, M.F.H.
1967 - S.P. THOMAS, ESQ.
1968 - C.G. PAYNE, ESQ.
1969 - H.B. MORGAN, ESQ. F.A.I.
1970 - J.A. FIELDEN, ESQ.
1971 - BRIG. E.B.W. CARDIFF, C.B. C.B.E.

1972 - DR. J.H.H. OLIVER, T.D. QHS. M.R.C.S. L.R.C.P.
1973 - CAPTAIN J.M.G. LUMSDEN.
1974 - J.E. BULMER, ESQ. M.P.
1975 - MISS M. ROUSE-BOUGHTON.
1976 - H.H. FERGUSON, ESQ. M.R.C.V.S.
1977 - M.T. MORGAN, ESQ.
1978 - REV. R.H. GARNETT.
1979 - J.V.T. WHEELER, ESQ.
1980 - B.M. ROBINSON, ESQ.
1981 - A.S.B. GASCOYNE, ESQ.
1982 - A.J. PARKIN, ESQ.
1983 - A.B. SANDERSON, ESQ. J.P.
1984 - T.F. HIGGINSON, ESQ.
1985 - J.H. NOTT, ESQ.
1986 - J. MCGRATH, ESQ.
1987 - P.R. SPAREY, ESQ.
1988 - G.E. BRIGHT, ESQ.
1989 - E.W. MORGAN, ESQ.
1990 - R.J. BRERETON, ESQ. M.R.C.V.S.
1991 - R.T. DAVIES, ESQ.
1992 - J.S. BLAKEWAY, ESQ.
1993 - D. PALMER, ESQ. M.F.H.
1994 - K.J. DAVIES, ESQ.
1995 - DR. R.J.A. LEAR.
1996 - P.J. UNDERHILL, ESQ.
1997 - LORD DARNLEY.
1998 - G. HUNTBATCH, ESQ.
1999 - P. JONES, ESQ.
2000 - MR. I. PUGH & MRS. A. PUGH.
2001 - MR. J.A. MEAD
2003 - MR. W.K. CROXTON
2004 - M. HOGAN, ESQ.
2005 - MRS. S. WILDIG.
2006 - J. GODDARD
2007 - MISS. M. MORRIS
2008 - J.B. ADAMS

NINE SECRETARIES

1858-1889 W. NORRIS
1899-1900 W. BALDWIN
1901- 1905 T.H. COOKE (LOWER ROCHFORD)
1905-1912 JOHN COOPER (AUCTIONEER)
1912-1914 W. BALDWIN
1919-1939 S.H. MATTOCK
1947-1966 H.B. MORGAN
1966-1970 P.W. BALDWIN
1970-1993 B.P. BUFTON
1993 N.C. CHAMPION

THERE WERE ONLY NINE SECRETARIES IN 150 YEARS.

The grass is always greener on the other side of the hedge.

T.A.S FARM COMPETITION

The Farm Competition was restarted in 1987 but, looking back through the old show schedules, it is clear that many such competitions were held in the past, proving the saying that farming and events go round in cycles.

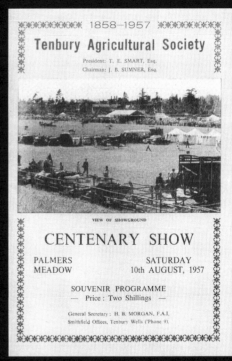

One of the main reasons why the Farm Competition was started again was to showcase the high standard of farming in the area. In addition to that it was thought the competition would add interest, encourage conservation and provide an opportunity for members of the Agricultural Society to be involved in an event between shows. It is now in its 21st year and between 40 and 50 farms compete annually in the 4 main classes, according to their acreage. Cattle - beef and dairy, sheep, most cereals, root crops and grassland are eligible to be entered. In 2008 a Diversification class was added as more and more farmers find other ways to make their farms viable. New Conservation classes have also been added to the existing ones and the photographs taken of the entries are inspiring. There is also a Best Whole Farm award in each of the four classes.

TAS Centenary Show programme

The rules are simple. To be eligible, competitors must be members of T.A.S. and their holdings must fall within a 10 mile radius of the Clock House, in Tenbury.

The judges come from far and wide, usually undertaking their task in June and July. The results are kept secret until the day of the Tenbury Show thus maintaining the element of surprise. Win or lose, it's the taking part that matters.

The Society runs various other events throughout the year including mouse racing, indoor horse racing, dances and a farm walk. The Annual Dinner is held in October at which the trophies, generously donated by local businesses over the years, and prize cards are presented.

Tenbury Agricultural Society is indebted to its members who take part and also to our judges. It is hoped the competition will continue to flourish so that it too may celebrate its 150th anniversary.

A LIST OF COMPETITION CLASSES FROM 1858 TO 1957

**TENBURY AGRICULTURAL SHOW ESTABLISHED 1858
FOR REWARDING GOOD PLOUGHMEN AND SERVANTS.
PRESIDENT – SIR W. SMITH, BART.
HON. SECRETARY – MR. W. NORRIS**

Committee – Colonel Rushout, M.P. (later, Lord Northwick). E.V. Wheeler.
Rev. H. Browne (Eastham). Mr. Bangham. Mr. Cooke (Hill Top). Mr. Drew.
Mr. Farmer. Mr. W. Giles. Mr. Moore. Mr. T. Price. Mr. B. Powis.
Mr. Winton.

Rule 1 - Annual Subscriptions – 10 shillings.

Rule 2 – The ploughing match and first meeting of this society for awarding prizes shall be on Wednesday 13th October 1858.

Rule 5 – That the A.G.M. and dinner shall be held at the Corn Exchange Hall in Tenbury on the day of The Annual Ploughing Match at which time the prizes will be awarded.

Rule 6 – That on the same day a dinner shall be given to each of the competitors in the ploughing and thatching class, later hedging, and to the successful competitors in the other classes.

PREMIUMS FOR 1858

Class 1 -   To plough ½ acre in 3½ hours with a swing plough with three horses abreast.

Class 2 -   To plough ½ acre in 3 ½ hours with a swing plough with two horses abreast.

Class 3 -   To plough ½ acre in 3 ½ hours with a swing plough with three horses at length.

Class 4 -   To plough ½ acre in 3 ½ hours with a wheel plough and three horses at length.

Class 5 -   To the man who has built his master's corn stacks in the best manner

Class 6 -   To the man who has built his master's hayricks in the best manner

Class 7 -   To the man who has thatched his master's hay and corn stacks in the best manner

Class 8 -   To the wagoner, cowman, or servant being a resident in his master's house for the greatest length of time

Class 9 -   The same as above, but not lived in.

Class 10 - To the female servant who has served longest

Class 11 - To the labourer who shall have brought up the largest family without parochial relief (except medical)

First and second prizes were awarded in each class – (generally £2 and £1).

Further classes were added to these in 1860, namely:-

Women's work is never done.

Class 1 - For the best crop of swedes on five acres of land - a silver cup (value ten guineas).

Class 2 – For the best cultivated farm within seven miles of the Corn Exchange – (Tenant farmers only).

Class 3 – For the best gallon of cider - (Subscribers to Society)

Class 4 – To the labourer who has polled the hop land best for his master in the best manner (Not less than three acres).

1861 £3 gift for the parish that had improved its roads most.

Schedules missing 1863-67.

1867 Dinner and A.G.M. at Swan Hotel 3s 6d (inc. dessert).
A silver cup for the best crop of mangolds -(min. two acres).
£1 for the best hogshead of cider – sample to be sent in a stone jar for judging (Corn Exchange).

£1 10s (The gift of Rt. Hon. Lord Northwick), for a boy who has served his master best, the candidate must also produce a certificate from the Clergyman of the Parish of his being able to read and write and work the four first rules of arithmetic.

1868 Hedging – Two perches (11 yards) of hedging (local) under 8 hours (2 prizes).

1870 Hedging – open to all England – £2 10s.
To the maker of the best of fence, of live stuff, not less than four feet high, no stakes or dead wood of any kind to be used and the local hedging class.

1871 Missing.

1878 To the blacksmith who shall make the best set of shoes and put them on a horse (provided) at the forges of Mr. Child or Mr. Blakeway in Tenbury.

1880 For several years there had been prizes for the neatest garden and homestead attached to a farm of not less than fifty acres.

1884 One guinea to the shepherd who has had the care of at least forty ewes, and who has reared the greatest number of lambs in proportion to the ewes, with the least loss of ewes.

1886 Hedging for juniors as well as seniors.
£1 to the man who has dried his master's hops best.
One guinea to the woman who has made the best pound of butter (Corn Exchange)
One guinea to the maker of the best cheese -(not less than 10 pound) (Corn Exchange).

1891 Sheep shearing classes for the first time –

To shear three sheep in the quickest time and best manner (open).
To shear three sheep in the quickest time (member of Society).
To shear three sheep in the quickest time and best manner (under 21).

Pot calling the kettle black.

1892	Best kept orchards by a tenant farmer (not less than three acres).
1896	£1 to a man under 23 years of age who shall graft a number of trees.
1897	To the man who shall judge nearest the weight of a fat beast (the animals were judged live and the carcass weighed after slaughter). To the man who shall judge nearest the weight of two fat sheep (the animals were judged live and the carcass weighed after slaughter).
1898	To man or boy to prune one old apple tree and one or more young trees and one or more gooseberry or currant trees.
1899	First Livestock Classes –

1899 continued:

Horses – Brood cart mare.
2 year old cart gelding or filly
Yearling cart colt or filly
Cart colt foal.
Cart filly foal.
Four yearling Hereford steers
Four yearling Hereford heifers
Four calves (any breed).
Pen of five Shropshire ewes
Pen of ten Shropshire lambs
The best sieve of apples (24 pounds).

1900	Best culinary apples, best dessert apples. Best cider apples, best perry pears.
1902	Best collection of soft fruits (plums, damsons etc).
1903	Best dairy cow. Schedule includes Tenbury & District Cottage Allotment Gardening Association (first time)- (later Horticultural 1921).
1905	Farmer of less than twenty acres – yearling heifer or steer.
1908	Most perfect wasps' nest. The employees were encouraged to get rid of wasps as they damaged the fruit. There were often ten or twelve entries in this class.
1910	Best bushel of wheat.
1912	Black oats – white oats (bushel).
1914	Yearling nag colt or filly. Best Hereford bull, cow and offspring. Best Hereford cow in calf or in milk.
1921	Best hunter, brood mare, colt.
1922	Five Ryeland ewes – five Ryeland lambs. Five ewes, any other breed – ten lambs
1923	Two pigs – middle white. Two gilt pigs – any other breed.

192

Clothes maketh not the man.

1927	Three Kerry ewes – three yearling ewes – three ewe lambs
	Yearling Clun ram – three ewes – three ewe lambs
	Sheep dog trials.

21.05.1933

Col. E.V.V. Wheeler dies. For nearly 50 years he was a TAS committee member.

1935   October - Annual Show of fruit and farm produce - Bridge Ballroom.

1951   Ploughing and hedging October 13th - Lower Berrington.

1957   Centenary Show.

Tenbury Wells Horticultural & Floral Society, (established 1843) separately.
Firstly as two shows - Summer and Autumn in a marquee at the Swan Hotel. Joined with TAS in 1921.

In 1954 Dr. Blundell-Williams was elected President and presented a Gold Medal to be awarded every third year to the member, who in the opinion of the Society, has in the past three years done most to further the practice and interests of Agriculture or Horticulture.

WINNERS
1955 - Archer Baldwin
1958 - Jim Nott
1961 - Ken Parry
1964 - Bill Sinnett
1970 - Gilmour Payne
1973 - Michael Morgan
1976 - Humprey Nott
1979 - Peter Sparey
1982 - Ray Evison
1985 - John Davies
1988 - Barry Bufton
1991 - David Powell
1994 - Ray Davies
1997 - Cyril Norman
2000 - David Spilsbury
2003 - Stan Yapp
2006 - Burgess Adams

Epilogue

WHAT OF THE FUTURE?

The past is written, the present is in hand but what of the future for Tenbury Agricultural Society? 150 years has seen highs and lows in farming and the virtual disappearance of the estates and these days most farms are owner occupied. Some have been bought by business people from cities as far away as London who are well able to commute to work by road or rail or work from home on the internet. Most of these new owners settle down to enjoy their new homes and the privacy their land gives them; they are not interested in farming it themselves and are quite happy to rent it out to a neighbouring farmer. During 2007, over half the farms sold were purchased by 'hobby' farmers, leaving fewer farms for the younger generation and, unless there is an opportunity to take on the established family farm, many farmers' sons and daughters are taking other careers.

Over the past 15 years livestock farming has gone through a very bad time. Major setbacks - B.S.E., Foot and Mouth disease twice, and the breakdown in herds of cattle with T.B. have been followed by the serious threat of Bluetongue. Recovery from these farming diseases is dependent upon positive government policies and support from the Department of the Environment, Food and Rural Affairs but this has been sadly lacking during this period. Records show that British dairy farmers are going out of business faster than ever chiefly because the price they are paid for milk is below the cost of production.

However, the future for the arable farmer looks distinctly brighter; this is mainly due to the developing countries buying more food on the world market and future prices which look set to remain at an economic level. The long term future of the many redundant farm buildings in and around the Teme Valley has been preserved by converting them into living accommodation, thus preserving the rural history of agricultural architecture for future generations.

During the lifetime of the Agricultural Society, Tenbury town has roughly doubled in size, and Burford, which once was a scattered village, is now virtually a small town in its own right. Long gone are the days when in the 1870s and 1880s the Tenbury steeplechases were held in the triangle of the A456, the Cleobury road and the recent Tenbury Agricultural Society showground. The entire area has since been used to build homes.

On a broader scale, over three quarters of Britain is farmland and small communities like Tenbury Wells need to make a living but pressure is building on farming families and, sadly, for some it is proving too great. Farmers are said to be among the occupational groups most at risk of suicide. After all, when a farmer is forced out of business, jobs are not only lost; family break up is inevitable and generations of agricultural knowledge lost.

Whichever way it is looked at, almost all farmers play their part in improving the environment and it is estimated that they carry out some £400 million of unpaid work as part of farm management.

To secure a safe future for farming communities, consumers should think carefully about the food they buy, how far it has travelled and how it was produced as well as whether it has been traded fairly to provide a farmer with a decent living. This is just as relevant to food produced in the United Kingdom as it is to food produced overseas. It is worth noting that there is a global trend for farmers to receive a lesser share of the consumer price, be it coffee, bananas, wheat or milk.

At a time when the government is worried about inflation, the rising cost of oil and fuel is higher than anticipated a year or two ago. Milk is up 13% in the

Let sleeping dogs lie.

last twelve months, and, due to the use of cereals for bio-fuel production, bread has risen sharply. Without doubt the higher price of grain is going to affect the livestock industry, particularly pig farming, forcing many pig farmers to cut back on numbers of breeding sows. It is almost certain that there will be a resulting world-wide shortage of pig meat.

The rising price of oil affects everyone, from domestic heating and cooking at home and in the work place to transportation and it will soon begin to show that the practice of flying food around the world is no longer sustainable. The 20th century brought an increase in world population, especially China and India where the daily diet of rice and wheat is changing to Western style dairy and meat. Over the last 150 years there was a time when Commonwealth countries supplied cheap food to Great Britain but those days are gone. Now many other nations are competing with us for food supplies and it is important that farming in the UK is encouraged to produce as much food as possible and still commit to looking after the environment.

Perhaps the future for farming begins at home where consumers are encouraged to support local farm shops and farmers' markets rather than shopping at the mighty supermarkets with their wasteful two-for-one offers. Helping farmers through hard times is where fair trade begins, at home, in places like the Teme Valley where the past hides in the patchwork of fields and hope is in the hands of future generations.

This then is the future role of the Tenbury Agricultural Society; will it last another century and is it safe in the hands of the next generations? Who really knows?

LAST WORD

Well, the tiddler lambs went to Ludlow Market this morning. A bit of a hard thing to do - taking your bottle reared sheep from the orchard where they've spent all their lives. There's no complaining though, that's why I was given them; I am after all marrying a farmer from near the 'town in the orchard' and hopefully there will be more lambs to take to market in the future. Three years ago they would have gone to our local market in Tenbury Wells but sadly that has closed and our 'market town' is now without its own livestock market.

Things do change and I suppose they always will. With the increasing influence of the European Union, greater production of crops grown for fuel, public awareness of how food is produced, problems with animal diseases and the English countryside to protect, we can look forward to some interesting years ahead. I know William and I have some challenges ahead and by the time you read this we will be married and trying to farm in a very different world to the one of just a few years ago.

Up, up and away - William Davies proposes to Samantha Jacobs

Samantha Jacobs
Oldwood Common
February 2008

P.S. I wonder how much the tiddlers made?

Curiosity killed the cat.

ACKNOWLEDGEMENTS

They say history often writes itself but sometimes it can use a bit of help. Vital help for this book has come from three major sources, Tenbury Museum, back copies of the Tenbury Advertiser and more important, a box full of memories, photographs and longstanding recollections of a remarkable farming community.

Tenbury Museum, housed in the old Goff School building in Cross Street, has a much sought after collection of local history and relics displayed in well filled show cases in one single room. They tell the story of the domestic, social and working life of a predominantly farming community from just about every angle and every museum volunteer is committed to preserving Tenbury's day to day heritage. It was also decided to resurrect the town's Civic Society in order to campaign for more protection of local town buildings, primarily the Grade II listed depleted Pump Rooms. During the 1990's the Tenbury Advertiser office needed more space and offered the museum its collection of old newspapers dating back to 1871 but deterioration of the news print caused serious problems. Thanks to a Heritage Lottery Fund grant of almost £50,000 in 2005, the newspapers were micro filmed and eventually transferred to CDs and have since become a dependable source of material for historical research.

More space is needed to cope with the existing collection and the regular donations of artefacts offered to the museum and the Museum Committee is currently looking for a permanent home for its growing collection. Hopes are running high for the more central Victorian Pump Rooms to become the natural home for a dedicated Tenbury Museum.

Jen Green and the Tenbury Agriculural Society Book Committee thank the following individuals for their generous contributions and help without which this book may not have been possible. John Asquith : Roger Bowkett : Pat Bradley : Bob Brown : Frances Bunn : Alison and Roger Chezoy : Nick Dunne : Ted Evans : Doris Griffiths : David Hambleton : Ronnie Hipkiss : Michael Hogan : Doris Hurds : Samantha Jacobs : Alf Jenkins : Maggie Kingston : Sir Richard Lloyd : Tim Mason : Ray Morris : Roger and Marion Morris : Kay Parkinson : Clive Powell : David Powell : Ivor and Ann Pugh : Rosemary, Giles & Andrew Pritchard : Bill Sinnett : Joyce Spilsbury : Dan Taylor : John Thacker : Pauline Vincent : John Wright : K. Stanley Yapp : Thelma Young : Jane Spilsbury : Helen and Neil from Orphans Press and the many other people who have helped along the way.

Source material from Atheneum Library : Hereford Times : New York Times : Tenbury Advertiser : Tenbury Historical Society : Tenbury Library : Tenbury Museum : Tenbury Press & News : Worcester Museum Worcester News : Worcester Records Office and A History of Buildings - Nigel Harvey: Discovering Traditional Farm Buildings J.E.C. Peters and the Harold Miller Archive. Every effort has been made to trace owners of source material.

Jen Green also wishes to acknowledge the substantial contribution from David Spilsbury and personally thanks him for his diligent research, patience and understanding needed to publish this work.

Cast no dirt into the well that gives you water.